New Spiritual Homes

INTERSECTIONS

Asian and Pacific American
Transcultural Studies

Russell C. Leong
General Editor

New Spiritual Homes

RELIGION AND

ASIAN AMERICANS

Edited by David K. Yoo

*University
of Hawai'i
Press
Honolulu*

*in association
with UCLA
Asian American
Studies Center
Los Angeles*

Library of Congress Cataloging-in-Publication Data
New spiritual homes : religion and Asian
Americans / David K. Yoo,
    editor
        p.   cm. — (Intersections)
    Includes bibliographical
references and index.
    ISBN 0–8248–2072–x (pbk. : alk.
paper)
    1. Asian Americans—Religion.
    2. United States—Religion—20th cen-
tury. 3. Asia—Religion. I. Yoo, David.
    II. Series: Intersections (Honolulu,
    Hawaii)
BL2525.N488   1999
200'.89'95073—dc21   98–35976
                                    CIP

Designed by Barbara Pope Book Design

Printed by Maple-Vail Book
Manufacturing Group

Contents

Acknowledgments

It is a genuine pleasure to acknowledge those who have been part of this collaboration. A conversation over five years ago with Russell Leong of UCLA helped spark this project, and it is fitting that this volume is joining Intersections, the series he is editing with the University of Hawai'i Press. Mary Kao, Glenn Omatsu, Darryl Mar, and Jean Pang Yip of UCLA have each helped this collection at various stages.

Institutional support has been important for testing out ideas for this book, and a symposium on race and religion in Asian America in October 1996 was sponsored by UCLA. I thank Don Nakanishi, director, and others at the Asian American Studies Center and those who participated in the conference. Oberlin College invited me to present the Mead-Swing Lecture in the fall of 1997, and conversations with students and faculty were quite helpful. Oberlin's Religion Department sponsored my visit, and I thank Paula Richman, James Dobbins, David Kamitsuka, and A. G. Miller for making my stay such an enjoyable one. Conversations with my colleagues at Claremont McKenna College and at the Claremont Colleges also informed this project.

The contributors to *New Spiritual Homes* of course deserve much thanks, for it is their scholarship that is the heart of this book's intellectual contribution. No doubt much more work on Asian American religions will be forthcoming, and no doubt many of the writers featured here will be responsible for the growth of this field. For comments and editorial suggestions on an earlier version of my introduction, I would like to thank Timothy Tseng and Jane Iwamura. On a personal note, I am grateful for the comments, support, and encouragement of Ruth Chung, my spouse and colleague. The birth of our son, Jonathan, and his presence in our life have added a chaotic joy that has kept this project and everything else in proper perspective.

New Spiritual Homes

Introduction:
Reframing the U.S. Religious Landscape

DAVID K. YOO

On 10 May 1869, a crowd gathered at Promontory Point, Utah, to witness the historic completion of the transcontinental railroad. The joining of the Union and Central Pacific symbolized a nation coming into its industrial own. Across its tracks, shipments of raw materials extracted in the West would head eastward to become the finished products that would then make their way back to consumers and to ships waiting to transport American goods to Asian markets. Begun in 1863 and heavily subsidized by the federal government, the transcontinental railroad symbolized promise and possibility for the United States. Accordingly, the laying of the final two lengths of rail and the driving of the last spike were cause for celebration. A photograph captured the well-known scene: men dangling from locomotives with champagne bottles, respective chief engineers shaking hands, and an impressive group of men gathered to mark the event. One observer, noting that Chinese and European immigrant laborers had laid the last rails, informed readers that "here, near the center of the American continent, were the united efforts of the representatives of the continents of Europe, Asia, and America—America directing and controlling."[1]

Despite the eyewitness report, no Chinese workers appeared in the famous photograph. They were relegated, as it were, to the space outside the frame of the camera's lens. The removal of Chinese from the scene, their services no longer needed, symbolically foreshadowed the nativist efforts that culminated in the passage of the 1882 Chinese Exclusion Act. Worth at least a thousand words, the photograph reminds us that what is omitted may be far more important than we realize. Chinese immigrants merit attention not for the sake of mere inclusion but because they are integral to the story of the railroads. The presence of Chinese Americans underscores how building the iron horse involved the international migration of peoples to the American West, a dual labor and wage system, racial politics, and tremendous human cost. To overlook these themes and connections is to have an impoverished understanding of the railroads and, by extension, our collective history as a nation.[2]

Promontory Point, by way of analogy, addresses the need to explore critically the obscure places that Asian Americans have occupied in the study of American religion. To that end, *New Spiritual Homes* asks how religious traditions, movements, and institutions have been vital for Asian Americans past and present. Through essays, poems, and resource materials, this volume casts a wide intellectual net to reframe the religious landscape to account for the experiences of Asian Americans. How has religion assisted people in dealing with the upheaval of migration and with rites of passage? At the same time, how has religion been the source of division, pain, and oppression? In what ways has religion been part of the identity formation of Asian immigrants and their descendants in the United States? How has religion played a role in the formation of Asian diasporas? These questions and many others emerge as the contributors explore how individuals and

David K. Yoo

communities have constructed worldviews in light of their religious commitments.

Although the range of peoples and traditions addressed here is impressive, *New Spiritual Homes* only begins to tap the depth and complexity of the subject. Indeed, it is difficult to imagine how any single volume could provide comprehensive coverage. Consequently, this collection represents just the first step in exploring the importance of religion for Asian Americans. While only a beginning, the scholarship presented in these pages testifies that the conversation has been long overdue.

A View from the Margins

By placing Asian Americans at the center of analysis, *New Spiritual Homes* shifts the narrative focus to the margins and provides an alternative vantage point to view the terrain of American religion.[3] An emphasis on the "unseen" underscores the incredible diversity that has characterized religion and society in the United States from the very beginning.[4] The breadth of Asian American religions alone suggests the limitations of viewing American religion through the lens of Euro-American Protestantism. In a provocative essay, religious studies scholar Robert Orsi has suggested that the study of American religion is in essence the study of improvisations. It is the instability, transience, and chaos of American social life that hold the greatest clues: "The real action in American religious history in [the twentieth] century . . . was happening not in the 'mainstream' . . . but out there on what has long been identified as the 'fringes.'" Orsi argues for a move beyond official creedal borders to look for religion in different kinds of spaces. The interpretive key can be found in the everyday lives of people and their engagement with material circumstances. New questions and answers unfold as one asks how people have negotiated the uncertainties of life. In the process, the "explosive creativity" of American religion is made manifest.[5]

As a largely untapped area of American religion, research on the experiences of Asian Americans can make an important contribution to a reconfiguring of the boundaries of the field. Perhaps most striking is the sheer diversity of traditions represented under the canopy of "Asian American religions." These traditions point to a far more varied and complex religious terrain than one might imagine when thinking of the United States. In this book alone, for instance, contributors explore Filipino folk religion, Chinese American Protestantism and Buddhism, Asian Indian Sikhism and Islam, Korean American shamanism and Christianity, as well as many other topics, including the interaction of religion with gender, colonialism, class, politics, and identity. The essays and poems reveal how immigrants from throughout Asia have transplanted their belief systems in the United States and, moreover, how those systems as well as the immigrants have undergone transformation in the building of new spiritual homes for themselves and successive generations. Along the way, our understanding of American religion is enriched, not by the inclusion of minor variants or exceptions to the rule, but by the challenge to rethink dominant paradigms and standard conceptual categories. Asian American religions remind us that religious belief and practice in the United States has always emanated from the confluence of many cultures, peoples, and places.

One of those places, the American West, a region typically noted for its perceived absence of religion, is reclaimed through the religious experiences of Asian Americans.[6] Although its physical grandeur has elicited allusions to the supernatural, the West for most Americans remains a place of cattle drives, gunfights, and brothels. Churches may appear in films and novels, but rarely are they more than window dressing, a vestige of civilization in an otherwise morally barren land. Popular culture is not the most reliable of guides, of

David K. Yoo

course, yet these persistent images illustrate the remarkable staying power and flexibility of the frontier vision given voice by Frederick Jackson Turner in 1893. Despite the "new" western history, the region continues to be vested with responsibility for the forging of the American character, made possible by the availability of "free land" and an encounter with wilderness.[7] It is worth noting, however, that neither Turner nor his critics devoted much energy to the topic of religion. Apart from passing references to the Mormons of Utah, the work of scholars in American history has followed Hollywood's lead more than anything else.[8] The ability to view the West as virgin territory, religious or otherwise, becomes considerably more difficult when one considers that the religions of Native Americans, Spaniards, and Mexicans had infused the area now referred to as the American West long before the arrival of the first Americans. The eventual encounters that would take place as well as the continued migration of people over the years have only added to the complex layering of religion in the West. Asian American religions, as part of this palimpsest, provide a point of entry into a region whose religious complexity and verve deserve as much scholarly attention as Puritan New England.

Religion and Race

Along with a greater awareness of the diversity and regional dimensions of American religion, Asian Americans uncover the deep ties between religion and race that can be traced to colonial times and Indian–European–African contact. Though interwoven throughout the American experience, stories of race and religion have only recently surfaced with the gradual decline of long-standing triumphalist narratives of a Protestant America. As in other areas of U.S. history, the issue of race raises troubling questions about our self-perceptions as a nation. When taken seriously, this issue provides an entry point into our past (and present) that seriously undermines the central ideals attributed to the founding of the nation. Albert Raboteau drives this point home in illustrating how the experience of African Americans contradicts the cherished myth of European migration to America as a journey into the Promised Land. The forced passage of African Americans was one from freedom into bondage, and what might have been the New Israel for one set of Americans was for another the New Egypt.[9] The case of Asian Americans problematizes the notion that religion has been the means by which immigrants gain eventual acceptance and access to American society and culture. Although Roman Catholics and Jews certainly faced their share of resistance, they have in time, according to sociologist Will Herberg, joined the mainstream once solely occupied by Protestants. This fundamental change in sensibilities reflected the role of religion in creating a triple melting pot.[10]

Adding Japanese American Buddhists to that group, however, would have weakened the force of Herberg's argument. Well outside the pale of a Judeo-Christian framework, Buddhists by their very presence may in fact have helped usher in the change noted by Herberg. Part of the American religious scene since the nineteenth century, Japanese American Buddhists discovered that the passage of time did little to remove the widespread suspicion that they could never really become part of the fabric of American life. Doubly marginalized by virtue of race and religion, Buddhists labored to educate others about their faith and to demonstrate its contribution to America. Six months before Pearl Harbor, as U.S.-Japan relations worsened, Young Buddhist Association president Manabu Fukuda anticipated the troubled times ahead: "Today we find ourselves in a difficult role of trying to strengthen the foundation of our religion and at the same time make our Occidental friends realize that the spirit of Buddhism shall in no way conflict with the ideals of American Democracy and the American Way." Such words fell on deaf ears. FBI agents rounded up Buddhist leaders in the aftermath of the bombing, having decided well before then that they constituted a special threat to national security. Federal authorities made little distinction between Shinto, the state religion of Japan, and Pure Land Buddhism: deviation from the norm (Christianity) was enough to render one suspect.[11] The experience of Japanese American Buddhists is but one illustration of the more or less permanent outsider status of many Asian American religions. The emphasis on difference has been further reinforced by the phenomenon of Americans seeking to reinvent themselves through the exotic and mysterious traditions of the Orient. Due to their proximity, Asian American religions have been included in this alternative search for self, representing as it were the treasures of Asia conveniently located in the United States.[12] In these ways, then, Asian Americans and their religions have been cast as the "Other," reinforcing the image of the "perpetual foreigner" and, in the process, ignoring how peoples and faiths have been part of larger sociocultural contexts in the United States.

For Asian American Christians, a shared faith with the dominant religious tradition of the nation has not been enough to bridge the gap created by race. Although the prevailing assumption is that Asian American Christians are more assimilated than their non-Christian counterparts, the fact remains that individuals and communities have consciously forged religious identities in opposition to the discrimination they have encountered despite shared faith with the majority of their fellow Americans. At the same time, the long-standing presence of independent racial-ethnic denominations attests to how Asian American Christians have created institutions that reflect their concerns and cater to their own needs. Separate racial-ethnic churches, programs, and governing bodies within majority Euro-American religious institutions, moreover, suggest the complex and contested nature of Asian American Christianity. In Christ there may be no

East or West, but for Asian Americans the observation made by the Reverend Doctor Martin Luther King Jr. still rings true: Sunday morning worship is the most segregated hour in America.[13] The privileging and power of the Euro-American Christian tradition have meant that all others, even coreligionists, have been relegated to second-class status. The challenge that remains is to situate Asian American religions within a multiplicity of sites that include race, migration, American culture and society, and transnational identities.

Asian American Studies

More than any other field, Asian American studies over the past three decades has unearthed, documented, and examined the experiences of Asian peoples who have migrated and settled in the United States. As the body of research has grown and matured, greater attention has been directed toward issues of gender, Asian-descent multiracialism, and the diversity of groups represented by the term "Asian American." An emphasis on diaspora has placed Asian America firmly within a global context, and innovative and interdisciplinary work within cultural studies is currently reconfiguring the field. In an effort to move beyond an Asian American/Euro-American dyad, comparative racial studies are now providing insights into interethnic and interracial relations. Amid such intellectual fervor in the field of Asian American studies, however, religion and religious experience continue to suffer from neglect.[14]

Apart from the difficulty of interpreting religion, Asian Americanists, by and large, have not been particularly interested in the subject.[15] There may be two reasons for this trend. First, the early philosophical underpinnings of the Asian American movement were influenced by Marxist thought—and despite the diversity of Marxist interpretations, religion generally has been cast as an opiate of the masses and ephemeral in nature. Second, the appeal of Marx and socialism as well as an embrace of "Asia" represented a conscious rejection of the United States as a capitalist, racist, and colonizing power that subjugated peoples of color both at home and abroad. As a key weapon in the social and cultural arsenal of the United States, religion has often been associated with Christian missionaries who linked arms with diplomats and businessmen to create an imperial apparatus that reaped huge profits for the United States while wreaking havoc in Asia.

While the biases against religion are understandable, they are nevertheless problematic in terms of social scientific theory and the characterization of Christianity in Asia. As we approach the twenty-first century, religion, in all its heterogeneity, continues to exert tremendous influence in the United States and abroad. Religion has not disappeared in a postmodern world. Though deeply enmeshed in social, economic, and political contexts, religion has its own integrity that is violated when subsumed under other categories of analysis. Similar to the argument for "race" as an independent variable, "religion" merits serious study in its own right as a force that shapes, transforms, and unifies as well as divides Asian American communities.[16] Furthermore, the identification of Christianity with the United States (and the West) has obscured the fact that Asian Christianity is not synonymous with the religion of missionaries. Upon closer examination, the history of the Roman Catholic church and American Protestant missions in Asia, while troubling in many respects, also contains stories of religious symbols and institutions appropriated by Asians for their own purposes. In short, Asians and Asian Americans, like people throughout the world, have made Christianity their own. Over the last two millennia, Christianity has taken a myriad number of forms and translations resulting in a legacy that defies any simple equation. The translation of the Bible into the vernacular languages of various Asian countries, in some cases, raised literacy rates, contributed to a disruption of class hierarchy, and fueled apocalyptic movements like the Taiping Rebellion.[17] The religion introduced by American Protestant missionaries gave rise to Korean (and Korean American) resistance to colonial rule during its thirty-five years of annexation by Japan (1910–1945).[18]

Religion can also expose the ways that shared ideas and institutions link Asian Americans to other communities within the United States. Exploring the Roman Catholic tradition among Filipino and Mexican Americans, for instance, may uncover the way these two groups interacted in the agricultural fields of the West Coast and show how religion influenced the formation of Filipino-Mexican households and networks. Catholicism and a Spanish colonial history offered these immigrants some common ground, even if their experiences within these institutions differed. Anthropologist Karen Leonard's study of Punjabi Sikh/Mexican marriages discusses the importance of religion and, in this case, the tensions that could arise in households where husbands and wives belonged to two separate religious traditions.[19]

Despite the important work taking place in Asian American studies, a reconceptualization of the field is necessary so that the serious treatment of religion becomes the interpretive rule rather than the exception. To overlook religion is to miss a critical feature of people's experiences and worldviews.

Narrative Matters

If scholars have failed to pay religion its proper due, Asian Americans themselves have certainly not followed the scholars. Religion has been intimately tied to how men and women have interpreted, ordered, and constructed their own worlds, especially in negotiating migration across the Pacific and establishing new lives in the United States. Raymond Brady Williams's study of Asian Indians and Pakistanis suggests that immigrants are often more religious than they were in their countries of origin. Presumably religion counters the frag-

David K. Yoo

mentation that individuals and families undergo and is an accepted means in the United States of developing a distinct identity. In the face of an epistemological crisis, religion provides a crucial narrative structure that calls upon a known world, even as that world shifts and adapts to new forces. Williams speculates that America's religiosity may stem from the central role that immigration has played in the peopling of the United States.[20]

The narrative role of religion underscores the human need for story. At a fundamental level, we discover who we are and define our relationship to the world around us through the stories we are given. In locating the self with the sacred, religious narrative touches upon our deepest myths, hopes, and fears. Given the pivotal opening that religion provides into the lives of Asian Americans, it is puzzling that religion has been largely omitted from narratives of American history and Asian American studies. As a consequence, we do not understand an essential aspect of how people structure their worlds. While these narratives cannot completely deny the efficacy of religious experience and meaning, their silence weakens the connections between people and communities and their larger contexts. The choices that are made, like the narratives themselves, matter because they are integral to the definition of the self and one's place in the larger scheme of things. And, of course, other questions naturally arise: Whose narratives are being told? How has the inclusion of certain narratives as well as exclusion of others affected the formation of individual and collective identity?[21]

About This Book

In an effort to highlight how religion can inform, enliven, and deepen our understanding of Asian America, *New Spiritual Homes* introduces readers to a wide range of writings. Those in search of a "master" narrative that integrates the individual pieces into a single composition will be disappointed. The content does not lend itself to such organization, since the term "Asian American religions" implies greater uniformity than is the case. And yet this collective terminology, however imprecise, does acknowledge that there have been common experiences among people of Asian ancestry in the United States. Rather than issuing a definitive statement, the objective of this book is to raise awareness, spark discussion, and encourage further study. To this end, the contributions are divided into three sections.

In Part I, "Foundations," the authors plumb the past and the present to discover how religious concerns have informed migration to the United States as well as a transnational consciousness among immigrants from China, the Philippines, India, and Taiwan. Part II, "Searching for Self and Soul," moves the discussion into the contemporary setting and asks how religion has informed the search for meaning that accompanies identity formation. Part III, "Creations of Spirit," turns to poetry and short stories in recognition of the fact that the study of religion must incorporate people's lived experiences. Asian American religions are more than an academic affair, and these contributions ground religion in the personal spaces that give it power and meaning. The book concludes with a selected bibliography, compiled by Marjorie Lee and Judy Soo Hoo, that represents a valuable resource on Asian American religions and points readers to additional sources.[22]

As the photograph of Promontory Point makes clear, so much of what we see (or don't see) depends on our vantage point. By focusing on the stories of Asian Americans, *New Spiritual Homes* challenges us to expand our frame of reference to take into account what has been relegated to the margins. The result is a much deeper and richer understanding of American religion. The task that remains is to continue a recovery of perspective that truly reflects the entire U.S. religious landscape.

David K. Yoo

Notes

1. Quote taken from Ronald Takaki, *Strangers from a Different Shore: A History of Asian Americans* (Boston: Little, Brown, 1989), p. 87. The Promontory Point photograph can be found in John Faragher et al., *Out of Many: A History of the American People,* brief ed., vol. 1 (Englewood Cliffs, N.J.: Prentice-Hall, 1995), p. 339.

2. Takaki notes that Chinese workers often had the most dangerous jobs (such as handling explosives) and were literally sacrificed for financial gain. Explosives not only maimed and killed Chinese but also triggered avalanches in the Sierra Nevada that buried workers alive. Since Chinese immigrants represented cheap, expendable labor, Central Pacific managers decided to blast tunnels during the winter rather than waiting until spring in order to capitalize on federal incentives measured by miles of track laid. Although they faced difficult odds, Chinese immigrants did fight for better wages and working conditions and engaged in resistance to better their material circumstances. See Takaki, pp. 84–87. For general background on the role of railroads in the West see Richard White, *It's Your Misfortune and None of Mine Own: A New History of the American West* (Norman: University of Oklahoma Press, 1991).

3. My observations about the study of American religion reflect my training as a U.S. historian whose primary entry into religious studies is through the field of American religious history.

4. See Charles H. Lippy and Peter W. Williams, *Encyclopedia of American Religious Experiences,* 3 vols. (New York: Scribner's, 1988), and Gordon Melton, *The Encyclopedia of American Religion,* 3rd ed. (Detroit: Gale Research, 1989).

5. Robert Orsi, "Forum: The Decade Ahead in Scholarship," *Religion and American Culture* 3 (Winter 1993):1–8. While Asian Americans are not specifically mentioned in Orsi's method, it seems clear that the study of Asian Americans can yield fresh insights about American religion.

6. Asian Americans have never been limited geographically to the American West, but it is there that they have predominantly settled.

7. Patricia Nelson Limerick et al., eds., *Trails: Toward a New Western History* (Lawrence: University Press of Kansas, 1991); Clyde A. Milner II, ed., *A New Significance: Re-Envisioning the History of the American West* (New York: Oxford University Press, 1996), especially the essay by Gail Nomura on Asian Americans. Turner's essay has been reprinted in Clyde A. Milner II et al., eds., *Major Problems in the History of the American West* (New York: Houghton Mifflin, 1989), pp. 2–21.

8. A number of essays in recent years have taken up the topic of religion in the American West. While providing helpful overviews of the lit-

erature, most authors have recognized the need for more research. See Laurie Maffly-Kipp, "Eastward Ho! American Religion from the Perspective of the Pacific Rim," in Thomas A. Tweed, ed., *Retelling U.S. Religious History* (Berkeley: University of California Press, 1997), pp. 127–148; Ferenc M. Szasz and Margaret Connell Szasz, "Religion and Spirituality," in Clyde Milner II et al., eds., *Oxford History of the American West* (New York: Oxford University Press, 1994), pp. 356–391; D. Michael Quinn, "Religion in the American West," in William Cronon et al., eds., *Under an Open Sky* (New York: Norton, 1992), pp. 145–166; Carl Guarneri and David Alvarez, eds., *Religion and Society in the American West* (Lanham, Md.: University Press of America, 1987).

9. Albert J. Raboteau, *A Fire in the Bones: Reflections on African American Religious History* (Boston: Beacon Press, 1995), p. 4.

10. Will Herberg, *Protestant-Catholic-Jew* (Garden City: Doubleday, 1955).

11. Quote taken from David Yoo, "Enlightened Identities: Buddhism and Japanese Americans of California, 1924–41," *Western Historical Quarterly* 27 (Autumn 1996):300. The roots of Japanese American Buddhism have been centered in the Pure Land sect. See Tetsuden Kashima, *Buddhism in America* (Westport, Conn.: Greenwood Press, 1977); Ryo Munekata, ed., *Buddhist Churches of America, 75 Year History, 1899–1974* (Chicago: Nobart, 1974); Shigeo Kanda, "Recovering Cultural Symbols: A Case for Buddhism in the Japanese American Communities," *Journal of the American Academy of Religion* 44 (December 1978):445–475. On the surveillance of Japanese Americans before the war see Bob Kumamoto, "The Search for Spies: American Counterintelligence and the Japanese American Community, 1931–42," *Amerasia Journal* 6 (1979):45–75.

12. Obviously not all non-Asian adherents of religious traditions based in Asia are motivated by the same concerns. My point is simply to highlight a process that has been happening in the United States for some time. See Victor Sogen Hori, "Sweet-and-Sour Buddhism," *Tricycle* (Fall 1994):48–63.

13. Two recent works include: Brian Hayashi, *"For the Sake of Our Japanese Brethren": Assimilation, Nationalism, and Protestantism Among the Japanese of Los Angeles, 1895–1942* (Stanford: Stanford University Press, 1995); Timothy Tseng, "Ministry at Arms' Length: Asian Americans in the Racial Ideology of Mainline American Protestants, 1882–1952" (Ph.D. diss., Union Theological Seminary, 1994).

14. The annual bibliography of *Amerasia Journal* testifies to the burgeoning literature. Also of interest are the journal's recent issues: "Thinking Theory," 21(1–2) (1995), and "No Passing Zone: The Asiatic and Discursive Voices of Asian-Descent Multiracials," 23(1) (1997). For

David K. Yoo

commentary on recent developments see Glenn Omatsu, "Asian American Studies and the Crisis of Practice," *Amerasia Journal* 20(3) (1994): 119–124.

15. Other works that have addressed Asian American religions include: Charles Prebish, *American Buddhism* (North Scituate, Mass.: Duxbury Press, 1979); E. Allen Richardson, *East Meets West: Asian Religions and Cultures in North America* (New York: Pilgrim Press, 1985); John Fenton, *Transplanting Religious Traditions: Asian Indians in America* (Westport, Conn.: Greenwood, 1988); Raymond Brady Williams, *Religions of Immigrants from India and Pakistan: New Threads in the American Tapestry* (Cambridge: Cambridge University Press, 1988).

16. For the argument that race is a central theme in the United States see Michael Omi and Howard Winant, *Racial Formations in the United States* (New York: Routledge, 1986). As Peter W. Williams points out, arguing for the integrity of religion stands apart from attesting to the ultimate validity of particular religious claims: *America's Religions: Traditions and Cultures* (New York: Macmillan, 1990), pp. vii–viii.

17. For a recent work on the subject see Jonathan Spence, *God's Chinese Son: The Taiping Heavenly Kingdom of Hong Xiuquan* (New York: Norton, 1986).

18. The role of Protestant Christianity and American missionaries in resistance to Japanese colonialism is not easy to decipher, but apparently some Koreans (and Korean Americans) did find in their religion a basis for their opposition to Japan.

19. Karen I. Leonard, *Making Ethnic Choices: California's Punjabi Mexican Americans* (Philadelphia: Temple University Press, 1992).

20. See Williams, *Religions of Immigrants*, pp. 3, 11–13, 24, and 31.

21. These ideas on the importance of narrative and religion have been influenced by my reading of Raboteau, *A Fire in the Bones*, pp. 2 and 6, and Tweed's introduction to *Retelling U.S. Religious History* pp. 2–3. Others have argued that religion itself has been subject to the same kind of neglect I have outlined for Asian Americans. See Bruce Kuklick and D. G. Hart, eds., *Religious Advocacy and American History* (Grand Rapids: Eerdmans, 1997).

22. Because of space limitations, only a portion of the references could be included in this bibliography. The complete listing, some fifty pages, is available on disk through the UCLA Asian American Studies Center.

PART I

Foundations

In this section of the book, four writers plumb the past and the present to probe how religious concerns have informed migration to the United States as well as a transnational consciousness among immigrants from China, the Philippines, India, and Taiwan. Although too late in periodization to deal with the events of Promontory Point, in Chapter 1 Timothy Tseng places Chinese Americans at the center of the frame in his case study of Christian nationalism among this population (1919–1923). Chinese American Christian leaders espoused views that contained seeds of revolution, but they also created an ideological structure with ties to Western imperialism, colonialism, and racism. How Chinese in the United States negotiated their religious convictions and sensibilities amid a pointedly anti-Western brand of nationalism makes for a compelling story. In Chapter 2, in roughly the same period, Steffi San Buenaventura's intriguing study of charismatic leader Hilario Camino Moncado and the Filipino Federation of America documents the transmission and transformation of folk spirituality as it made its way from the Philippines to California and Hawai'i and, eventually, back to its original source. San Buenaventura's cultural and religious history fills important gaps in Filipino American studies by highlighting aspects of the lives of laborers in the 1920s and 1930s. In Chapter 3, Vinay Lal's essay on a recent court decision involving a Sikh family in California raises issues of religion, law, and pluralism. The Cheema family's desire to have their children carry the kirpan *(small knife or dagger) for religious purposes provides Lal an opportunity not only to analyze the legal side of the story but to place the situation in a much broader context. Lal ties the Cheema case to the history of the Sikh religion in India and suggests how events in California may model a politics of diversity. In Chapter 4, the final essay of this section, Irene Lin writes about the Hsi Lai Buddhist Temple in Hacienda Heights, California, the largest Buddhist temple in the United States. Lin examines how a major religious institution and its vast range of religious activities and social services have helped its members to hold together multiple identities that involve religious, national, and transnational affiliation. More recently, the Hsi Lai Buddhist Temple has been part of the media reportage on Democratic Party fundraising.*

Chapter 1

Chinese Protestant Nationalism in the United States, 1880–1927

TIMOTHY TSENG

In a few of the oldest Chinese Protestant churches in the United States, recollections of the Chinese Republican era are preserved in congregational histories and the memories of their elder members.[1] As the revolutionary years recede into the past, the story of early-twentieth-century Chinese Protestants in America and their search for a republican and Christian China remains buried, neglected by religious historians and Asian Americanists alike. But if unearthed, their stories may shed some light on the history of the Chinese community in America. This exploratory probe into that history provides a glimpse of an era when Chinese Protestants were considered political radicals and social progressives. Indeed, years before the collapse of the Qing regime in 1911, and for many years afterward, Chinese Protestants were among the most outspoken supporters of Sun Yat-sen and revolutionary republicanism. Him Mark Lai has noted: "A few Chinese, mostly Christians who were more sympathetic towards Western concepts of representative government, supported his cause, but conservative Chinese in America were still unprepared to espouse his radical political solution for China, particularly since Sun was of plebeian origin and was outwardly so Westernized."[2]

Though never a significant proportion of the Chinese population anywhere, Chinese Protestants in the late nineteenth and early twentieth centuries were influential among the Chinese in American and in Chinese politics.[3] The three daughters of the American-educated Methodist missionary, publisher, and revolution financier Charlie Soong married Sun Yat-sen (Qingling), Chiang Kai-shek (Meiling, "a Wellesley college graduate of 1917, YWCA activist"), and industrialist and YMCA director H. H. Kong (Ailing). T. V. Soong, the most prominent of his sons, became the finance minister under Chiang.[4] Sun Yat-sen, himself a professing Christian, noted shortly after the overthrow of the Qing regime that it was "mostly from the church that I learned the truth of revolution. The establishment of the Republic today is due, not to my efforts, but to the service of the church."[5] In the United States, Chinese activists, many of whom were Christians, collaborated with Protestant clergy and lawyers to fight discriminatory practices and exclusionary immigration laws.[6] Presbyterian minister Ng Poon Chew (Wu Panzhao), founding editor of the *Chung Sai Yat Po* (China-West Daily), was one of the strongest advocates of Chinese republicanism and Chinese American civil rights. Ng and the *Chung Sai Yat Po* embodied Chinese Protestant participation in the politics of Chinese nationalism. From protesting Chinese exclusion in 1902 to the promotion of a liberal, multiparty democracy in China, Ng was a leading Chinese American voice. Through the *Chung Sai Yat Po* he denounced foot binding, polygamy, opium smoking, and queue wearing while advocating progressive reform in America's Chinatowns, education, modernization, and integration into American society.[7] Finally, notwithstanding their hierarchical racial ideology and condescending attitudes, white Protestant matriarchs of "rescue

Timothy Tseng

homes" were also, to some degree, sources of empowerment for many Chinese women in San Francisco. Hence the Protestant influence among Chinese women must be taken into account.[8] In retrospect, it is clear that these politically astute Chinese Protestants were greatly influenced by their religious outlook.

This study explores the ideology of Chinese Protestant nationalism in the United States between 1880 and 1927.[9] During the first twenty-two years of this period, Chinese immigrants were victims of brutal atrocities instigated by populist anti-Chinese movements.[10] But after 1902, when Chinese laborers were permanently banned from entry into the United States, the public perception of the Chinese slowly improved. China, after all, appeared to be modernizing while the Japanese "menace" now received greater attention. During these two periods, an iconoclastic religious nationalism emerged among Chinese Protestants in the Pacific diaspora and the Americas.[11]

Responding to the changing social and political circumstances in China and the United States, Chinese Protestant nationalism underwent two significant transformations over the years: a phase of evangelical piety and one of revolutionary politics. Prior to 1900, Chinese Protestants in the United States were, for the most part, apolitical with regard to China.[12] The sociopolitical climate in China was not yet open to critics and reformers such as Chinese Protestants. In the meantime, Chinese Protestants concentrated on proselytizing and strengthening their religious institutions in China. Yet beneath their evangelical rhetoric, revolutionary fervor lay dormant, ready to be awakened at the proper moment. That moment arrived in the mid-1890s. Following its defeat by Japan, China faced the possibility of partition by the European powers. Under these circumstances an intellectual and political ferment erupted and dramatically altered China's political climate. The doors now were open for reform and, perhaps, revolution. The previously quiescent Chinese Protestants in the United States were transformed into major political players in the reform efforts. In fact, soon the strongest proponents of replacing the Qing monarchy with a democratic, republican state were vocal Chinese Protestant leaders in southern China, the Pacific diaspora, and North America who financed and provided leadership for reform and revolution until the ascendancy of the Chinese Communists.

Before the May Fourth movement of 1919, Chinese religious nationalism drew from Western cultural, political, and religious sources for the sake of equality in the United States and national salvation overseas.[13] Chinese Protestants in America worked closely with white Protestants to battle racial discrimination and immigration exclusion and to advocate for the evangelization of China. Like their white coreligionists, Chinese Protestants were sharply critical of America's exclusionary immigration legislation.[14] Yet because they were convinced that America's democratic values, republican government, and modern lifestyle were outgrowths of Christian influence, they sought to guide twentieth-century China along a similar path. A Christian China that sat at the table of modern nation-states would earn the respect of Westerners and help end the inequities Chinese immigrants experienced in the United States. This form of nationalism was a significant precursor to the nationalism of the 1920s.[15]

During the May Fourth movement in China, a new form of antitradition, anti-imperialist, and antireligious nationalism appeared among many young Chinese intellectuals. Consequently, Chinese Protestants, now accused of being the "running dogs" of Western imperialism, were placed in an extremely vulnerable position. Their religious beliefs and accommodating nationalism were rejected as anachronisms that, like Confucianism, were deemed oppressive. Chinese Protestants were forced to choose between identifying themselves as anti-imperialist nationalists or as the lackeys of foreign oppression. Many left the faith. Those who remained underwent a second transformation. They became fiercely anti-imperialist and pressed for independent Chinese churches. These developments in China had a profound impact on Chinese Protestants in the diaspora. In San Francisco, this new form of Chinese Protestant nationalism erupted just as white Protestants began to consolidate their Chinatown missions and intensify their crusade against the Chinese tongs and prostitution rings. The origins of Chinese Protestant diversity, worldwide today, can be traced to the development of Chinese religious nationalism and its transformation in the late nineteenth and early twentieth centuries.

Evangelical Piety and the Leavening of Chinese Protestant Nationalism: 1880–1902

Few studies have addressed the nature and function of Christianity among non-European peoples. To view Christianity as essentially a European religion ignores the agency of non-European subjects who creatively appropriated the symbols of Christianity for their own social and political purposes. In discussing African American Christianity, for instance, Charles Joyner notes: "The slaves did not simply adopt the God and the faith of the white missionaries. In establishing a spiritual life for themselves, they reinterpreted the elements of Christianity in terms of deep-rooted African religious concerns." Thus he concludes: "The originality of African-American Christianity, then, lies neither in its African elements nor in its Christian elements, but in its unique and creative synthesis of both."[16] Similar dynamics lie behind the Chinese adaptation of Protestant Christianity for the purpose of creating a nationalist ideology.[17]

A better understanding of how religion shaped the social and political consciousness of Chinese Protestants and their leaders will provide a clearer picture of the character and development of Chinese Protestant nationalism. This is especially true prior to 1900 when political engagement was not a viable option. Despite the criticisms of anti-Christian Chinese nationalists in the 1920s, Protestant Christianity did not function as an "opiate" or a "denationalizing" ideology. Rather, it was a catalyst that propelled many Chinese onto the paths of social activism, Chinese nationalism, and revolutionary politics. One central function of religion is to provide a structured, meaningful, and persuasive worldview for people. Such an "ordered outlook" is mediated through symbols, rituals, and doctrines. Christianity introduced to Chinese Protestants "new symbolic resources" that enabled them to see "an alternative way of looking at the world and themselves."[18] For many Chinese immigrants in late-nineteenth-century America, Protestant Christianity provided the spiritual and emotional resources to cope with the disruptions caused by racism and social dislocation.

The evangelical rhetoric of lost souls—mired in sin and darkness and in desperate and immediate need of Jesus Christ's redemptive power—introduced an outlook that enabled converts to look anew at their own spiritual condition as well as that of their fellow Chinese. The speech of Fung Chak, a missionary on the Pacific coast in the 1880s and 1890s, appealed to the religious sensibilities of his hearers at the 1882 annual meeting of the American Baptist Home Missions Society, but it also revealed a quasi-nationalistic concern for the Chinese: "The Chinese must not be wholly left without the Gospel. Whatever may be, do not think of helping the Chinese less. Think of thousands of souls without the Gospel, without one voice to warn them from the vortexes that yawn on every side to engulf them, and drag them down to endless ruin."[19] For most Christians, a religious message that succored the individual's thirst for spiritual uplift and salvation sufficed. While the same can be said of most Chinese Protestants, they also exhibited an almost obsessive concern for their fellow Chinese and China. This protonationalistic concern was crystalized by an evangelical rhetoric that continues to sustain many Chinese churches today. In a time of painful social upheaval in China—and brutalities against Chinese immigrants in the western United States—Protestant Christianity provided for many Chinese people a new outlook and hope for personal and national salvation.

This appeal is seen clearly in the pages of *The American Missionary,* one of the few nineteenth-century missionary periodicals to reproduce the sermons and letters of Chinese Protestants. Owing to its abolitionist commitments, evangelical fervor, and the insistence of the Reverend William C. Pond (1830–1925), a missionary to the Chinese in San Francisco, Chinese Protestant voices, though circumscribed by the periodical's evangelical outlook, were heard by supporters of the Congregational American Missionary Association (AMA).[20] The AMA missions to the Chinese in California focused on English education classes in order to avoid competing with Presbyterian efforts to build churches. In the long run, such an arrangement benefited the Presbyterians, whose missions eventually developed into established Chinese congregations. Nevertheless, this approach freed AMA resources to organize educational programs all over the Bay Area, a strategy that proved most useful to the transient young Chinese men who needed a quick introduction to the English language and American society.[21] Pond's articles and reports for *The American Missionary* were replete with his Chinese assistants' letters and sermons as well as his own sympathetic observations and opinions about the Chinese and the political affairs affecting them. In early 1880, Pond reported that a convert, Chin Fung, had said to him, "I have wished very much that I could be prepared to go as a missionary to my countrymen at home." At first Pond did not realize how "deep that feeling was," but Chin Fung demonstrated his intentions to receive missionary training by saving his money, despite the "slender earnings of his work as a houseservant" and disregarding his family's request that he return to China to be married. Pond admitted that Chin Fung was an exception, but he remarked that expressions of the desire to become missionaries to their fellow Chinese "were frequent among our brethren, and I never have doubted their sincerity."[22]

Even more telling was a sermon by Jee Gam (Chu Jin) published in the October 1880 number of *The American Missionary*. Arriving in San Francisco in 1863, Jee Gam converted seven years later and became William Pond's most versatile and articulate "helper."[23] Expounding on the epistle to the Hebrews 10:38, Jee Gam exhorted his listeners to "get faith." By faith, Moses rejected the wealth and idolatry of Egypt, Daniel performed an act of civil disobedience, and Martin Luther broke with the Roman Catholic church. The rejection of the world and sin was the first step to acquiring saving faith. But Christian faith was not limited to certain people. Everyone could have this faith, "be he white, black, red, or yellow. . . . The beggar can have it as well as the king. The poor can have it as well as the rich; and the negro, the Indian and the Chinaman." Having argued for the universality of Christianity and its relevance for Chinese people, Jee Gam then linked his desire to Christianize China to its potential global status: "And by faith I venture to say right here that China will, before long, become a Christian country, and rank high when compared with all her sister nations."[24]

Accompanying this quest for a Christian China was a powerful iconoclasm, as seen in Jee Gam's earlier call to reject evil.[25] But this iconoclasm suggests a concern for, not a rejection of, China. While many white Protestants sought the destruction of traditional Chinese religions in order to reshape the Chinese Protestants in their own images,[26] Chinese Protestants advocated the destruction of idols for the sake of China's future. In one of the AMA schools, a classroom debate ensued about whether Christianity ought to be brought to China. An antagonist found biblical support (Matthew 9:17) for rejecting Christianity: "China . . . is an old bottle, very old; you must not put this new doctrine into it; it will burst." Hong Sing, a Christian student, offered this rebuttal: "It is not China that is old and weak, but our hea- then customs of worshipping ancestors and buying luck at the shrine of Joss, etc., etc. Put the doctrine of Christ into these and it will burst them certainly; but put it into China, and it will make her stronger and fairer than ever."[27] On another occasion, Pond published a letter from Fong Get Loy, who had returned to China for a visit and found himself in a heated argument with his family. When he refused to vener- ate his ancestors and insisted on removing the family idols, his family warned him, "You no worship idol, by and by you have no house, no children, no money." In response, Fong pointed out that "other nations that not worship idols have more money and better houses than any we have in China. . . . We do not have to worship idols to get money."[28] He then proceeded to rid his household of traditional Chinese religious practices.

The iconoclastic rejection of traditional religion among many Chinese Protestants was lauded by white Protestants, who highlighted numerous episodes similar to Fong Get Loy's story in order to refute the charge that Chinese converts were "rice Christians." It is not likely that Chinese Protestants separated themselves from their non-Christian peers as dra- matically as white Protestants imagined. Nevertheless, there were conflicts between converts and traditional values. Pres- byterian minister Huie Kin (Xu Qin), recalling the difficulty of reconciling Confucianism with Christianity, noted that "we were torn between appeals for our loyalty to the Word of God on the one side and on the other to the age-old wis- dom of our national sage."[29] Often converts had to choose between their newfound faith and the happiness of their non-

Christian family.[30] Occasionally tensions between Chinese Protestants and the Six Companies did erupt. On 14 August 1881, the Six Companies posted a placard at the location in Sacramento's Chinatown where Lem Chung usually conducted street preaching. Accusing the preacher of avarice, the Six Companies warned the Chinese to stay away from this "new false religion." After dismissing Christian claims about Jesus, an edict was issued:

> Notice is hereby given that such of the Chinese people as have been converted to Christianity must not follow that way any more. Moreover, this religion must not be preached any more on the street, and if any shall do so they shall be arrested by the Six Companies and punished for preaching false doctrines and deceiving the people. They shall be given eighty lashes, and then dragged to the grave-yard and buried alive; their bones shall not be taken back to China, but shall remain foreign ghosts forever; and then they can believe in Jesus all they are a mind to. Whosoever shall dare to take this white notice down shall be the son of no father.[31]

Lem Chung removed the poster and the warning turned out to be an empty threat. Nevertheless, such incidents indicate the tensions between Protestants and traditionalists in the Chinese communities. The presence of Chinese Protestants pointedly revealed a growing religious diversity within Chinatowns in America. Later, as more families converted, Chinese Protestants would create their own subculture and a distinct ethnoreligious identity. Eventually, Chinese Protestants would represent one of several "public spheres" in larger communities such as San Francisco's Chinatown. As such they were able to mediate between the white and the non-Christian Chinese communities and between traditionalist and modernist advocates. This helped set the stage for the elevation of a few Chinese Protestant leaders to prominence in the

United States and in China in the early twentieth century.[32] In the United States, white Americans respected Protestant Chinese more than the "heathen Chinee." In China, as reform and revolution advocates gained strength, doors were opened to Western-educated Chinese Protestants.

Beyond the pages of *The American Missionary,* the evangelical rhetoric of iconoclastic religious nationalism could also be found among most other Chinese Protestants before the turn of the century. In Fung Chak's 1882 report to the American Baptist Home Mission Society, he proclaimed that in the midst of all the "turmoil and strife raised by the 'Chinese Question,' there is being laid foundation work in the minds of the Chinese population." In the near future, he predicted, this work "is going to revolutionize and shake from circumference to centre the hoary Empire from which they come; and if we Baptists want to plant a pure Gospel all over that then rejuvenated Empire, *Now* and *Here* is the time and place to begin the work."[33] Fung Chak's vision for revolutionary change in China was premature.[34] Political circumstances there were not yet ripe for reform or modernization.

In the meantime, Fung Chak's Protestant peers focused on evangelizing Chinese immigrants and strengthening the Christian movement in China. Once again the focus was on China, not the United States. The Baptist mission in Portland, for instance, supported a Chinese missionary to China as early as 1881.[35] That same year, the Chinese affiliated with William Pond's California Chinese Mission requested that the AMA organize a Congregational mission station and seminary in Hong Kong so that converts who returned to China "would be made firmer in faith, and more earnest in leading others to Christ." The Chinese themselves pledged to provide most of the financial support for this mission.[36] Although the AMA followed their policy of confining their missions to the United States, Congregationalist Chinese were delighted to learn that the American Board of Commissioners for Foreign Missions (ABCFM) agreed to cosponsor the mission in Hong Kong.[37] According to Wesley Woo, most Chinese Protestants were poor.[38] Yet their eagerness to support mission work in China, often at the expense of their own missions in the United States, gave the impression that Chinese Protestants did not want to mature into self-sufficiency. "I sometimes think that we do not get enough from the Chinamen themselves," one Presbyterian executive complained.[39] Given their limited financial resources, U.S. statutes prohibiting their immigration and naturalization, and an emerging nationalist consciousness, one can understand why Chinese Protestants felt a stronger obligation to "take care of churches in China."[40]

Progressive Protestantism and Revolutionary Politics: 1900–1919

The evangelical rhetoric and practices of nineteenth-century Chinese Protestants had a leavening effect on their political consciousness. By the turn of the century, Chinese Protestants carried the banner of progressive political and social activism in America's Chinatowns.[41] During the first two decades of the twentieth century, Chinese Protestants played a significant role in persuading Chinese Americans to opt for a republican government for China.[42] Protestant attempts to depose the Qing regime can be traced back to Sun Yat-sen's efforts to create the Hsing-ching Hui (Revive China Society), a revolutionary party in Hawai'i in 1894. Supporters of Sun argued that Chinese culture itself had to be renewed by Christianity and modernization if China was to join the family of modern nation-states. When his Canton coup failed a year later, Sun's stature diminished for several years.[43] But by the turn of the century, the fortunes of the revolutionaries would change.

The closing years of the nineteenth century were marked

by serious setbacks for China and the Qing rulers. Humiliated in the Sino-Japanese War, many Chinese leaders became convinced that social and political reforms appropriating Western sources were needed for national survival. Kang Yu-wei, one of the leaders of the reform movement in Beijing, sought to employ the Japanese model of adapting Western technology while retaining Confucian philosophy. Though he had the support of the young emperor early in his reform efforts, when the emperor's mother, the conservative empress dowager, seized the reins of the imperial government, Kang was exiled and several of the reformers were executed in 1898. Kang then traveled throughout the Chinese diaspora and organized the Pao-huang Hui (Protect the Emperor Society). Eventually this party supported constitutional monarchy and grew in prestige when the empress dowager conceded certain reforms in 1905.[44]

In the United States, the Geary Act of 1892 and China's defeat had important repercussions for the Chinese communities. The general discontent with the Qing regime and the failure of the Six Companies to defeat the Geary Act led to increasing friction between different factions in the Chinese communities. The decline of the Six Companies left a vacuum to be filled by a plethora of reform organizations who sought to modernize China and end anti-Chinese discrimination in the United States. The circumstances were now ripe for Chinese Protestants to enter the political arena.

As Chinese Protestants entered the fray, they continued their evangelical rhetoric of criticizing a backward, pagan China but now linked Christianity to modernization, democratization, and republicanism. This progressive political ideology proved useful for Protestant political activists, who were convinced that the drama of Christian redemption had undeniable social and political implications. "The immediate aim of our effort is the salvation of souls by the preaching of the Gospel," Huie Kin remarked in 1917. "The ultimate aim is the redemption of China through the earnestness of our converted young men when they return to the homeland." After the May Fourth movement, he still maintained that "more young Christian leadership in China is needed. It is the only sort of leadership for the salvation of the Republic, as is being realized more and more by the Chinese themselves."[45]

Led by Ng Poon Chew, Chinese Protestant forays into Chinese politics became visible when the *Chung Sai Yat Po* declared itself a pro–Pao-huang Hui newspaper in 1900. Apparently Kang Yu-wei had agreed to drop the language of Confucian veneration in the founding constitution of the Pao-huang Hui. While most of the Chinese were content with the merchant-dominated Pao-huang Hui, Protestants, partially owing to their iconoclastic outlook, gradually turned pro-revolution.[46] In 1904, Ng Poon Chew and the *Chung Sai Yat Po* broke with the Pao-huang Hui and tipped the scales toward the resurgent revolutionary politics of Sun Yat-sen.[47] From this point on, Chinese churches in America became safe havens where Sun could rest, promote revolution, and raise money.[48]

After the *Chung Sai Yat Po*'s break with the Pao-huang Hui, the voices of revolutionary Protestants intensified. Fung Yuet Mow, pastor of the Chinese Baptist mission in New York's Chinatown, now proclaimed: "All China is looking for change and desirous of adopting Western education and of reforming China as Japan did."[49] In the 4 September 1908 issue of the *Chung Sai Yat Po* the editor (presumably Ng Poon Chew) ostensibly celebrated the newly rebuilt Chinese Baptist mission in San Francisco but in fact argued that republican governments were based on Christianity. First, the editorial defended Christianity as a universal religion that has "no race distinction, yellow and white alike; no national distinction, Americans and Chinese are alike all disciples of Jesus Christ." But it also advanced the idea of a republican government for China:

Timothy Tseng

The Christian teaching brings the idea of a republican form of government such as we find in the United States and in some parts of Europe. . . . The people make their own laws. Both high and low have common rights. . . . The Chinese wish very much that they had the republican form of government today, but they have not learned and do not understand it, so how can we legislate laws? . . . Are we going to continue to have a monarchy? Monarchies will never bring prosperity and freedom.[50]

The editor praised the self-sacrifice of white missionary teachers, particularly those who worked at the Baptist mission, but criticized the Chinese inability to provide a progressive education for their own children. "Oh, my countrymen," he exclaimed, "are you not aware that without education you will be ignorant and cannot be prosperous?"[51] This rhetorical strategy of measuring everything by Christian convictions of a universal and equitable brotherhood in Christ—hence his praise of dedicated white Christians—was used to prod apathetic or conservative Chinese toward a revolutionary stance, to gain the support of white Protestants, and to offer a subtle Christian apologetic.[52] No self-denigration appears among any of the statements of Chinese Protestants of this period. Rather, Chinese Protestants were remarkably similar to the leaders of the May Fourth movement a decade later. They too "opposed Chinese culture out of love for the Chinese nation."[53]

The Republican Revolution in 1911 triggered a momentary euphoria among Chinese and American Protestants. Martha Ames, veteran missionary in San Francisco's First Chinese Baptist Church, observed how Chinese Protestants of all denominations gathered one afternoon "to pray for the prosperity of China and the advancement of the gospel there" prior to a large community celebration for the new republic. "Idolatry . . . is passing away . . . the prejudice against Christianity is to a large extent gone," she exclaims, and "the Chinese wish to be as much like Americans as possible."[54] Ames's assertions were undoubtedly exaggerations. But between the revolution and the May Fourth movement, not much is known about the views of Chinese Protestants in America. The generation to which Jade Snow Wong's father belonged slowly disappeared from the purview of mainline Protestants, who were now less interested in the Chinese revolution or that generation of Chinese Protestants.[55]

In the meantime, reports of Donaldina Cameron's exploits against Chinese tongs and prostitution rings in San Francisco gained much public notoriety. Women missionaries who taught in the many mission schools and developed community service centers for the Chinese children began to speak in terms of the Americanization of the second-generation Chinese.[56] The first generation appeared hopelessly unable and unwilling to assimilate, but their American-born children were a different story. White Protestants now believed that the Chinese missions needed to move in a different direction. Christian education and religious programs were now to be used to "Americanize" the second-generation Chinese.[57] Meanwhile, looming in the background, East Coast Protestant leaders studied the Chinese situation in the United States, particularly in San Francisco, and prepared to consolidate the missions and crusade against the tongs.[58]

An Angry Resurgence: Chinese Protestants in the 1920s

The failure of the Treaty of Versailles to dismantle Western and Japanese imperialism in 1919 triggered a new iconoclastic Chinese nationalism in the May Fourth movement. This cultural movement, led by young intellectuals, gave birth to a renewed hope for a modern China based on Western (that is, modern) scientific principles rather than superstitious religions and traditions such as Christianity or Confucianism.[59] Disillusioned by Confucian culture and frustrated by Western

Timothy Tseng

imperialism, its leaders soon became hostile toward Christianity. During the 1920s, Chinese Protestants struggled, on the one hand, to justify their relevance to China and, on the other, sought to gain control of the religious institutions run by Western Christian missions.[60]

Infected by the winds of change in China, the Chinese diaspora, including the American Chinatowns, became increasingly polarized along the same lines that divided the May Fourth movement into Marxist and liberal camps.[61] It is not yet clear how the May Fourth movement and its subsequent cleavage affected Chinese Protestants in the United States. White Protestants were accentuating the divisions between the first and second generation as evidence of the Americanization of the American-born.[62] But among the first-generation Chinese Protestants, it appears that the earlier nationalism was yielding a new variety that was critical of white Protestants.

A few missionary comments about the Chinese community in the 1920s hint at a growing hostility toward America and Christianity. This animosity can be detected by comparing the observations of white women missionaries from two generations. In 1898 Florence Ford, a missionary at the Chinese Baptist mission school in San Francisco, noted that many of the Chinese "are coming to see the superiority of American customs in many things." Yet she hoped that "through the Holy Spirit they may be able to discern that it is the Christ in our civilization that makes our way better than theirs in whatever respects they are better."[63] Her Chinese Protestant contemporaries would probably have agreed. By 1926, however, the women missionaries in the same mission school now exclaimed: "If only in [the Chinese people's] minds we could separate Christ from American!"[64] Identifying Christianity too closely with things American was now perceived to be a stumbling block for evangelism.

A year later, with the Guomindong's ascendancy in the

backdrop, Charles R. Shepherd, superintendent of the Chinese Baptist missions on the West Coast, commented on the hostility against Christianity: "The Chinese in the United States have naturally become interested in the affairs in China to the point of absorption and obsession. . . . With the exception of a small minority, their attitude toward Christianity ranges from cold, placid indifference to aggressive hatred and opposition. Their objection and animosity is not to Christianity per se, but as practised by so-called Christian nations."[65] This was an accurate assessment. Over the years, Protestants and non-Protestant Chinese have continuously made white Protestants aware of the discriminatory treatment received at the hands of white Americans.[66] For Chinese Protestants in the 1920s, however, Christ remained central for China's national salvation. In 1925, Dr. Mabel Lee of the Chinese Baptist mission in New York City was still able to declare that "Christianity is the salvation of China" despite being "deeply wronged by various governments."[67] What had changed for Chinese Protestants was a decisive rejection of the earlier desires to emulate the Euro-American model. Thus one young Chinese Protestant declared to his missionary teacher: "China must have Christianity, but it must be its own Christianity, not what some one else thinks."[68]

The most direct consequence of this development was an independence movement among Chinese churches in China and America that intensified conflicts with white Protestants.[69] Most independent (or indigenous) Chinese churches had their origins in the May Fourth period.[70] Driven by an "incipient" Chinese nationalism and a fundamentalist reaction against Protestant liberalism, indigenous churches, usually led by charismatic leaders, disavowed any affiliation with Protestant denominations.[71] Because most Chinese missions in the United States depended on the support of mainline Protestant denominations, conflicts between white Protestants and Chinese Protestants, influenced by the indigenous movement in China and anti-Western nationalism, were bound to erupt.[72]

Between 1920 and 1923, white Protestants attempted to consolidate the Chinese missions in the United States, in particular, San Francisco. In 1919, however, after noting a decline in the Chinese population, an alarming level of denominational competition, and much administrative inefficiency, mission society executives and missionaries determined to reorganize the Chinatown missions. Rather than perpetuating the seventeen separate and overlapping religious and community service agencies in San Francisco's Chinatown, they decided to unite their missionary work. This way, it was hoped, the Chinese would more quickly become self-supporting.[73] Their heavy-handed approach, however, alienated the now independent-minded Chinese.[74] In the end, Chinese resistance made it impossible for white Protestants to accomplish their goals in San Francisco, though amalgamation succeeded in cities with smaller Chinese populations.[75] Later, white Protestant leaders would blame the "antichurch" movement in China for the failure. "Self-support has been set back from ten to twenty years because of the antichurch feeling abroad which is reflected in this country," they noted.[76] Also blamed was the growing independent and antidenominational spirit of the Chinese churches.

Conclusion: Toward Chinese Protestantism

In the 1920s, Chinese Protestant nationalism in the United States broke from its earlier critical view of China and expressed more vocal dissatisfaction with white Protestant control of Chinese religious organizations in China and the United States. White mainstream Protestants, taken aback by this sudden rebellion, also experienced a transformation of outlook. By the end of the decade, cultural relativism and "modernist" theology had become predominant among the younger generation.[77] Younger Protestants no longer viewed Chinese culture as an idolatrous or heathen relic to be destroyed.[78] Chinese Protestants began to view their own culture more favorably, as well, though the fundamentalists among them continued to retain a "dualistic system" with the capacity to critique either culture, Chinese or American.[79]

These changes warmed relations between Chinese and white Protestants in the 1930s. Chiang Kai-shek's conversion to Methodism in 1930 also helped. As relations between China and the United States grew friendlier in the 1930s, Chinese hostility dissipated and once again Chinese nationalism converged with a positive view of the United States. But among older Chinese Protestants in the United States, being Chinese no longer meant denigrating one's own culture, for they were convinced that China was now on the road to modernization.[80] In 1932, Huie Kin, now retired, expressed great pride in modern China: "In spite of her present sorrows and difficulties . . . my faith in China's future remains unshaken." He continued:

> Since the opening of the Century, which marked the birth of the modern era in our country, I see China marching steadily forward in the fundamental things which pertain to a nation's real greatness, education, agricultural and economic improvement, communications, public health, municipal reform, growing strength of public opinion through an enlightened press, and the new national life symbolized in the Nanking Government.[81]

The transformation of Chinese Protestant nationalism in the United States accompanied the emergence of a modern China. Shaping and responding to the political and social changes in China and America, Chinese Protestants worked with, and sometimes against, white Protestants toward nationalistic ends. In the shadow of Chinese exclusion and segregation in America, Chinese Protestants creatively appropriated

Timothy Tseng

the symbols of Christian faith in order to cope with the terrors of physical and social dislocation and gradually established a new sense of identity. As a result, they created space for themselves to develop a Chinese Protestant church without yielding to pressures either to Americanize or to conform to traditional Chinese culture.[82]

Notes

1. I intentionally use the term "Protestant" as opposed to "Christian" in order to distinguish the Chinese Protestants from their Roman Catholic coreligionists.

2. Him Mark Lai, "The Kuomingtang in Chinese American Communities Before World War II," in Sucheng Chan, ed., *Entry Denied: Exclusion and the Chinese Community in America* (Philadelphia: Temple University Press, 1991), p. 174. See especially L. Eve Armentrout Ma, *Revolutionaries, Monarchists, and Chinatowns: Chinese Politics in the Americas and the 1911 Revolution* (Honolulu: University of Hawai'i Press, 1990), who gives more detailed coverage of Chinese Protestant involvement via the daily newspaper *Chung Sai Yat Po*.

3. In 1900 the Presbyterian missionary Ira Condit estimated that 1,600 out of the 100,000 Chinese in the United States were Protestants. (Some 4,000 Chinese had been baptized since Protestant mission work started in 1851.) By 1910, of the 71,531 Chinese in the United States, 6,500 were Protestants. An exhaustive survey conducted in 1920 revealed sixty-seven Chinese churches or missions and 3,072 members, reflecting a population decline. By 1923, owing to unions and mergers, there were now forty-one Chinese Protestant churches and missions. By 1930, thirty-eight Chinese churches and missions were reported by only fourteen denominations. Presbyterians and Methodists alone (representing twenty-six of the churches and missions) reported 1,589 members. One can surmise that several independent Chinese churches were not included. Sources: Wesley Woo, "Chinese Protestants in the San Francisco Bay Area," in *Entry Denied*, p. 217; Ida Condit, *The Chinaman as We See Him and Fifty Years of Work for Him* (Chicago: Revell, 1900), p. 233; George W. Hinman, ed., *Directory of Oriental Missions* (New York: Home Missions Council and Council of Women for Home Missions, 1921), p. 16; J. S. Tow, *The Real Chinese in America* (New York: Academy Press, 1923), p. 112; William M. Gilbert, "Report on Mission Work Among Orientals in the United States," in *Databook (vol. I) for the Use*

of Delegates to the North American Home Missions Congress to Be Held in Calvary Baptist Church, Washington, D.C., Dec. 1–5, 1930 (New York: Home Missions Council and Council of Women for Home Missions, 1931), pp. 135–136.

4. Jonathan D. Spence, *The Search for Modern China* (New York: Norton, 1990), pp. 228, 297, and 363. Like many Chinese Protestants, the Soongs became conservative in the 1920s and 1930s.

5. Sun Yat-sen, *Tsung-Li ch'üan-shu* (Complete works of the president), 12 vols. (Taipei: Central Committee of the Kuomintang, 1956), 7A: 144; translated by Chester C. Tan in his *Chinese Political Thought in the Twentieth Century* (Newton Abbot: David & Charles, 1971), p. 150; quoted in Wing-Hung Lam, *Chinese Theology in Construction* (Pasadena: William Carey Library, 1983), p. 148.

6. Charles McClain shows how the Chinese worked with Methodist missionary Otis Gibson and Presbyterian missionaries William Speer and Augustus W. Loomis in their struggle against discriminatory legislation. See *In Search of Equality: The Chinese Struggle Against Discrimination in Nineteenth-Century America* (Berkeley: University of California Press, 1994), pp. 19–20, 23–24, 49, 51, and 63–64. See also Timothy Tseng, "Ministry at Arms' Length: Asian Americans in the Racial Ideology of American Mainline Protestantism, 1882–1952" (Ph.D. dissertation, Union Theological Seminary, 1994), pp. 44–46 and 186–214.

7. Ordained in 1896 as a minister at the Chinese Presbyterian mission in Los Angeles, Ng would leave the ministry in 1900 to start the *Chung Sai Yat Po* in San Francisco. The previous year he lost his clothing and furniture in a fire, leaving him and his family next to destitute. Despite financial help from Christians in Los Angeles, this event coincided with a Presbyterian Board of Foreign Missions' decision to stop supporting Chinese missions outside of San Francisco that year. Because the Los Angeles presbytery was unable to provide an adequate salary on its own for Rev. Ng, he resigned to start the Christian newspaper. White Presbyterians were delighted that six-sevenths of the stockowners were Christians and that the paper did not publish on Sundays. In San Francisco, however, he continued to volunteer his services in the Chinese Presbyterian church as a teacher of an infant Sunday school class and church organist. That church helped fund his 1901 national tour opposing Chinese exclusion and discrimination. Sources: *1896 Annual Report of the Board of Foreign Missions of the Presbyterian Church in the United States of America* [henceforth *BFM 1896 AR*], p. 251; *BFM 1899 AR*, p. 281; *BFM 1900 AR*, p. 280; *BFM 1901 AR*, p. 323; *BFM 1902 AR*, p. 310; Woo, "Chinese Protestants in the San Francisco Bay Area," pp. 235 and 237–238; Shih-shan Henry Tsai, *The Chinese Experience in America*

(Bloomington: University of Indiana Press, 1986), pp. 129–130; Corrinne K. Hoexter, *From Canton to California: The Epic of Chinese Immigration* (New York: Four Winds Press, 1976).

8. Peggy Pascoe, *Relations of Rescue: The Search for Female Moral Authority in the American West, 1874–1939* (New York: Oxford University Press, 1990); Judy Yung, *Unbound Feet: A Social History of Chinese Women in San Francisco* (Berkeley: University of California Press, 1995); Judy Yung, "Unbinding the Feet, Unbinding Their Lives: Chinese Immigrant Women in San Francisco, 1902–1913," in Shirley Hune et al., eds., *Asian Americans: Comparative and Global Perspectives* (Pullman: Washington State University Press, 1991), pp. 69–85; and Judy Yung, "The Social Awakening of Chinese American Women as Reported in *Chung Sai Yat Po*, 1900–1911," in *Chinese America: History and Perspective, 1988* (San Francisco: Chinese Historical Society of America, 1988), pp. 80–102.

9. The paucity of sources in Chinese or English makes historical investigation of Chinese American Christianity a difficult task. Hence this chapter is based largely on a critical reading of the subtexts of white Protestant observations of the Chinese and the Chinese Protestant voices that were permitted to be heard. As new sources are recovered and as oral histories and ethnographic studies are developed, the study of Chinese American Christianity and Asian Pacific American religions will deepen our insights into the religious experiences of Asian and Pacific Islander Americans. Some efforts have already been initiated: Wesley Woo, "Chinese Protestants in the San Francisco Bay Area," pp. 213–245, and "Protestant Work Among the Chinese in the San Francisco Bay Area, 1850–1920" (Ph.D. diss., Graduate Theological Union, 1983); Wilbur W. Y. Choy, "Strangers Called to Mission: History of Chinese American United Methodist Churches," in Artermio R. Guillermo, ed., *Churches Aflame: Asian Americans and United Methodism* (Nashville: Abingdon Press, 1991), pp. 65–90; Barbara B. Zikmund, "Chinese Congregationalism," in *Hidden Histories in the United Church of Christ,* vol. 2 (New York: United Church Press, 1987), pp. 168–188; Diane Mei Lin Mark, *Seasons of Light: The History of Chinese Christian Churches in Hawaii* (Honolulu: Chinese Christian Association of Hawai'i, 1989).

10. See Elmer C. Sandmeyer, *The Anti-Chinese Movement in California* (Urbana: University of Illinois Press, 1991).

11. Because Chinese were not permitted to immigrate or naturalize whereas their white missionary contacts frequently traveled between China and the United States, the assumption that the Chinese missions were "Americanizing" institutions must be questioned. Although their "Americanizing" function was what white missionaries hoped for during

this period, in reality the missions should be seen as transnational centers for an emerging international Chinese Protestant community.

12. In their struggling against discrimination in the United States, however, the Chinese community can hardly be described as apolitical. See McClain, *In Search of Equality.*

13. Stevan Harrell argues that the Christian "civilizing project" in nineteenth-century China led to a hostile backlash by proponents of the Confucian "project." But for groups on the periphery of Chinese society, the religion of the "civilizers" was adopted to renew or create a new ethnic identity. Christian converts were also given voice, but within the acceptable framework of Western missionaries. I argue that Chinese Protestant nationalism is a variant of this process of ethnogenesis and vocality. See Stevan Harrell, "Civilizing Projects and the Reactions to Them," in Stevan Harrell, ed., *Cultural Encounters on China's Ethnic Frontiers* (Seattle: University of Washington Press, 1995), pp. 3–36; and Nicole Constable, *Christian Souls and Chinese Spirits: A Hakka Community in Hong Kong* (Berkeley: University of California Press, 1994). For discussions about the civilizing project of white American Protestants see William R. Hutchison, "A Moral Equivalent for Imperialism: Americans and the Promoters of 'Christian Civilization,' 1880–1910," in Torben Christensen and William R. Hutchison, eds., *Missionary Ideologies in the Imperialist Era: 1880–1920* (n.p.: Aros, 1982), pp. 167–177; and William R. Hutchison, *Errand to the World: American Protestant Thought and Foreign Missions* (Chicago: University of Chicago Press, 1987).

14. The article of Congregationalist minister Jee Gam in *The American Missionary,* an organ for the American Missionary Association, illustrates this point well. See "Chinese Exclusion, From the Standpoint of a Chinese Christian," *American Missionary [AM]* 56(2) (February 1902): 99–108; Tseng, "Ministry at Arms' Length," pp. 186–225.

15. The political discourse and activities of the Chinese Hand Laundry Alliance of New York are described by Renqui Yu, *To Save China, To Save Ourselves: The Chinese Hand Laundry Alliance of New York* (Philadelphia: Temple University Press, 1992). Evelyn Brooks Higginbotham's notion of the "politics of respectability" as a way of resolving W. E. B. DuBois' description of the African-American experience of "double-consciousness" is helpful here. See *Righteous Discontent: The Women's Movement in the Black Baptist Church, 1880–1920* (Cambridge, Mass.: Harvard University Press, 1993).

16. Charles Joyner, " 'Believer I Know': The Emergence of African-American Christianity," in Paul E. Johnson, ed., *African American Christianity: Essays in History* (Berkeley: University of California Press, 1994), p. 37.

Timothy Tseng

17. In her study of a contemporary Hakka Christian community in Hong Kong, Nicole Constable argues that the Hakka Christians were not syncretistic. Rather, they remained staunchly orthodox in their Christian beliefs by secularizing and relativizing Chinese traditional religions: "Christian practices are maintained as strictly orthodox, and Chinese practices and festivals that have not been reinterpreted as secular are criticized, avoided, or deemed of little concern." As a result, a "dual system of belief" and a new ethnoreligious identity is created. Similar dynamics appear frequently among the Chinese Protestants in this study. See Constable, *Christian Souls and Chinese Spirits*, pp. 98–99.

18. Pui-Lan Kwok adds that "in the process of adaptation to the Chinese context Christian symbolism was feminized in order to increase its appeal to both Chinese men and women." See *Chinese Women and Christianity, 1860–1927* (Atlanta: Scholars Press, 1992), p. 187; Clifford Geertz, "Religion as a Cultural System," in *The Interpretation of Culture* (New York: Basic Books, 1973), pp. 87–125.

19. *Baptist Home Missions in North America 1832–1882* (New York: Baptist Home Mission Room, 1883), pp. 98–99.

20. The American Missionary Association, organized in 1846 to protest the reluctance of the American Board of Commissioners for Foreign Missions to ban slaveowners from the mission field, became one of the most vocal abolitionist religious agencies in America. During Reconstruction it became prominent for its efforts in educational missions among freedmen. See James McPherson, *The Abolitionist Legacy: From Reconstruction to the NAACP* (Princeton: Princeton University Press, 1975); see also *History of the American Missionary Association* (New York: American Missionary Association, 1891).

21. See Zikmund, "Chinese Congregationalism," and Woo, "Protestant Work Among the Chinese."

22. William C. Pond, "The Santa Barbara Mission—Chin Fung," *AM* 34(1) (January 1880):24.

23. Jee Gam and Pond worked together for forty years. Both retired in 1910. That same year, Jee Gam died on route to China. A biography of Jee Gam can be found in Woo, "Chinese Protestants in San Francisco," pp. 222–223.

24. "Sermon by Jee Gam," *AM* 34(10) (October 1880):311.

25. Destroying idols (as Sun Yat-sen is reported to have done upon his conversion) was common and statements like these were widespread: "Our people [the Chinese] are in very darkness indeed, worshipping idols" (*AM* 34(3) (March 1880):85); "I am obliged to leave the idols and come to worship the true God. . . . The people of China are great superstitious" (*AM* 35(7) (July 1881):214).

26. Protestants disagreed on this point. In 1904, noting the ambiguity of Chinese assimilation, one writes: "The Chinese do not readily assimilate; perhaps never would in a measure. But for all that they may make excellent citizens of the [U.S.] Republic. They possess qualities and aptitudes and capacities for service which America needs." See *Baptist Home Mission Monthly* [*BHMM*, organ for the American Baptist Home Mission Society] 26(12) (December 1904): 447. Two years later, in contrast, another missionary who exoticized the Chinese expressed disappointment that most Chinese children dress in American fashion, "which is horribly commonplace and ugly compared with the Chinese dress. Really, it seems a pity to change the dress, but that goes doubtless with Americanization." See "The Morning Star Christmas," *BHMM* 28(2) (February 1906):74.

27. *AM* 41(2) (February 1887):55. For an excellent study of white Protestant women missionaries in China see Jane Hunter, *The Gospel of Gentility: American Women Missionaries in Turn-of-the-Century China* (New Haven: Yale University Press, 1984).

28. *AM* 35(10) (October 1881):312.

29. Huie Kin, *Reminiscences* (Beijing: San Yu Press, 1932), p. 32.

30. One perturbed young convert presented his dilemma to Pond: "I do so love your Jesus, but my family be angry. What shall I do?" *AM* 41(6) (June 1887):175.

31. William C. Pond, "Steadfast, Immovable," *AM* 35(10) (October 1881):311.

32. Evelyn B. Higginbotham argues that the social dynamics of "multiple publics" and "mediating organizations" were present among black Baptist women leaders during the same period. See *Righteous Discontent*, p. 10ff. Wesley Woo cautions against assuming that the intercultural mediatory roles of Chinese Protestant leadership reflected the concerns of the "average person in the pew." He proposes that Chinese-centered Protestant organizations such as the Youxue Zhengdaohui served as an alternative social locale for Chinese who were neither interested in the dominant Chinese groups nor alienated from white Protestant control of the missions. See "Chinese Protestants in San Francisco," pp. 218 and 225–234.

33. *BHMM* 4(6) (June 1882):176.

34. In 1881, at the age of twenty-three, Fung Chak was appointed to the Chinese Baptist Mission in Portland, Oregon. For the next twenty years he labored there before returning to China permanently in 1901. See *BHMM* 23(10) (October 1901):289; Anna Gilchrist Petty, "Unto the Third and Fourth Generation," *Missions* (Northern Baptist) 13(8) (September 1922):474–475.

35. Ibid.

Timothy Tseng

36. Jee Gam, "Jee Gam on the Mission in China," *AM* 35(6) (June 1881):179–181.

37. *American Missionary Association 1882 Annual Report*, p. 15. Presbyterians also spoke frequently about the special concern that Chinese Protestants had for the Chinese in China. See *BFM 1897 AR*, p. 217; *BFM 1899 AR*, p. 280, in particular.

38. Woo, "Chinese Protestants in San Francisco," p. 220.

39. Abram Halsey to Quick, 10 June 1916; Presbyterian Historical Society [PHS], RG81-1-5.

40. "A Joint Meeting of the Commission, the Oriental Mission Council, and the Chinese Christian Union," 21 February 1923; PHS (Philadelphia Archives), RG301.7-2-1 (Box 11, No. 15), "Oriental Work, 1923–1939."

41. For standard histories of Protestant progressivism see Timothy S. Smith, *Revivalism and Social Reform: American Protestantism on the Eve of the Civil War* (Baltimore: Johns Hopkins University Press, 1980); Charles H. Hopkins, *The Rise of the Social Gospel in American Protestantism, 1865–1915* (New Haven: Yale University Press, 1940); and Robert T. Handy, *A Christian America: Protestant Hopes and Historical Realities*, 2nd ed. (New York: Oxford University Press, 1984), pp. 101–158. See also Shirley S. Garrett, *Social Reformers in Urban China: The Chinese Y.M.C.A., 1895–1926* (Cambridge, Mass.: Harvard University Press, 1970), for similar developments in China.

42. See Ma, *Revolutionaries, Monarchists, and Chinatowns,* and Lai, "The Kuomingtang in Chinese American Communities Before World War II."

43. The roots of Chinese Protestant revolutionary politics can be traced to both Chinese and Western sources. While Christianity made a powerful impact on the worldview of the Chinese Protestant, it did not obliterate the Chinese cultural and political heritage. The anti-Manchu sentiment among Triad secret societies in Kwangtung and the creative synthesis of Christian and Chinese perspectives in the Taiping Rebellion also influenced persons like Sun Yat-sen. Sun's iconoclasm reveals an eclectic borrowing from various sources for the purpose of revolution. For Protestant theological sources for revolutionary politics see Hill, *Puritanism and Revolution*; Michael Walzer, "Puritanism as a Revolutionary Ideology," *History and Theory* 3 (1964):59–90; and Nathan O. Hatch, *The Democratization of American Christianity* (New Haven: Yale University Press, 1989).

44. By 1908 the Pao-huang Hui was in decline as revolutionary advocates became dominant in the Chinese communities in North America. See Ma, *Revolutionaries, Monarchists, and Chinatowns,* pp. 125–131.

45. *BFM 1917 AR*, p. 193; *BFM 1920 AR*, p. 189. Huie Kin pastored

the Presbyterian mission in New York City between 1886 and 1925. There he became acquainted with many young Chinese students who studied in East Coast colleges and attended the mission during the 1900s and 1910s. Many eventually became prominent in China. Though not a student, the most prominent figure to stay at the New York mission was Sun Yat-sen himself. See *BFM 1916 AR,* p. 192; *BFM 1919 AR,* p. 154; *BFM 1922 AR,* p. 192.

46. Ma, *Revolutionaries, Monarchists, and Chinatowns,* p. 58. Huie Kin observed that the reform agenda of the Pao-huang Hui was dominated by the business interests, whereas Sun Yat-sen had a following among students and laborers. See Kin, *Reminiscences,* pp. 70–71.

47. Ibid. Ma also notes that editorials in the *Chung Sai Yat Po* became increasingly anti-Manchu and "claimed that Cantonese were inherently superior." See *Revolutionaries, Monarchists, and Chinatowns,* p. 97. This provides further evidence of the process of "ethnogenesis" that Stevan Harrell describes in "Civilizing Projects."

48. Tsai, *The Chinese Experience in America,* p. 94. Sun made a practice of staying with Chinese Protestants in America. During one stay at the Chinese Presbyterian mission in New York, Huie Kin received a letter threatening a boycott of the mission if Sun were not ousted. See Kin, *Reminiscences,* pp. 70–71.

49. Fung Yuet Mow, "China as Seen by a Chinaman," *BHMM* 27(5) (May 1905):205.

50. "A Confucian Chinese Editor's View of Christianity," *BHMM* 30(12) (December 1908):482–486.

51. Ibid. Similar reformist-revolutionary discourse can be found among many Chinese Protestant women as well. Lowell High School student Yuk Ying Lee's 1905 article for the Chinese Students' Alliance of America expresses this newfound confidence in the Protestant ability to transform China, particularly in women's education. "Now is the time," she exclaimed, "that the womanhood of my people need the helping hand of Christian lands. Christianity and the right kind of education will be the only instruments that can raise it from idolatry and superstition as they have done in other nations." While it is not clear whether Yuk Ying Lee was a Christian, Peggy Pascoe and Judy Yung's studies show that Chinese women converts found themselves freed of the traditional Chinese gender systems. Ironically, many of these converts also found themselves circumscribed by American racism. See Yuk Ying Lee, "Education of Christian Woman," in *Chinese America: History and Perspective, 1988* (San Francisco: Chinese Historical Society of America, 1988), p. 106 (originally published in *The Dragon Student* [San Francisco: Chinese Students' Alliance of America, 1905]); Pascoe, *Relations of Rescue;*

Yung, "Unbinding the Feet, Unbinding Their Lives" and "The Social Awakening of Chinese American Women."

52. Jee Gam and Ng Poon Chew use a similar strategy to argue for the repeal of Chinese exclusion. See Gam, "Chinese Exclusion, From the Standpoint of a Chinese Christian"; Patrick J. Healy and Ng Poon Chew, *A Statement for Non-Exclusion* (San Francisco, 1903).

53. Lucien Bianco, *Origins of the Chinese Revolution, 1915–1949* (Stanford: Stanford University Press, 1971), p. 42.

54. *Missions* 4(1) (January 1913):51.

55. There are hints of the continued activism of this generation of Chinese Protestants in America. In Jade Snow Wong's description of her father's religious activities, she notes that "Daddy seldom hesitated to stick his neck out if he thought social action or justice were involved. For instance, he was on the founding board of the Chinese YMCA and fought for its present location [in San Francisco's Chinatown]." See Thomas C. Wheeler, *The Immigrant Experience* (New York: Dial Press, 1971), pp. 113–114, cited in Edwin S. Gaustad, ed., *A Documentary History of Religion in America Since 1865*, 2nd ed. (Grand Rapids: Eerdmans, 1993), p. 38. See also Jade Snow Wong, *Fifth Chinese Daughter* (Seattle: University of Washington Press, 1988). Protestant missionary hopes for China dissipated as warring factions after the revolution failed to establish a republican government. See Murray A. Rubinstein, "Witness to the Chinese Millennium: Southern Baptist Perceptions of the Chinese Revolution, 1911–1921," in Patricia Neils, ed., *United States Attitudes and Policies Towards China: The Impact of American Missionaries,* (Armonk, N.Y.: M. E. Sharpe, 1990), pp. 149–170. The anti-Japanese movement on the West Coast, tensions with Japan, a resurgent nativism, and World War I also preoccupied many Protestants at this point. The appearance of Sidney Gulick on the scene diverted much of Protestant attention away from the Chinese and toward the Japanese crisis and nativism. See Sandra C. Taylor, *Advocate of Understanding: Sidney Gulick and the Search for Peace with Japan* (Kent: Kent State University Press, 1984); Roger Daniels, *The Politics of Prejudice: The Anti-Japanese Movement in California and the Struggle for Japanese Exclusion,* rev. ed. (Berkeley: University of California Press, 1977).

56. Tseng, "Ministry at Arms' Length," pp. 91–136.

57. See, for example, George W. Hinman, *The Oriental in America* (New York: Missionary Education Movement of the United States and Canada, 1913).

58. Tseng, "Ministry at Arms' Length," pp. 137–185.

59. Vera Schwarcz, *The Chinese Enlightenment: Intellectuals and the*

Legacy of the May Fourth Movement of 1919 (Berkeley: University of California Press, 1986).

60. Lam, *Chinese Theology in Construction,* pp. 5–26; see also Samuel D. Ling, "The Other May Fourth Movement: The Chinese 'Christian Renaissance,' 1919–1937" (Ph.D. diss., Temple University, 1981), pp. 21–59; and Jessie G. Lutz, *Chinese Politics and Christian Missions: The Anti-Christian Movements of 1920–28* (Notre Dame: Crossroads Books, 1988).

61. Peter Kwong, *Chinatown, N.Y.: Labor and Politics, 1930–1950* (New York: Monthly Review Press, 1979), pp. 45–67.

62. By the early 1930s, Albert Palmer, the president of Chicago Theological Seminary, was convinced that second-generation Asian Americans would abandon their ethnic "ghettos" provided that barriers to their employment in the mainstream could be torn down. See Albert W. Palmer, *Orientals in American Life* (New York: Friendship Press, 1946).

63. *1898 Annual Report of the Woman's Baptist Home Mission Society* (Chicago: Women's American Baptist Mission Society, 1927), p. 40.

64. *From Ocean to Ocean 1926–27,* p. 207.

65. *American Baptist Home Mission Society 1927 Annual Report,* p. 37.

66. C. H. Hsia, probably a student at the University of Michigan, wrote a revealing letter to Charles D. Hurrey, general secretary of the YMCA's ministry to foreign students. Formerly a Christian, Hsia decided to become a Confucianist because of his experience at the Angel Island "prison" and other instances of discrimination toward Chinese. "I believe that the Brotherhood taught in Christianity is less universal than that taught in Confucianism," he noted. "Do you suppose people will believe in Christianity while Christinity [*sic*] is not practiced by Christians in a wholly Christianized nation?" C. H. Hsia to C. D. Hurrey, undated (received 20 June 1918); PHS, RG81-29-4.

67. Dr. Mabel Lee, daughter of Rev. Lee To, the pastor of the Chinese Baptist mission in New York and one time president of New York's Consolidated Chinese Benevolent Association, completed her doctorate at Columbia in 1922 before assuming her father's mantle at the mission. A close friend of Hu Shih, she also associated with future Kuomingtang leaders such as T. V. Soong and H. H. Kung. See Mabel Lee circular letter (addressees unknown), 3 July 1925; letter located in the First Chinese Baptist Church, New York City.

68. *From Ocean to Ocean, 1926–27,* p. 212.

69. Reflecting a heightened sense of racial and cultural consciousness, Chinese Protestants increasingly called for a break from Western missionary control of educational institutions, hospitals, and social service agencies. A growing number of Chinese theologians in the 1920s began to articulate an indigenous theology that critiqued the Western

Timothy Tseng

theological constructs while supporting Chinese nationalistic aspirations and making Christian theology more culturally relevant to the Chinese people. See Lam, *Chinese Theology in Construction*; Ling, "The Other May Fourth Movement"; and Lutz, *Chinese Politics*.

70. The True Jesus Church was founded in 1917, the Jesus Family in 1921, and the "Little Flock" in 1922. See Philip L. Wickeri, *Seeking the Common Ground: Protestant Christianity, the Three-Self Movement, and China's United Front* (Maryknoll: Orbis Books, 1990), pp. 157–170.

71. Charles Shepherd did not look favorably upon one of these groups, the Trust in God movement. Rather than cooperating with other churches, these self-supporting churches are "satisfied to have a rather one-house affair that is their own." See C. R. Shepherd to Frank A. Smith, 3 July 1934, American Baptist Historical Society (Valley Forge), G. Pitt Beers files, Group 4, Box 5, "Bilingual Chinese Corres Chas. R. Shepherd, 1932–1946." Huie Kin, however, was quite drawn to this movement during his visit to China: "I was gratified to find two churches maintained in Shanghai by the people of my province, the Cantonese Union Church and the Cantonese Baptist Church." See Kin, *Reminiscences*, p. 89. In 1923, six of the forty-one Chinese Protestant churches and missions in the United States were independent. In 1955, of the sixty-six Chinese churches in the United States, twelve were independent. In 1982, there were an estimated 468 Chinese churches and only a minority were affiliated with any denomination. Since then the number of Chinese churches in the United States has more than doubled. See J. S. Tow, *The Real Chinese in America* (New York: Academy Press, 1923), p. 112; Horace R. Cayton and Anne O. Lively, *The Chinese in the United States and the Chinese Christian Churches* (New York: National Council of Churches, 1955); Gail Law, ed., *Chinese Churches Handbook* (Hong Kong: Chinese Coordination Centre of World Evangelism, 1982), p. 243.

72. Conflicts between Chinese Protestants and missionary executives had flared up occasionally in the past, but without the strong anti-Western nationalism of the Chinese. In 1880, for instance, Methodist missionary superintendent Otis Gibson was distraught over a "native preacher" whose ambition was "to set up an independent Chinese Church, with himself at the head." The preacher was finally "excluded" from the Methodist mission and peace was restored. See *62nd Annual Report of Missionary Society of the Methodist Episcopal Church, 1880*, p. 204; see also Woo, "Chinese Protestants in San Francisco," pp. 218–219 and 231–234.

73. Minutes of the "Committee on Orientals and Hawaiians of the Home Mission Council," 12 March 1920; PHS, RG81-25-11.

74. Charles R. Shepherd's book, *The Ways of Ah Sin: A Composite*

Narrative of Things as They Are (New York: Revell, 1923), was meant to be an exposé of the tong and prostitution problem in San Francisco's Chinatown. Written with the intentions of helping the "innocent" Chinese, it created a furor among the Chinese community, including many Chinese Protestants, for its perpetuation of Chinese stereotypes. Shepherd and Donaldina Cameron's campaign against Chinese tongs actually led to the tightening of Chinese immigration restrictions in 1924. Shepherd's book, as well as his and Cameron's friendlier attitude toward the state, was not viewed favorably by many Chinese. See Tseng, "Ministry at Arms' Length," pp. 137–185; Sue Fawn Chung, "The Chinese American Citizens Alliance: An Effort in Assimilation, 1895–1965," in *Chinese America: History and Perspective, 1988* (San Francisco: Chinese Historical Society of America, 1988), pp. 48–49; and Pardee Lowe, *Father and Glorious Descendent* (Boston: Little, Brown, 1943), pp. 199–208.

75. Today the Chinese Christian Church of New England (Boston), the Chinese Christian Church in Philadelphia, and the Chicago Chinese Union Church are results of this "federating" effort. The Japanese Union Church of Los Angeles is another example of this effort. See Tseng, "Ministry at Arms' Length," pp. 164–165. For a detailed study of Japanese Protestant churches in Los Angeles see especially Brian Hayashi, *"For the Sake of Our Japanese Brethren": Assimilation, Nationalism, and Protestantism Among the Japanese of Los Angeles, 1895–1942* (Stanford: Stanford University Press, 1995).

76. Gilbert, "Report on Mission Work Among Orientals in the United States," pp. 138–139.

77. Peggy Pascoe argues that in the 1920s and 1930s, the emergence of an attitude of "cultural relativism" undermined the assimilationist aspirations of many women missionaries. See Pascoe, *Relations of Rescue,* pp. 198–201. Pardee Lowe rejected the narrow Protestant perspective in which he grew up. He came to define his Protestantism as principally good works and became a universalist with respect to other religions. See Lowe, *Father and Glorious Descendent,* pp. 165–169, 173, and especially 308.

78. There was even an exoticizing appreciation of "difference" among some white Protestants. See Carl Click, *Shake Hands with the Dragon* (New York: McGraw-Hill, 1941).

79. Especially helpful for understanding Chinese theological diversity in the 1920s to 1940s is Lam, *Chinese Theology in Construction.*

80. This helps to explain how Jade Snow Wong's father was able to be "as serious about Christian precepts as he was intent on Confucian propriety." Among American-born Chinese, however, pride in being Chinese was more problematic. Inculcated in an American education sys-

tem, the second generation sought to demonstrate their Americanness. Ministries to second-generation Chinese in the 1930s to 1960s reflected this assimilationist orientation—giving sociologists like William C. Smith and Rose Hom Lee the impression that Chinese churches were institutions of "assimilation." See Wong, *Fifth Chinese Daughter,* p. 73; Tseng, "Ministry at Arms' Length," pp. 226–277; William C. Smith, *Americans in Process: A Study of Our Citizens of Oriental Ancestry* (Ann Arbor: Edwards Brothers, 1937); Rose Hom Lee, *The Chinese in the United States of America* (Hong Kong: Hong Kong University Press, 1960).

81. Kin, *Reminiscences,* p. 112. Throughout Huie Kin's career, he identified Protestantism with modern civilization and appropriated both toward nationalistic ends; see pp. 51 and 53–54.

82. Rejecting "essentialist" or "circumstantialist/instrumentalist" understanding of religious and ethnic identity formation, Constable argues that the Hakka Christians she observed displayed a "primordialist/sentimentalist" strategy of ethnogenesis. The Hakka Christians she studied understood their Protestant identity through a sense of "shared" history rather than by a shared political or manipulative strategy ("circumstantialist/instrumentalist") or cultural or physical markers ("essentialist"). The Chinese Protestants examined here exhibit a "circumstantialist/instrumentalist" strategy, but by the 1930s the "primordialist/sentimentalist" strategy becomes visible. See Constable, *Christian Souls and Chinese Spirits,* pp. 10–16.

Chapter 2

Filipino Folk Spirituality and Immigration: From Mutual Aid to Religion

STEFFI SAN BUENAVENTURA

The Filipinos who journeyed to the United States at the beginning of the twentieth century were mostly young, single men from the rural areas of the Philippines. They came with little or no formal schooling and became indispensable workers on Hawai'i's plantations and California's farms. Much of their story, however, remains untold. What has been written about them has come from a limited perspective focused primarily on their sociodemographic profile and the inadequacy of their adaptation to the oppressive conditions they faced in white American society. While it has been necessary to place the early history of the Filipinos in the United States in this factual context, this single framework of interpretation has nevertheless contributed to creating a static, if not stereotyped, image of the early Filipino immigrants.[1] The legacy of their experience is rich, however, and deserves to be studied from more innovative sources of analysis.

One of the untapped areas of inquiry in Filipino American studies can be found in the cultural traditions that accompanied the pioneering immigrants on their voyage overseas. As the turn of the century ushered in a second phase of colonial rule, the new American colonists promised an irresistible offer of benevolence and opportunities of equality.[2] The early Filipinos crossed spatial and social boundaries eagerly in search of a modern experience in the United States. Despite their initial exposure to Americanization in the Philippines, they came essentially as they were: the product of a deeply ingrained indigenous culture combined with more than three centuries of Spanish colonial tradition. The story of the early Filipino immigrants, therefore, should be as much a narrative of the cultural world they brought with them as it is an account of their life in the new country.

Undoubtedly many of the pioneering Filipinos used their indigenous resources to face—and even shape—their destiny in America. A dynamic force underlying their cultural heritage, for example, has been their religious belief system. This chapter offers a new interpretation of this subject. It is part of a larger research project that analyzes the history of a group of Filipino immigrants whose interaction with America was based on their spiritual beliefs and practices.[3] Through the instrument of their native mysticism they formed a mutual aid organization and shaped it into a socioreligious phenomenon: a stateside messianic movement that evolved in California in the mid-1920s, spread to Hawai'i in 1928, and was introduced in the 1930s to the Philippines, where it became an established, albeit minor, religious sect. This study discusses the roots of this phenomenon. It looks at a tradition of folk religion that was very much an integral part of the early Filipino immigrants' identity. It interprets how this folk spiritual tradition transformed a mutual aid society into a Filipino American syncretic religion. It also shows how a "Filipino religion"—founded on nativist spirituality but made in America—came full circle, back to the home country, but only after having incorporated elements of American culture and the Filipino immigrant experience.

Filipino Folk Spirituality and Immigration

Filipino immigration to America began to increase with the arrival of 2,426 Filipinos in San Francisco and Los Angeles in 1923; 85 percent of them came from Hawai'i's plantation workers *(sakada)*. In *1929,* some 5,795 entered California, half of whom sailed from the Philippines, the other half from Hawai'i.[4] The rise in the Filipino immigrant population was accompanied by an increase in the formation of small home-town associations and mutual aid societies.[5] These organizations served many necessary functions: above all, the new arrivals needed a surrogate family support system to provide them with basic human care away from home. Thus these organizations became an extension of a highly valued Filipino tradition of mutual help *(tulungan)* in which assisting kin, neighbors, friends, and those in need came naturally and with reciprocal benefits. The sojourners saw these associations as the ideal instrument for preserving their ethnicity and celebrating their cultural heritage in the new land.

Among these numerous organizations, two stood out: the Caballeros de Dimas Alang and the Legionarios del Trabajo (and, to a lesser extent, El Gran Oriente). These were pseudo-Masonic fraternal groups that originated in the early 1900s in the Philippines and were introduced abroad as early as 1921 by members who came to Hawai'i and California.[6] Filipino expatriates welcomed the familiar groups, which retained much of their original objectives and structure. Thus even as they celebrated their new life in America, members of the Caballeros and Legionarios continued to practice the traditions of the organizations observed in the home country.[7]

Filipino Federation of America: "Clean and Moral"
On 27 December 1925, a new mutual aid organization was formed in Los Angeles under the name of the Filipino Federation of America. It competed against the Caballeros and

Legionarios for immigrant membership and for leadership in the Filipino community. In contrast to the Philippine fraternal groups with Spanish names, the Federation carried a "Filipino American" identity—indicated by the circumstances of its inception in California, its name in English, and its orientation toward the immigrant situation in the United States.

The Caballeros, Legionarios, and Federation shared certain basic principles: they embraced the idea of the supreme power of God, the sanctity of human brotherhood, and the obligation to care for and help one another (the spirit of *tulungan*). Politically they were committed to promoting "friendly relations" between the Philippines and the United States and were strongly in favor of the immediate independence of the Philippines.[8] These organizations ambitiously expanded their membership base outside of Hawai'i and the West Coast by establishing branches in cities like Chicago and New York where there were clusters of Filipino population. Significantly, their popular appeal revealed another important function of mutual aid organizations: as formal institutions that sought to project a collective voice of Filipinos and present a unified image of the group to the outside world.

Despite these common features, the Federation stood out as a separate and distinct entity from other Filipino organizations—not only in form but in substance. One factor that differentiated the Federation from its counterparts was its aim "to encourage clean living in accordance with the principles of strict morality."[9] It was a "clean organization," the members claimed, because they did not drink, gamble, smoke, or patronize taxi dance halls—"not like the Dimas Alang and Legionario," they said. This distinction was essential to the Federation's objective to show white America that the organization's members were a solution to, not part of, "the Filipino problem." Not only were they capable of taking care of themselves, they were also "morally clean" in the Christian meaning of the phrase. This moral stand was taken seriously by the membership. It was one of the main reasons why so many joined the organization—suggesting that not all Filipinos danced, gambled, and drank. There were those who upheld a contrary lifestyle.

Manifest Objectives: Acculturation, Approval, Acceptance

The Federation appealed to many Filipinos who wanted to be part of America. For one thing, the organization's activities expanded their vista of American experiences. With annual regularity, members led by the Federation Band marched in Fourth of July parades in their special regalia;[10] they also attended anniversary banquets and watched impressive tableaux, such as the one presented in December 1930 extolling George Washington and José Rizal, the Filipino national hero, all in one breath.[11] At a later time, the Federation would incorporate golf into its annual celebrations. The Federation was equally impressive in the amount of promotional materials it produced: books, essays and speeches, brochures, anniversary programs, manuals, newsletters, and pamphlets. It published *The Filipino Nation,* a monthly newsmagazine in English, which reported the activities of the Federation branches in California and Hawai'i, recorded events in various Filipino communities across the country, featured American and Philippine government officials on its covers, and debated issues in Philippine-U.S. relations, particularly the question of Philippine independence.[12]

Many joined because of this political agenda. They were told that the Federation was working for the independence of the Philippines and that their help was needed to win this fight. By exploiting this issue to the fullest, the organization essentially offered its members a participatory role in a patriotic cause that was in the traditional domain of the formally educated Filipino—the government-sponsored student *pensionado,* for example, or members of the political elite—to debate and advocate.[13] And the more the members became involved in this ultranationalistic issue, the more they began

Steffi San Buenaventura

to form the perception of their indispensable role in obtaining the independence of their country when it finally came. These activities, particularly the publications, were intended to engrave a lasting impression of the Filipino Federation of America not only on its membership but in the public consciousness. They exposed the members to the thinking of white America. Through the constant underscoring of the organization's objectives—especially those that called for "[loyalty] to the U.S. Constitution," "[developing] true Christian fellowship," "[showing] a real humanitarian spirit," and "[being] an active agency of the solution of Philippine problems"—outsiders were reminded of how attuned the Federation was with American values and expectations.[14]

Hilario Camino Moncado and the Federation Leadership

To Federation observers it was immediately evident that its founder and president, Hilario Camino Moncado, was the central figure in the movement. He put the organization together with unprecedented temerity and flamboyance: stepping outside his own ethnic boundaries, he unabashedly worked his way into the world of the white American establishment at a time when there was much prejudice and discrimination against the Filipinos.[15] Claiming to lead an organization with a large and loyal following, Moncado convinced segments of the white community, especially members of the business establishment (such as farm growers), who now saw Moncado as an "agency of social control."[16] They supported the Federation's policy against organized labor and lauded Moncado's directive to his members not to participate in strikes. Moncado's personality, ideas, and leadership style defined every aspect of the Federation's character, agenda, and activities to the point where outsiders saw the Filipino Federation of America and Moncado as one entity.

Despite Moncado's center stage position, the limelight ought to be shared by the founding members with whom he started the movement. He could not have gone far without them. This core group had talented and dedicated individuals with remarkable leadership skills and organizational abilities and was directly responsible for the rapid growth of membership in the early years. The members of the charter lodges— men such as Andres Darilay, Francisco Manigo, Cornelio Clenuar, Fabian Banguis, and Lorenzo de los Reyes—oversaw the establishment and day-to-day management of the Federation offices in Los Angeles, Stockton, and other branches in addition to undertaking special duties, especially in Moncado's absence. These men met in America. A few may have known each other back home: some were recruited by friends and fellow townsmen who joined the organization before them; others were Moncado's compatriots (from the Cebuano-speaking region) who, like himself, worked briefly as *sakadas* in Hawai'i's plantations before heading for the West Coast. They came from poor rural families in the Philippines. Some received only a few years of elementary education, but they came to America with big dreams just the same. They worked in the fields of California, in the canneries of Alaska, and as busboys, dishwashers, cooks, janitors, bellboys, servants, and menial laborers in the cities.[17]

A number of them, however, managed to finish high school, enroll in automotive and vocational programs, and take adult education evening classes and even college courses while working. Moncado himself succeeded in getting a law degree from Southwestern University in Los Angeles in 1928 by the time the Federation was at its peak of popularity. He also managed to obtain an honorary "doctor of laws" degree from a very short-lived "Olympic University" in Los Angeles.[18] Thus Moncado and his cofounders belonged to a group of Filipinos—living primarily in urban centers—who called themselves "self-supporting students" (as distinct from *pensionados*). Having acquired some formal education helped them to understand mainstream American ideas and introduced them to the acculturating effects of the educational system. Their education also placed them among the "educated" immigrants who resided in the cities and thus maintained their distance (figuratively and literally) from the majority of workers in the fields. Members of this upwardly mobile group easily emerged as heads of organizations and acquired leadership status in the Filipino community.[19] Choosing not to turn their backs on their *sakada* origins, Moncado and his immediate circle knew only too well that they needed the support of their coworkers.

Recruiting Among the Filipino Laborers

Motivated by a zealous belief in the uniqueness of their organization, the pioneering members of the Federation campaigned actively for new recruits, starting with the agricultural communities in the San Joaquin Valley where many of them had been working. They concentrated on Stockton, which had the largest population of Filipinos in California.[20] They visited labor camps, taxi dance halls, gambling joints, pool halls, barbershops, and restaurants owned and frequented by Filipinos to persuade their compatriots to join. Their "campaign" (a Federation term) inevitably stressed everything that was different and special about the Federation, starting with its moral character and its much deeper involvement in the struggle to obtain Philippine independence. Moncado's speeches during the public celebrations of the Federation also attracted attention. Regino Tutor, for one, remembered his personal reaction when he heard Moncado's passionate appeal for support in the fight for Philippine independence:

> When Dr. Moncado told me that as a member of the Federation I must fight for Philippine independence, I asked, "How can that be? I am only one person and I am here in America, so far away from the Philippines. How can I fight for Philippine independence all by myself?" Dr. Moncado told me, "No, you

don't have to go to the Philippines. I will go for you. I will fight for you. But you, as a member of the Federation, must work hard to support this object."[21]

In the intimate seclusion of the labor camps, the campaigners began disclosing the "mysterious" aspect of a quasi-religious Federation—a reference often made about the organization in its literature but just now being explained. They revealed that the Federation was more than a mutual aid group: it was a *"misterioso"* organization guided by the principle of *doce-doce* (Spanish for "twelve-twelve"). They explained that only "1,728" members—the nucleus—were needed to complete the "special mission" of the organization. This "mystical" number (1,728) was the sum of the membership structure of the Federation, which was organized around the number twelve: it would be composed of twelve divisions, each division would have twelve lodges, and each lodge was to be composed of twelve members.[22]

Membership in the Federation demanded the renunciation of "all vices." While this stipulation prevented many from taking the organization seriously (many indeed ridiculed it), it did attract the "select few." The membership fee to become one of the 1,728 "matriculate" members was just as prohibitive: a $100 ("lifetime") fee plus a mandatory $10 for the Federation pin. This sum obviously discouraged a rush of prospective members, but given the option to pay by installment, many managed to come up with the full amount. When twelve people had each contributed the required sum, a lodge was formed.

The Doce-Doce *Organization and Rizal*

A crucial instrument in convincing many to join the movement was a photograph of twelve men. Six of them stood, shoulder-to-shoulder, on each side of a tall man in the center. Their arms were crossed against their chests and their hands were linked. These men were the first to form the *doce-doce* organization—members of Lodge 1, Division 1. The commanding figure in the middle was the six-foot-tall Moncado.

This image, linked with the number twelve, struck a deep emotional chord among the Filipino immigrants. Many were stunned at encountering a Philippine folk symbol here in America. They recalled the mystical symbolism that the old folks back home had given to *doce*—a number associated with Jesus Christ and his twelve apostles and consequently with the political martyr José Rizal, who was said to have had his own following of twelve Filipino patriots. They remembered their elders telling them that the number twelve signified Rizal's organization.[23] Fernando Blas, for example, recalled his grandmother specifically instructing him, when he was growing up in the Philippines, to join any organization associated with twelve: "She said Rizal's work was not finished because he was executed by the Spaniards. But Rizal lives. A new organization will come to continue his work, my grandmother said. But the organization will not be in the Philippines but in a foreign land. It will finish the work that Rizal began. That's why I joined the Federation and became a follower of Dr. Moncado."[24]

Folk tradition had already laid the foundation for the religious beliefs about Rizal's "sainthood" and his "reincarnation." After he was executed by the Spaniards, nativistic movements sprouted all over the Philippines, dedicated to the worship of Rizal as the immortal Filipino fighting oppression. The cult of Rizal permeated deeply into folk spirituality and popular culture.[25] Moreover, the Filipinos who came to America in the early decades of the twentieth century lived in close historical proximity to the death of Rizal in 1896. Many were young children at that time whose parents (and even grandparents) had certainly felt the impact of the political martyrdom of the Filipino hero. Rather providentially, the Federation's popularity was launched by a successful 1926

Filipino Folk Spirituality and Immigration

Rizal Day celebration in Los Angeles led by Moncado. The momentous event, in effect, associated Moncado and the Federation with the national figure. This Rizal Day was directly instrumental in the instantaneous growth of the organization: its membership rose from 36 in December 1926 to

740 by December 1928.[26]

A "Trinity of Doce-Doce"

The members were awed by the charismatic persona of Moncado. Outwardly and materially, they gave Moncado total loyalty, financial support, and the mass following he needed to promote his activities. They were impressed by his accomplishments. He had more education than they could ever hope to have. He spoke with such articulation and wisdom. He was not intimidated by white people. Internally and spiritually, they felt early on that he was "not an ordinary human being" *(ibang tawo siya)* because he had *kalaki* or *gahum* (power, charisma). They became convinced of this not only from what they observed but from what they experienced about him in their *damgo* (dreams).[27]

The symbolism of the *doce-doce* photograph pointed to a "remarkable" comparison between Moncado and Rizal. Two additional images circulated among the members. One was a photograph of Rizal, seated in a group, with "Twelve Ilustres." (The correct term is *ilustrados,* the Filipino educated or "enlightened" class, of which Rizal was a part.) The second picture was the familiar image of the Last Supper depicting Christ and his twelve disciples.[28] Then a third photograph emerged, especially composed, synthesizing this "trinity with a following of twelve" in linear order and in three contiguous columns: first the image of Christ (with the word "ALPHA" and a portrait of the Last Supper), followed by a portrait of Rizal (with the word "AND" along with the "Twelve Ilustres" group photo), and ending with a photograph of Moncado (accompanied by the word "OMEGA" and the *doce-doce* picture of Lodge 1, Division 1). At the bottom space, the words read: "THE BEGINNING AND THE END, THE FIRST AND THE LAST."

The belief had evolved that Moncado possessed a "divine" persona reincarnated from Rizal, who in turn was a reincarnation of Christ. Rizal's special mission was to free the Filipinos but his death prevented him from doing so. Moncado was going to make this happen, starting with the independence of the Philippines. And as Regino Tutor concluded: "Everything Dr. Moncado said really happened."

The Material and the Spiritual

Because of this selective process, those who joined the Federation did so with a strong moral commitment and with great personal and financial sacrifice. Through self-selection they essentially became the chosen ones—ready and willing to dedicate everything to the Federation's teachings and "principles of morality" *(principios)*. Not only did the temporal and highly visible (that is, material) activities of the Federation draw them as one body, but their participation in the development of their organization's hidden (that is, spiritual) dimension gave them a closer and stronger bond beyond fraternal relationship and ethnic pride, a bond approaching a deep religious experience.

From the moment they began to form a lodge, members were given what amounted to a set of spiritual instructions *(instruksyon)* on a sheet of paper. These instructions were essentially guidelines telling them what prayers to say, when, and how many times in a twenty-four-hour day. The prayers consisted of short phonetically strung words that outwardly seemed meaningless plus prayers for avoiding temptations written in chantlike phrases that were to be invoked as protection against persons and situations with intent to harm.[29] They were there "to protect," explained Alfonzo Nagal, a spiritual member in Hawai'i since early 1930: "It is just like in the Catholic [religion], to protect if you believe all the prayers that can help you from any bad habit that can control you if you depend on the prayers you have. . . . If you want to change your habit . . . being a gambler . . . if you believe on it, everything, you can take it away—smoking, drinking, any kind vices you can take it out. . . . If your spirit is in the Federation for real, there is no hardship to take every bad habit, all vices."[30] Furthermore, they were encouraged to fast for three days after officially entering the Federation. Those who were spiritually inclined took these instructions to heart and kept the sheet folded and wrapped in a protective cover attached to a cord. This they wore around the neck as spiritual protection (like the Catholic scapular) or as an *anting-anting* (talisman).

Although the *instruksyon*, prayers, and fasting were part of the initiation process, members were never forced to observe these rituals. Officers of the respective branches and others who were engaged in public activities often chose not to follow these spiritual guidelines because of their visible role in the community; some simply did not believe in them. But they all actively supported Moncado and worked behind him in pushing the Federation's political agenda. Clearly they were doing important "material" work. Thus they were referred to as "material" members of the Federation.

Others were drawn more to a developing religious philosophy. Preferring obscurity to public exposure, these members emphasized prayer and fasting, followed a strict vegetarian "raw food" diet, and performed "physical culture" (their version of yoga), all in guarded secrecy. These "spiritual" members intensified the religious experience by elaborating on the rituals and weaving mystical meanings into them. With every step of their creation, the deification of Moncado took a more distinct shape. Unlike the material group, the spiritual members' work was "hidden underneath" *(tago sa ilalim)*. Equally veiled in their mysterious world was the quiet presence of their spiritual leader and teacher: Lorenzo de los Reyes, a Tagalog mystic from the Philippines and one of the original members of the *doce-doce*—Lodge 1, Division 1.

Lorenzo de los Reyes: Spiritual Founder

Because of Moncado's dominant presence, few outsiders were aware of Reyes' indispensable position in the movement. From the beginning he was involved with Moncado in planning the creation of a quasi-religious organization.[31] It was Reyes who put together a body of doctrine and rituals for the Federation in keeping with this identity. He headed and trained the campaigners to recruit members. Through his spiritual role, he prepared the way for the coming of Moncado and led the members to recognize Moncado's charisma. By assuming the role of a John the Baptist, he gave impetus to the creation of a Filipino nativistic (that is, messianic) movement in America.[32] It was a role for which he was trained very early in life; it was the calling that brought him overseas to America.

Even members who knew Reyes and worked closely with him in the early years of the Federation in California and Hawai'i could say very little about his personal background.[33] All indicated that "Mr. Reyes" (they also addressed him as "Papa Reyes") was gentle, quiet, soft-spoken, and chose to remain in the background, a mysterious figure. They knew about his mystic work in the Philippines primarily from Andres Darilay's three-page "Biographical Sketch of Lorenzo Delos Reyes" that appeared in the "Blue Book" edition of *Every Day New and Wonder,* published by Reyes himself in 1931 in Los Angeles. Circulated only among the spirituals who kept its content a secret all these years, this "Blue Book" (its cover was blue as distinct from the earlier "red" and "white" editions) became the catechism of the Federation's teachings and *principios.* It contains sketches of selected "mystical" episodes in Reyes' childhood, a description of his inventions, interpretation of millenarian visions, numerous photographs and images of the spiritual members in the practice of their rituals, and, of course, numerous references to the "supernatural" persona of Moncado.

No record exists of when Reyes was born. Darilay writes that Reyes had no formal schooling. It can be safely assumed that he was a minor (say, fifteen or sixteen) when he sailed to Hawai'i in May 1910 because he came as a "surrogate dependent" of a *sakada* couple recruited by the Hawaiian Sugar Planters' Association (HSPA). "In Hawai'i," Darilay narrates, "young Reyes worked in the sugar plantation with some children. His salary was fifty cents a day." (Adult workers were officially paid $1 a day.) In the early part of 1911, he sailed for San Francisco where he met Moncado, unplanned, in the summer of 1916—a year after Moncado arrived in California from Hawai'i. "Both were young and full of ambition for their future," Darilay continues. "After their informal meeting, they parted from each other with the unwritten promise that they would sacrifice, regardless of hardship, for the betterment of their beloved country, the Philippines in particular, and to humanity in general." In 1920, Reyes moved to Southern California at Moncado's request and they held a "mutual conference" in Los Angeles where Moncado was now residing. In the early morning of 4 October 1924, while living in Bakersfield, Reyes had a dream calling him to become "a servant to humanity." Darilay suggests that this dream was the sign for the Filipino Federation of America to be organized and says that preparations for this special task had begun a few years before the dream occurred.[34]

The Roots of Reyes' Mysticism

Reyes was part of the first wave of Filipinos who began the early journey to America during the first decade of the 1900s. He was present at the beginning, in 1910, of the large annual *sakada* movement to Hawai'i and the mainland. Unlike his cohorts who came primarily for economic gains, however, Reyes made his pilgrimage to America for spiritual reasons.

Born to a poor rice-farming family, Reyes was raised in the heart of the Tagalog region that has been the major center of native mysticism—in the contiguous provinces of Batangas, Laguna, and Tayabas (later renamed Quezon) surrounding Mount Banahaw. According to his biography, after the age of six "he began to study the movement of the earth and the Universal Mysteries, under the tutorship of a Mystic Professor, an intimate friend of his father. This professor at that time was 250 years old, and had done a great deal of traveling all over the world. His residence is in the mountain of Banahaw." The biography continues:

> The first instruction given to Mr. Reyes was A, J, S, instead of A, B, C. He memorized these by heart before having other lessons. Besides these he studied Latin, the five wounds of Christ and the twenty-four instructions equivalent to twenty-four hours in a day, signifying action. That is why Mr. Reyes is willing to work and serve the world in morality.
>
> After obtaining this knowledge, hundreds of visitors, men and women, came to see Mr. Reyes, especially on Holy Friday, to ask for the knowledge he had acquired from the unknown professor.
>
> When the father of Mr. Reyes was at the point of death . . . he told him . . . to travel abroad to look for a man who may some day lead the world in morality.

Reyes had to know "the twenty-four spaces of the world" as part of learning the "twenty-four instructions." (The number twenty-four naturally suggests a connecting pattern to *doce-doce*.) Drawings in the "Blue Book" also depict Reyes as a boy being given a drink of "the holy water" by his mystic father (illustrated with a short beard). Halley's Comet appeared in early 1910. A mystical omen in the Philippines, it was also the sign for Reyes to leave.

These glimpses into Reyes' mystic past, though brief and

incomplete, reveal a background rich in folk spirituality. This tradition has roots in the merging—over more than three centuries—of an indigenous animistic belief system with the Western Catholicism introduced by Spanish colonization, resulting in what has commonly been referred to as Philippine "Folk Catholicism" or "Folk Christianity."[35] This religious syncretism became clearly pronounced in popular movements in the second half of the nineteenth century, beginning with the Apolinario de la Cruz/Cofradia de San José "religious uprising" of the 1840s in Tayabas (Quezon) province. After the death of de la Cruz (killed resisting the Spaniards), the movement hid on Mount Banahaw. The original and second-generation followers canonized their charismatic founder and renamed the Cofradia as the Colorum Society in 1870.[36]

"Colorum" became the generic term for similar messianic phenomena. These peasant-based social movements were forms of religious protest and were threatening to church and government. They also symbolized powerful political articulation of liberation against the established order. Mainstream society considered these movements as fanatic manifestations of peasant ignorance, superstitions, and banditry and attempted to eradicate them and their charismatic leaders.[37]

The Colorum *Tradition in America*

The life of Lorenzo de los Reyes was molded by religious elements of the *colorum* tradition: the presence of charismatic figures (usually Christlike); the quest for the power of the *anting-anting;* the practice of sacrifice and meditation; the recitation of secret prayers in the vernacular languages combined with Latin words and phrases; the use of holy water as a medicinal cure; the unraveling of cosmic mysteries; the significance attributed to natural events, disasters, dreams; the imparting of folk wisdom and philosophy; the pursuit of the secrets of the supernatural world and its magical powers; the role of the old and the wise as teacher. Reyes brought these elements to America with him in search of the fulfillment of his mystic mission.

Given the thousands of the Filipino folk population arriving annually in Hawai'i and America at this time, it is not surprising to find a Filipino mystic like Reyes among them. In fact, hundreds of others must have had links with the *colorum* tradition. Regino Abarquez, a Federation member from Stockton, remembered having been brought to a *colorum* organization called Doce-Pares (Pair of Twelve) at the age of seven in his native province of Cebu. In Hawai'i, there has been evidence of *anting-anting* among the possessions of *sakadas*. According to Faustino Felipe, a lifetime spiritual Federation devotee in Hawai'i, while working on the plantation he heard that members of a *colorum* group from the Philippines had come to Hawai'i as plantation laborers. Other records tell of charismatic leaders of popular *colorum* movements in the Philippines who worked as *sakadas* in Hawai'i, such as Pedro Calosa.[38]

Those who joined the Federation recognized the familiar symbols of their native mysticism and Reyes' legitimate place in that world. They accepted his tutelage and nurtured these indigenous resources as the foundation of their unique legacy. In the context of the *colorum* social movement, the phenomenon that Reyes, Moncado, and the Federation members created was essentially an extension of this indigenous culture in the immigrant crossing to America.

Spirituals: Men, Women, and Children

The mystical foundation of the Federation was established in Stockton, where Reyes lived from 1927 until 1930. As the site of its first branch office the Federation had purchased a house and property on San Joaquin Street (where the Federation headquarters still stands today). Branch manager Clenuar carried out the material business of the organization, and Reyes conducted the spiritual training of members in what he called his "College of Mystery." In Stockton, Reyes lectured, supervised the fasting of members, took care of the sick, and promoted a healthy diet for body, mind, and spirit. A few devoted students of Reyes became known for the length of their fasting—as exemplified by Geraldo Alvaro, who "completed his two years and a half without eating." Others, like Arcadio Amper, practised *sacrificio* (a combination of prayer, fasting, and meditation) and went into the mountains *(namundok)* of Santa Maria to test their spiritual prowess, a hermitlike practice *(nag-ermitanyo)* that the spirituals would pursue in Hawai'i in the coming years. The spirituals also chose celibacy; many began to grow their hair long.[39]

There were women in the Federation, as well, many of whom came from Hawai'i as wives and children of *sakadas* who joined the organization in California. By the latter part of 1928, a number of these women had formed perhaps three "women's lodges."[40] They too became spiritual members, joined Reyes' group in Stockton, and observed the same practices as the men. Their leader was Luisa Cortez, who became known as "Mama Luisa." The women and children in the Federation are featured prominently in the "Blue Book."

Material members, however, began to voice disapproval of the spiritual practices. They accused Reyes of hindering the Federation's progress and giving it the bad image of a *colorum* organization. In 1930, the growing conflict forced Moncado to instruct Reyes and his group to move to Hawai'i, where the Federation had opened two branches. This relocation of Reyes' group resulted in the formal creation of a "spiritual division" in Hawai'i. The "material division" remained in California. It turned out to be a wise move. The Federation flourished on the islands because of Reyes' presence and a *sakada* population that shared his mystic proclivities. He started to develop a core group of 144 spirituals—single *(soltero)* men, including those who came from Stockton— who dedicated everything to the Federation and Moncado. In

Steffi San Buenaventura

addition, Reyes built a loyal following of *miembros* (a term they used) among most of the material members (men and women), many of whom did *sacrificio* regularly, unlike those in California. In the tolerant and open landscape of Hawai'i and the rural isolation of the plantations, the spiritual practices of the Federation grew richer and stronger. The *miembros* themselves elaborated some of the practices and offered new interpretations, which Reyes encouraged. These additions—such as the saying of novenas on Fridays and observing certain rituals on Good Friday—were very similar to the folk religious observances in the Philippines.[41] The difference between the material and spiritual *miembros* in Hawai'i may have become blurred, but the chasm between the Federation in Hawai'i and California had become even more pronounced at this point.

The Federation's Doctrine

The core of the Federation's body of beliefs and practices was extracted from Filipino nativism and the *colorum* tradition, but elements of American Protestantism, cabala and numerology, popular culture, health fads, and certain works of fiction found their way into the formation of its doctrine. Some ideas came from Moncado's lectures. The uniqueness of the Federation phenomenon resides essentially in this syncretism and in the subtexts of these mergings between the Filipino and the American. Here are some of the beliefs that Federation members held sacred and secret in the privacy of their mystic world.

"Master E. F. B." Moncado was referred to as "Dr. Moncado" when the members addressed him as president of the organization. At the spiritual level he was called "Master E. F. B."—"Master Equi Frili Bricum," which is the human persona, and "Master Equi Frili Brium," the supernatural. The acronyms stand for: EQUI—Equality, FRILI—Fraternity,

BRIUM—Liberty. The iconography of "E. F. B." shows a photograph of Moncado (face close-up) juxtaposed against a background of angels and a big star (Halley's comet), with the words printed above his head: "Master Equifrilibrium." The words "Master Equifrilibricum" are written at the bottom of the portrait. Even today the Federation's dwindling loyal members (including second-generation followers) pray to this image and invoke the name "E. F. B." in the same way that Filipino Catholics have been invoking the name of "Jesus, Mary, Joseph" ("Hesus, Maria, Hosep").[42]

"Alpha and Omega." The logic of Moncado's reincarnation from Christ via Rizal (whose reincarnation from Christ had been established earlier in folk belief) is "proved" in this idea of alpha and omega. The basis of this thinking is embedded in the belief that Moncado's "fight for Philippine independence" was to be the fulfillment of Rizal's aborted mission to gain Filipino freedom from Spain. As one spiritual said: "The next God after Christ is a brown God. Moncado is God." Just as Christ came to save, Rizal came to save the Filipinos; his unfinished mission will be accomplished by Moncado. He added: "Those who are not Filipinos, like the white people, can also be saved *(ligtas)* if their heart is like a Filipino."

"The New Continent" and the Millennium. The millenarian theme is integral to the Federation's beliefs. At the material level, it was manifested at the very beginning in the planned return of Federation groups to the Philippines in order to establish colonies in Mindanao—the unexplored, rich frontier in the southern region of the Philippines. Spiritually the members speak of the "Second Coming" and refer to the return of "Master E. F. B." at the millennium in which the new "Equifrilibrium Religion" will replace Christianity. There will literally be a "new land" (said to form underneath Lake Lanao in Mindanao) that will emerge with the new religion—the "World Coming Religion."

"Vrilya." When Moncado claimed that he had a million followers, the members understood that the Master was talking about the *vrilya*—invisible, good, little people who changed their appearance in front of human beings. Considered protectors of the Federation, the idea of the *vrilya* was further developed in Hawai'i, where the spiritual followers claimed to have seen "plenty *vrilya*" in various forms and circumstances.[43]

"Serve Humanity; Humanity Be Served." Reyes saw his mission as one of service to humanity, and he urged the members to be "Willing to Work and Serve" (one of Reyes' mottoes). Members referred to Reyes as the "World Coming Servant." Thus the members who gave their life commitment to the Master and the Federation, who practised *sacrificio* and physical culture, who worked hard, materially and spiritually, in helping others and promoting the Master's political work were performing their mission as servants of humanity. Reyes taught them: "Serve ye but ye not be served."

"Divinity of Woman." In 1925, Moncado wrote a booklet of about seventy pages with the title *Divinity of Woman* ("and her superiority over man"). Members philosophize among themselves why woman is special; they point to the word "woman," which they say is "complete" because it also contains the word "man." The members have always been proud that Moncado urged "all women of the earth to take the leadership of the world." The Master's prophesy has come true, they assert, as they enumerate the names of Golda Meir, Indira Gandhi, Margaret Thatcher, and Corazon Aquino.[44]

"Man's Moral Concept." As "Master of Morality," Moncado composed a 230-word essay, "Man's Moral Concept," in 1947 in the Philippines. This postwar addition to the "principles of clean living and morality" and the moral teachings of Reyes elaborated in the "Blue Book" was instantly integrated into the Federation's moral teachings as if it had been there from the beginning. Members recite "Man's Moral Concept"

as a form of prayer during meetings and spiritual gatherings. In part, it says:

> Moral . . . is a great divine power to achieve all things on earth. . . . Man is God's human mechanism in His wisdom. Because without man on earth there is no God on earth. . . . The moral of a man is against all earthly vices. All vices are destructive to man's physical fitness—and, therefore, man should fight against all vices. . . . God is moral. Moral is man, and man is God. . . . Morality is but man's divine service for humanity. Humanity be served is a moral virtue of every man to achieve in life.

Most of the members shared these beliefs and contributed to their formulation even if they did not belong to the spiritual group.

The Federation's Practices

The Federation's practices were observed mostly by the spirituals in Hawai'i. These practices reflected Reyes' earlier philosophy about the balance between "physical, mental, moral, and spiritual" but underwent transformation in Hawai'i.

"Sacrificio." The spirit of *sacrificio* dominated the lives of the members, especially the spirituals. Consistent with their commitment to giving and serving and their chosen life of self-deprivation and abstinence, the *miembros* understood the idea and practice of sacrifice, a predominant theme in Catholic teaching and worship. A practice that began in Stockton, *sacrificio* essentially meant fasting (for as many consecutive days as possible and on a regular basis). Fasting was usually accompanied by prayers and meditation; dreams during this exercise were monitored and given greater significance. By depriving the body of material nourishment, the members used *sacrificio* as a means to gain spiritual strength.

"Suroy-Suroy." A more challenging form of *sacrificio* was

expanded by the spirituals in Hawai'i. This time they combined fasting with secret pilgrimages into the mountains (*namundok, nag-ermitanyo,* or, as they said humorously, *nag suroy-suroy,* "to wander about"). This challenging undertaking served as a test *(tahas)* of spiritual prowess: as a member said, he did it "to get power." These were spiritually, mentally, and physically trying experiences that became the magical moment for discovering potent *anting-anting*.

Raw Food. The daily regime of the spirituals centered on eating only raw food and a vegetarian diet. In Stockton they developed their own special recipe for peanut juice *(mug-mug)* and their version of "prepared" raw food they called *simento* (a compressed "cementlike" mold of oats, honey, and raisins cut into small slices). Material members ate regular, cooked meals but limited their meat to poultry. By mastering fasting and eating only raw food, the members were convinced they could survive any calamity because they had trained their bodies and minds and strengthened their spirit.[45]

Physical Culture. This practice consisted of yoga-like exercises that the members attempted to do daily. Said Nagal in an interview: "If you have good training in your stomach you can prevent your hunger and you can eat wind, too, not only water but you can put air in your stomach. . . . If you have good physical training you can swallow air and then your stomach will be full."[46] Nagal further revealed: "During the early days of the Federation that is our secret. Our neighbors are surprised why we are making noise in the room, sometimes . . . even how careful we move they still can notice that we are doing counting."

Sunday Schools. As they became exposed to Protestant church services, homilies, fellowships, and Bible meetings, the Federation's members began to absorb the religious messages and form of worship they had witnessed. They began to refer to their regular Sunday gatherings as their "Sunday School." Attended heavily by material members, these were occasions to deliver homilies, philosophize on spiritual matters and native mysticism, and interpret biblical passages. They sang hymns (primarily Protestant) and gave homage to E. F. B. The Federation's Sunday School became a regular weekly service of the materials who shared the basic beliefs about the Master but not the spiritual practices.

Evolution of a Religion

The seeds of a Filipino American religion had been planted from the time Lorenzo de los Reyes created the spiritual component of the Federation in California. After the spirituals converged in Hawai'i in 1930, the movement accelerated. In June 1932, Reyes and a group of members (called *destinos*) left Hawai'i, on Moncado's order, to expand the "Moncado Colonies" in the Philippines. The colonists in Mindanao worked hard to convert others (including Muslim Filipinos) to join their movement. Their efforts were primarily financed by the spirituals in Hawai'i, who continued to support the Mindanao colonies even after Reyes' death on 21 August 1937. In 1946, the spiritual division bought land and built a church in Kalihi Valley in Honolulu.

The membership base of the Federation and other Filipino organizations shrank when Filipino immigration ended with the Tydings-McDuffie Act of 1934. Despite these changes, there were probably a few hundred Federation members in Hawai'i and California who remained devoted followers of Moncado and supported his ventures into Philippine politics from 1933 until after the war. In 1948, Moncado returned from the Philippines, where he was stranded during the war, to reside in Los Angeles. With his immigration status in jeopardy, he chose to leave the United States in 1954 rather than face deportation. He lived in Baja California, Mexico, while awaiting passage of a special congressional bill to grant him U.S. residency.

On 4 April 1956, in what was to be his last visit to Los Angeles, he met with a small group of his quasi-spiritual followers over supper and said: "The work of the Filipino Federation of America is finished. Our work now is Religion." Moncado died on 8 April. On 27 May, Ansie Lara Mariano (a second-generation Federation member) started Sunday services in Moncado's home in Los Angeles. She began a religious gathering of members, as an act of obedience "to the Last Command of the Master,"[47] and founded the Equifrilibricum World Religion, a move that augmented the earlier development of a "Moncado religion" already started by some colonists and *destinos* after Reyes died. The Moncado group in Mindanao became known as "Moncadistas" (and not "Federation spirituals") by outsiders, who were aware that the group belonged to a "religious cult" and were followers of a "Filipino living in America" who was their "Filipino God."[48]

The introduction of the "Moncado religion" in the Philippines marked a turning point in the movement, which had now come full circle. The cultural landscape had changed from America back to the immigrant country of origin. What had evolved as a Filipino American social movement was now reintroduced as a millenarian religion centered on the formal worship of E. F. B. and the doctrine of "Man's Moral Concept." By the time Ansie Lara Mariano went to Mindanao to spread the religion, it had already begun to acquire another coating of syncretism. Founders and new followers of the E. F. B. religion—consisting of early Federation members and their local converts who had never been to America—added new symbols of mysticism, this time taken from Filipino culture in situ.

The "Moncado religion," nurtured on Philippine soil, developed into a small religious sect associated with a cluster of small, independent churches: Equifrilibricum Iglesarium (1945), Equifrilibricum World Religion (1956), Moncadian

Sheepfold Equi Frili Bricumian Gospel (1958), Moncadian Church of the Philippines (1959), and Universal Religion of the Equifrilibricum Universum (1959).[49] In 1971, Dominga Aniasca Ramos, a second-generation member, started the Equi Frili Brium Iglesarium with her husband, Agapito, from their home in Honolulu. In 1979 she established the church in Moncado's hometown, in Balamban, Cebu. Her church is "part of the E. F. B. World Religion," she declared, except that hers is a "church of God" because she used the name "Equi Frili Brium" whereas Mariano's is a "church of man" because she used the name "Equi Frili Bricum."[50] The impetus for institutionalizing the E. F. B. churches came from the younger, second-generation material members, who now included more women.

Although the spiritual division broke up into several factions after Moncado's death, the old members kept their reflections focused on the Master. Clemente Ogatis, in one of his homilies as presiding "priest" in the Kalihi church, expressed a fundamental belief they shared: "Si Master ang atong Diyos. Buhi. Buhi na buhi. Sabi ni Master: 'ang Diyos dili mamatay.'" (Master is our God. He is alive. Very much alive. For Master said: "God does not die.") Nor could they separate the Master from Lorenzo de los Reyes: "Si Master ug si Reyes, usara" (Master and Reyes are one), said Ted Dumaran.[51] Reyes' special role as "E.F.B.D." (the "Door to E. F. B." in Reyes' own phrase) opened the way for the collective membership's inclusion in the shaping of the Filipino immigrant experience. Together Moncado and Reyes created a phenomenon that melded the power of their folk spirituality with the vitality of their American experience. The faith of Federation members had withstood the tests of time. Over several decades, they remained steadfast under vicious attacks from within and without: their Master was publicly berated as a fool and accused as a crook; they were mocked as ignorant and illiterate and ostracized by their own people; their organization was ridiculed as a "fake," as "superstitious," as a "suspicious" movement.[52] These condemnations only strengthened the Federation members who likened themselves and their Master to the persecution of Christ and his followers.

The legacy of the Federation has spanned three generations and two continents. Only a handful of the pioneering members are still alive today. As a unique episode in nearly one hundred years of Filipino interaction with America, this phenomenon signifies the flow of Filipino cultural identity and its power of continuity. As a social movement, it celebrates the culture of folk spirituality and wisdom—which energized a group of immigrants to triumph over the hardships of their collective struggle and to bear the spirit of their Filipinoness into the realm of native mystical empowerment. The Master empowered them, of course, but they empowered the Master.

Notes

A postdoctoral fellowship and an additional research grant from UCLA's Institute of American Cultures in the Asian American Studies Center in 1991–1992 made it possible for me to update this research, do fieldwork in selected Filipino American communities in California, and gather data from several archival collections. I wish to thank Don Nakanishi, Russell Leong, Valerie Matsumoto, Enrique dela Cruz, Tania Azores, and Herminia Menez for their warm and generous support and Yuji Ichioka for being a mentor and friend.

1. Some of the pioneering work on the history of the early Filipino immigrants has come from H. Brett Melendy, for example, the section on "Filipino-Americans," in *Asians in America: Filipinos, Koreans, and East Indians* (Boston: Twayne, 1977), and from Howard DeWitt's series of articles on the labor struggle of Filipino farmworkers in California before World War II. But Carlos Bulosan's fictive narrative, *America Is in the Heart* (Seattle: University of Washington Press, 1973), has been the single most popular work that has shaped our image of the Filipinos in the 1920s and 1930s. Ronald Takaki's narrative on the Filipinos is based almost entirely on the "Bulosan model"; see "Dollar a Day, Dime a Dance," in *Strangers from a Different Shore* (New York: Penguin,

1990). Fred Cordova's pictorial essay, *Filipinos: the Forgotten Americans* (Dubuque: Kendall/Hall, 1983), provides fresh glimpses of a more balanced "Pinoy" life, pre-1965, viewed by an American-born Filipino. Philip Vera Cruz's life story is significant because his experience began with the same Bulosan cohort but became integrated with the postwar farm labor movement. See Craig Scharlin and Lilia V. Villanueva, *Philip Vera Cruz: A Personal History of Filipino Immigrants and the Farmworker Movement* (Los Angeles: UCLA Labor Center, Institute of Industrial Relations, and UCLA Asian American Studies Center, 1994).

2. Steffi San Buenaventura, "Filipino Immigration to the United States," in Franklin Ng, ed., *The Asian American Encyclopedia* (New York: Marshall Cavendish, 1995), pp. 439–453.

3. This research began in 1976 with visits to the "Moncado colony" in Honolulu and informal interviews of its members. In 1979, through a small Luce Foundation grant from the University of Michigan's Center for Southeast Asian Studies, a historian friend, Michael Cullinane, and I did a dozen extensive oral histories of the members of the Filipino Federation of America in Honolulu. Beginning in 1980 I expanded the research to the Federation communities on Oʻahu and the neighbor islands and in California. See Steffi San Buenaventura, "Nativism and Ethnicity in a Filipino-American Experience" (Ph.D. diss., University of Hawaiʻi, 1990), and "The Master and the Federation: A Filipino-American Social Movement in California and Hawaii," *Social Process in Hawaii* 33 (1991): 169–193; and Steffi San Buenaventura-Smith, "A Filipino Socio-Religious Movement: Ethnic Identity and Creative Response in America" (paper presented at the American Studies International Conference, Berkeley, September 1980). See also Michael Cullinane, "The Filipino Federation of America: The Prewar Years, 1925–1940—An Overview," *Crossroads* 1 (1983):74–85.

4. State of California, *Facts About Filipino Immigration into California,* Special Bulletin 3 (San Francisco: California State Printing Office, April 1930); San Buenaventura, "Filipino Immigration," pp. 445–446; Jonathan Y. Okamura, "Filipino Americans," in *Asian American Encyclopedia,* pp. 429–439.

5. See Roman R. Cariaga, *Filipinos in Hawaiʻi: Economic and Social Conditions 1906–1936* (Honolulu: Filipino Public Relations Bureau, 1937), pp. 62–63; Ruben R. Alcantara, *Sakada: Filipino Adaptation in Hawaiʻi* (Washington, D.C.: University Press of America, 1981), pp. 57–58; Jonathan Y. Okamura, "Filipino Organizations: A History," *The Filipinos in Hawaiʻi: The First Seventy-Five Years* (Honolulu: Hawaiʻi Filipino News, 1981), pp. 73–76; Dean T. Alegado, "The Filipino Community in Hawaiʻi: Development and Change," *Social Process in Hawaiʻi* 33 (1991):

16–17. Edwin Almirol was an early contributor to the literature on Filipino voluntary organizations; see, for example, *Ethnic Identity and Social Negotiation: A Study of a Filipino Community in California* (New York: AMS Press, 1985).

6. The Caballeros de Dimas Alang was first established in San Francisco on 14 December 1920 by Pedro Loreto and incorporated on 22 January 1921. It originated from a Philippine organization, Gran Orden de Caballeros de Dimas-Alang (Dakilang Hanay ng mga Kaginoohan ng Dimas Alang), inspired by José Rizal and his nom de plume (Dimas-Alang) and founded by Patricio Belen at the turn of the century. See Jose (Pepe) A. Paman, "Caballeros Springs from Revolution," *History of the Caballeros de Dimas-Alang, Inc.* (San Francisco, 1979), pp. 10–11, in the private collection of Frank and Leticia Perez. The Legionarios del Trabajo was formed by members from San Francisco and Stockton in 1924. Founded in Manila in 1919 by Domingo Ponce, the organization sought to honor the brotherhood of workers *("kapatiran . . . anak-pawis")*. See LDT's *Aklat na Guinto* (Golden Book), pp. 1–15, published in Manila in 1919, in Leo Giron's private collection; Bart R. Navarro, "A Brief History of the Legionarios del Trabajo in America," in *Legionarios del Trabajo Blue Book* (Stockton: LDT, 1975), p. 10; see also Melinda Tria Kerkvliet, *Manila Workers' Unions, 1900–1950* (Quezon City: New Day Publishers, 1992), p. 40. El Gran Oriente, a Masonic organization in late-nineteenth-century Philippines, also became popular in America but was not established until the late 1920s. See the *Souvenir Book and Program,* Most Worshipful Grand Lodge of the Gran Oriente Filipino, 1982 Grand National Convention (Seattle), in Urbano Barcenas's private collection.

7. Original documents of the Caballeros and Legionarios published in the early 1900s in Manila, such as handbooks and secret rites, were written in Tagalog. Their programs and the names of their lodges were all Philippine-related (names of national heroes, historic places, events). Leo Giron, a member of the Legionarios in Stockton, provided rich insights and information during our long talks (winter and spring 1992).

8. From the Caballeros, Legionarios, and Federation articles of incorporation and anniversary programs.

9. Hilario C. Moncado, presidential address at the opening of the national convention of the Filipino Federation of America, 26 December 1929 (Los Angeles). Reprinted in *Mabuhay General Hilario Camino Moncado,* compiled by Fabian L. Banghuis (Los Angeles, 1946), p. 13; San Buenaventura-Smith, "Filipino Socio-Religious Movement," p. 4.

10. *Filipino Nation* (May, June, August 1928); San Buenaventura, "Nativism," pp. 243–245.

11. *Philippine Republic* 8(1) (January–February 1931):12; San Buenaventura, "Filipino Socio-Religious Movement," pp. 6–7.

12. The bibliographic references on pp. 487–493 in San Buenaventura, "Nativism," list some of these Federation documents; for information on *The Filipino Nation* (published 1928–1932) see pp. 245–250.

13. The *pensionados* who were enrolled in prestigious U.S. universities wrote regularly for Filipino newspapers and magazines and debated the issue of Philippine independence among themselves and in public.

14. San Buenaventura, "Nativism," p. 160.

15. Ibid., pp. 216–221.

16. David E. Thompson, "The Filipino Federation of America," *Social Process in Hawai'i* 7 (1941):24–35; San Buenaventura, "The Master," p. 170. Moncado worked as an "office boy" for a Los Angeles attorney, Luke McNamee, who became his mentor. McNamee presumably introduced him to individuals like William Shaefle, publisher and editor of the *American Globe,* who devoted entire issues of his "financial magazine" to feature stories about Moncado and the Federation. The publisher and editor of the *Philippine Magazine,* Clyde Tavenner, did the same thing out of his Washington D.C. publishing office. Presidents of local Chambers of Commerce, like Edgar E. Parsons of San Fernando Valley, attended and gave speeches at Federation banquets. See *American Globe* 28 (January 1931):5.

17. Reyes met Darilay in 1919 in San Francisco while both were "working in the shipyard of the Schawbacher Company," according to Darilay's biography by Nemesio Limbaga in Lorenzo de los Reyes, *Every Day New and Wonder* (Los Angeles: n.p., 1931), pp. 207–209. Darilay recruited Santiago Ayaay, a coworker in Hawai'i who sailed with him to California; Manigo recruited a few of his friends to join, men like Fausto Villanueva, and so on. Information about members of the Federation comes from both oral and written accounts.

18. For details on Moncado's educational background see San Buenaventura, "Nativism," pp. 192–199.

19. Helen Borough, who worked closely with Moncado and the Federation officers, expressed a strong dislike for the *pensionado* elite group because of their arrogant attitude and behavior (interviews, Honolulu, 3–5 March 1984). This congregation of Filipino "students" and "leaders" was concentrated in cities like Los Angeles. Together with the small group of *pensionados,* they were the writers, publishers of newspapers, entrepreneurs, labor agents, union organizers, and artists. See P. C. Morantte, *Remembering Carlos Bulosan* (Quezon City: New Day Publishers, 1984). On the East Coast, the student group, dominated by the *pensionados,* was busy publishing the *Filipino Student Bulletin,* for exam-

ple. For a glimpse of how Filipino students affected the Filipino community see Barbara M. Posadas and Roland L. Guyotte, "Unintentional Immigrants: Chicago's Filipino Foreign Students Become Settlers," *Journal of American Ethnic History* 9 (Spring 1990):26–48.

20. For a description of Stockton during this period see Carol Hemminger, "Little Manila: The Filipino in Stockton Prior to World War II," *Pacific Historian* 24 (Spring 1980):21–24 and (Summer 1980): 207–220.

21. Interviews, Stockton, 18–30 August 1980.

22. San Buenaventura, "Nativism," pp. 168–173.

23. This belief in the *"doce-doce"* should be investigated further to determine its provenance and its prevalence in particular regions of the Philippines. Members of the Federation may very well have learned about this from one another.

24. Interview, Stockton, 20 August 1980.

25. For an illustration of this phenomenon see Marcelino Foronda, *Cults Honoring Rizal* (Manila: n.p., 1961), and "The Canonization of Rizal," *Journal of Philippine National Historical Society* 8 (1960): 93–140; San Buenaventura, "Nativism," pp. 82–92.

26. Hilario Camino Moncado, *1926 Rizal Day Organization: Breaks All the Records of Any Filipino Rizal Day Celebration in America* (Los Angeles: West Coast Publishing, 1927); Filipino Federation of America, *Handbook* (Los Angeles, 1928); interviews with Helen Borough; telephone interview with Francisco Manigo (8 November 1989); San Buenaventura, "Nativism," pp. 173–179.

27. Many members believed in the meaning and message of dreams. Some indicated they had dreamed of the Master—especially after hearing Moncado give a mystical discourse and while they were fasting.

28. It is not known if Reyes or anyone in the Federation constructed this photograph of Rizal with Filipino patriots, not all of whom belonged to the *ilustrado* class; the revolutionary hero Andres Bonifacio, for example, was not an *ilustrado*. The Caballeros de Dimas Alang had a different photograph of "Rizal and the Twelve *Ilustrados*" circulating among their members on the cover of *The Caballero* 1 (July–August 1952). The caption says "Filipino Immortals" and identifies each individual in the photograph. Rizal and Bonifacio are shown seated front center, but others in the photo include "minor" national figures (such as Pedro Paterno) and some of Rizal's *ilustrado* cohorts are excluded (compared to the photo circulated by the Federation thirty years earlier).

29. A common example is "SATOR/AREPO/TENET/OPERA/ ROTAS"; see San Buenaventura, "Nativism," pp. 306–308. The Reverend

Nicolas C. Dizon, a leading critic of Moncado in Hawai'i, exposes some of these "prayers" in his anti-Federation treatise, *The Master vs. Juan de la Cruz* (Honolulu: Mercantile Press, 1931).

30. Interview, Honolulu, 31 August 1979.

31. San Buenaventura, "Nativism," pp. 260–262.

32. "The Master," p. 174; Thompson, "The Filipino Federation."

33. San Buenaventura, "Nativism," p. 254ff.

34. Reyes, *Every Day,* p. 10; San Buenaventura, "Nativism," p. 163ff; see also Cullinane, "The Filipino Federation." Before the Federation was formed, Moncado published a newspaper in 1924 called *Equifrilibricum News Service* that Reyes may have supported. The title and format changed to the *Filipino Nation* in 1928.

35. John Leddy Phelan calls this phenomenon the "Philippinization of Catholicism" in his seminal work, *The Hispanization of the Philippines* (Madison: University of Wisconsin Press, 1959). For an especially revealing source of native religious and cultural practices at the point of Spanish contact see Pedro Chirino, S.J., *Relacion de las Islas Filipinas* (Account of the Philippines), trans. Ramon Echevarria (Manila: Historical Conservation Society, 1969). See also Vicente L. Rafael, *Contracting Colonialism: Translation and Christian Conversion in Tagalog Society Under Spanish Rule* (Ithaca: Cornell University Press, 1988).

36. For the seminal work on this subject see David R. Sturtevant, *Popular Uprisings in the Philippines 1840–1940* (Ithaca: Cornell University Press, 1976). See also Reynaldo Clemena Ileto, *Pasyon and Revolution: Popular Movements in the Philippines* (Quezon City: Ateneo de Manila University, 1979). The term *"colorum"* comes from the Latin phrase *"per omnia secula secolorum."* What began as a local resistance led by Apolinario de la Cruz in 1840 against church injustice and abuses gained instant peasant support and triggered what historians consider the beginning of the rise of popular, nativistic movements in Philippine rural society in the mid-nineteenth century.

37. *Colorum* movements have always been viewed negatively and with a strong class and cultural bias. Ileto's work is critical of Sturtevant's for this reason. Ileto presents these popular movements from the perspective of those "from below" and argues their significant connection with indigenous values. I share Ileto's position. *"Colorum"* has been part of the language of Philippine popular culture and has retained negative connotations of "illegal," "fake," "imitation," "not true."

38. Abarquez interview, Stockton, 21 August 1980. I came across an *anting-anting* in the form of a *libreto* or *orasyon*—a miniature handmade "book," which fits in the palm of the hand, with handwritten prayers in combined Latin, Tagalog/Cebuano, and Spanish words—in the private

Steffi San Buenaventura

collection of Angel Ramos in Kahuku, Oʻahu. Felipe interview, Honolulu, 24 August 1979. Calosa was a famous, charismatic leader of the historic Tayug *(colorum)* uprising of 1931 in Pangasinan province. He was a *sakada* in Hawaiʻi for ten years, became actively involved in the plantation strikes, and was deported in 1927. See Sturtevant's interview of Calosa in *Popular Uprisings,* pp. 183 and 272. Sebastian Foronda, who joined the spirituals around 1963, was a roommate of Calosa on a plantation. He remembered that in one of the strikes Calosa easily escaped the plantation police because he had an *anting-anting* that made him invisible. According to Foronda, Calosa was right there but the police could not see him. Foronda interview, Honolulu, 16 September 1979.

39. Reyes, *Every Day,* p. 244; Amper interview, Honolulu, 10 September 1979.

40. 1928 *Federation Handbook.* Angie Orlanes, a second-generation member living in Los Angeles, indicated that she belonged to the last women's lodge (Lodge 6) formed on 3 July 1944 in California.

41. San Buenaventura, "Nativism," pp. 318–322.

42. Although it is very likely that "Equifrilibrium" was inspired by the word "equilibrium," the only time I came across "equilibrium" was in Diosdado Yap's interview with Leon Vaguios in *Every Day,* p. 201, where Vaguios mentions "material and spiritual equilibrium." None of the members I talked with ever mentioned "equilibrium."

43. The *vrilya* are subterranean figures in Edward George Bulwer-Lytton's novel *The Coming Race* (London: Routledge, 1847). Moncado had read the book and shared the story with the members in his lectures. Darily mentions Bulwer-Lytton; so does Reyes in *Every Day.* Who incorporated it into the Federation's "doctrine" is not clear. See San Buenaventura, "Nativism," pp. 346–351.

44. See San Buenaventura, "Nativism," pp. 296–300. The recitation of the names of the women world leaders came especially from Ted Dumaran, Federation member from Waianae, Oʻahu, who died in 1993.

45. Natural health food restaurants featuring "raw food" in downtown Los Angeles ran ads in the *Filipino Nation.*

46. Interview 31 August 1979.

47. Ansie Lara Mariano, "Brief History of How the Religion Came into Being," in *The Seven Years Struggle, 1956–1963* (Los Angeles: Equifrilibricum World Religion, 1963).

48. The term "Moncadista" originated in 1934 when Moncado ran for political office against Tomas Cabili, a "local son" in Lanao, Mindanao. Followers of Cabili became known as Cabilistas and followers of Moncado were called Moncadistas. See Victoria V. Flores-Tolentino, "The 'Moncadistas' of Mindanao: A Study of a Religious Movement,"

Kinaadman (Wisdom) 4 (1982):1–36. Tolentino's article (and the original master's thesis) documents the religious practices of the Moncadistas in the colonies.

49. Douglas J. Elwood, *Churches and Sects in the Philippines: A Descriptive Study of Contemporary Religious Group Movements* (Dumaguete City, Philippines: Silliman University, 1968). See San Buenaventura, "Nativism," pp. 426–431.

50. From several conversations with Dominga Ramos in Honolulu in the early 1980s.

51. Ogatis gave this homily on 5 December 1979. The information about Moncado and Reyes came from Ted Dumaran: in one of Moncado's visits to Hawai'i after the war, Dumaran said, Moncado uttered this phrase about him and Reyes.

52. Moncado and the Federation had a long list of critics, Filipinos and non-Filipinos, in the United States and the Philippines. His most vicious attacks came from Primo E. Quevedo in Los Angeles, who wrote and published *Read the Truth About Hilario Camino Moncado: The Greatest Impostor the World Has Ever Known* (1931), and from Rev. Nicolas C. Dizon from Honolulu, *The Master vs. Juan de la Cruz*. For the criticisms against Moncado and the Federation see San Buenaventura, "Nativism," pp. 432–445. (Quevedo was not a *pensionado* as I earlier indicated in "The Master" article (p. 184). He was a "working student" in Los Angeles who actively and openly opposed Moncado. I was very fortunate to have interviewed Quevedo in February 1992 at the age of ninety-seven. He died in the summer of 1993.)

Chapter 3

Sikh Kirpans *in California Schools:*
The Social Construction of Symbols,
the Cultural Politics of Identity, and
the Limits of Multiculturalism

VINAY LAL

In recent years American courts, as well as numerous government institutions and public bodies, have deliberated on what would appear to be an esoteric issue but in fact directly addresses the right to free exercise of religion guaranteed by the Bill of Rights and subsequent legislation. Across the state of California, certain children of the Sikh faith have been wearing to school, in accordance with the tenets of their faith, a small knife or dagger that the Sikhs call a *kirpan*.[1] In January 1994, three siblings, Rajinder, Sukhjinder, and Jaspreet Cheema, were observed to be wearing a *kirpan* under their clothes while at school and were at once suspended on the ground that a *kirpan* fell within the definition of a weapon offered in the California Penal and Education Codes and other regulations, which make it a criminal offense, subject to specified exceptions, to bring or possess specified weapons, including knives and daggers, upon the grounds of, or within, a public or private school. Subsequently the superintendent of the Livingston Union School District in Merced County, where the Cheema family has been residing for some years, was approached by the American Civil Liberties Union with a request that the school district reconsider its position, but the members of the school board refused to lift the ban on *kirpans* or to allow the Cheema children to attend school while the matter was under dispute. On 15 April 1994, the Cheema family filed suit and sought a preliminary and permanent injunction preventing the school district from excluding Sikh students from attending school without violating their right to the free exercise of religion. Such an injunction was denied by the district judge; but the U.S. Court of Appeals, Ninth Circuit, subsequently reversed and remanded the district judge's decision. On remand, the district judge ordered that the Cheema children be allowed to carry, subject to certain conditions, *kirpans* to school. Matters were not to end there, however, as a bill that was unanimously passed in the California Senate—which would have allowed Sikh children to carry *kirpans* to school on the ground that possession of such *kirpans* constituted an integral part of a recognized religious practice—was vetoed by Pete Wilson, governor of California, who declared himself unable to "abandon public safety to the resourcefulness of a thousand school districts."[2]

As one of the first cases to be tried under the Religious Freedom Restoration Act (RFRA) of 1993, *Rajinder Singh Cheema, et al., v. Harold V. Thompson, et al.* is a case of unusual legal importance. The provision in the Bill of Rights allowing for the free exercise of religion has been one of the most keenly contested aspects of American constitutional and political history, and the enactment by Congress of the Religious Freedom Restoration Act of 1993, which was struck down as unconstitutional by the Supreme Court in 1997, suggests that the duties of the state in matters pertaining to religion will continue to be a matter of controversy and subject to continuous (and conflicting) interpretation by the courts. I propose, in the first instance, to sketch a history of the *kirpan* and then to locate sociologically and historically the claims pursued by both parties to the conflict. As I shall argue at some length, the politics of Sikhism in the diaspora cannot be divorced, as it was in the arguments of both the defense and the prosecution in the Cheema case, from the politics of Sikhism in the land of its birth. I then proceed to explore the moral and political complexities of a problem in which the religious convictions of a particular community, when their exercise has not been shown to be detrimental to the rights of other members of society, are nonetheless posited against the consideration, preeminent as it must be for any state, of public safety.

As I shall suggest, the complex legal arguments establishing that the Livingston Union School District was not entitled to prevent the Cheemas from the free exercise of their religious convictions and obligations are persuasive, but our endorsement of the right to the free exercise of religion need not hinge upon an acceptance of the arguments presented by the plaintiffs' attorneys. It must be unequivocally clear that our acceptance of the right of the Cheemas, and thus of all Sikh children, to be in possession of *kirpans* while at school must be forthcoming even if the legal interpretation of the Religious Freedom Restoration Act does not support such a right, as the Supreme Court has now ruled. While I am not yet prepared to advance, at least in the confines of this study, an argument for an unconditional right to self-determination, or even an argument for some unadulterated and transcendent notion of "rights," dominant communities must, it appears, learn to dispossess themselves of their privileges. Situations such as those in which the Cheema children found themselves, and in which a thousand others are placed daily, provide the only test, not merely of a culture's capacity for resilience, but of its willingness to be chivalrous, its ability to live with some discomfort, its adherence to the ethos of cultural pluralism and accommodation, its celebration of the plurality of knowledge, and its readiness to create the conditions for the survival of plurality.

The history of Sikhism is a subject that has been detailed in innumerable monographs and learned studies. And while this history need not detain us, certain elementary—though not always incontestable—statements of "fact" need to be set out.³ The Sikh religion was founded in India by Guru Nanak (1469–1539) nearly five hundred years ago. Born in the Punjab, Nanak rebelled against the obscurantism and ritualism of Hinduism and questioned the authority of India's sacerdotal caste, the Brahmins. Nanak preached a simple faith shorn of idolatry and predicated on the equality of all men. He perceived God as *sat*—epistemologically "truth," ontologically "being," the supreme reality, omnipotent and omniscient. An itinerant master of monotheism, Nanak roamed the Punjab and gathered a number of disciples, or *shishya*, from which the word "Sikh" was ultimately derived. For Nanak there were neither Hindus nor Muslims, but when he died adherents of both faiths laid claim to his remains. In the words of one couplet:

> *Guru Nanak, the King of Fakirs.*
> *To the Hindu a Guru, to the Mussulman a Pir.*⁴

Nanak chose as his successor Angad (1504–1552), the second guru of the Sikh faith, who was followed in turn by eight others. Angad developed the Gurmukhi script and collected the writings of Nanak; the fourth guru, Ram Das (1534–1581), founded the holy city of Amritsar, where his successor Arjan (1563–1606) built a *gurdwara* (literally, "doorway to the guru") or Sikh temple. Guru Arjan also engaged in the construction of numerous other *gurdwaras* and gave definite shape to the compilation of Nanak's writings, which along with the hymns of Hindu and Muslim saints and the writings of the other gurus were constituted into the Adi Granth or

Vinay Lal

Guru Granth Sahib, the holy book of the Sikhs. The Sikhs thereby became, in the words of one scholar, a "textual community."[5] Guru Arjan's efforts to put his faith on a firm basis and secure for it an organizational structure attracted the attention of India's Mughal dynasty, and he was consequently put to death in the city of Lahore. This was, by the conventional account, also the fate of Tegh Bahadur (1621–1675), the ninth guru, who refused conversion to Islam. His son, Gobind Singh (1666–1708), having assumed the leadership of his people at the age of ten, conceived a plan in his later years to save the Sikhs from possible extinction and safeguard the interests of the community. He initiated five of his followers —known as the Panj Pyaras, or Five Beloved—into a new brotherhood that he called the Khalsa: the Pure.[6] Like any monks joining a Hindu order, they were given new names to each of which was attached the suffix "Singh," or lion. (Khalsa Sikh women receive the name "Kaur.") They were also enjoined to wear, as a mark of their devotion to the faith and an indication of their membership in the Khalsa, *panj kakke,* or five symbols: *kes* (uncut hair), *kangha* (a comb), *kara* (a steel bangle), *kirpan* (a sword or knife), and *kachcha* (special breeches or undergarments). Having further commanded them to abstain from tobacco, alcohol, and *halal* meat (that is, meat ritually slaughtered in the Muslim manner), Gobind Singh then baptized the five men and was in turn baptized by them. Thus was formed the Khalsa.

As every Khalsa Sikh male was henceforth to be known as a Singh, or lion, Gobind Singh in one stroke had not only signified his radical commitment to equality by the obliteration of the mark of caste identification,[7] but he also prepared the Khalsa for a life of militant devotion to their faith. While the reasoning that prompted Gobind Singh to command the Khalsa initiates to embrace the *panj kakke* is less certain, the scholar Jit Singh Uberoi has offered what is undoubtedly a compelling interpretation of the five symbols and their place

Sikh Kirpans *in California Schools*

within Sikhism. He suggests that we view Guru Gobind Singh's injunctions in relation to certain rites of renunciation *(sannyasa)* that were prevalent throughout the Punjab (and indeed the rest of India) in his time. In the initiation rites undertaken by the Hindu *sannyasi,* he would—having found a guru—have his beard, mustache, and head entirely shaved. The neophyte of the Jogi order, says Uberoi, "is first made to fast for two or three days. A knife is then driven into the earth, and the candidate vows by it not to (1) engage in trade, (2) take employment, (3) keep dangerous weapons, (4) become angry when abused, and (5) marry."[8] Such a life could only signify disinvestiture and renunciation. But Guru Gobind Singh, in requiring Sikh men to keep their hair long, clearly intended the Sikh initiation rite to be understood as an investiture and act of affirmation standing in antithesis to the rites of Hindu renunciation. The antidepilatory taboo, argues Uberoi, is to be understood "as a specific inversion in symbolic terms of the custom of total depilation" enjoined by *sannyasis,* Jogis, and others—indeed as the "permanent renunciation of renunciation," the "negation of the negation."[9] Uberoi's argument is complicated by the circumstance that in some Muslim and Hindu orders the hair is worn long; but, as he notes, it is then worn as matted hair, dressed in ashes. In the Sikh conception, the function of "constraining the hair and imparting an orderly arrangement to it" falls upon the comb: thus the *kes* (uncut hair) and *kangha* (comb) form a unitary and complementary pair. A similar complementary pair is formed by the *kirpan* (sword) and *kara* (steel bangle). Uberoi suggests that "the steel bracelet imparts the same orderly control over the sword which the comb does the hair."[10]

Uberoi admits that "the custom of wearing long and unshorn hair *(kes)* is among the most cherished and distinctive signs of an individual's membership of the Sikh Panth, and it seems always to have been so."[11] Long hair—because it is distinctive, particularly when rolled up in a turban, as it is among modern-day Sikhs—appears to be the most characteristic sign of a Khalsa Sikh male. A recent piece of legislation, the Delhi Gurdwara Act 82 of 1971, went so far as to define a Sikh as a "person who professes the Sikh religion, believes and follows the teachings of Sri Guru Granth Sahib and the ten Gurus only *and keeps unshorn hair.*" If it had to be ascertained whether a person were a Sikh, the act further states, the person in question would be required to make the following declaration: "I solemnly affirm that I am a Keshadhari Sikh, that I believe in and follow the teachings of Sri Guru Granth Sahib and the ten Gurus only, and that I have no other religion."[12] Keshadhari, or orthodox, Sikhs keep their hair long. But as Uberoi argues, and as Sikh scholars would indubitably agree, despite the preeminence seemingly attached to *kes* or unshorn hair the five symbols are of a piece and together constitute "the authenticating sign and seal of Sikhism."[13] They were almost certainly seen as belonging together on the person of the Sikh. In one of the earliest colonial accounts we have of the Sikhs, the Khalsa Sikhs were described thus: "The disciples of Govind were required to devote themselves to arms, always to have steel about them in some shape or other, to wear a blue dress, to allow their hair to grow, to exclaim when they met each other, *Wa! Guruji ka khalsah! Wa! Gurji ki futteh!*" ("The Khalsa are the chosen of God! Victory be to our God!")[14] Indeed colonial officials—who were predisposed toward viewing Sikhs as one of India's preeminent "martial races" and saw in the support rendered to the British by the Sikhs during the difficult days of the Indian rebellion of 1857–1858 the vindication of their views—considered the observance of the symbols among Sikhs as not only a true sign of their faith but as conferring upon them the military prowess for which they were esteemed. "The best practical test of a true Sikh," wrote the author of a manual intended for army officials, "is to ascertain whether calling himself a Sikh he wears uncut hair and abstains from smoking."[15] Only those Sikhs who faithfully observed the Khalsa symbols were recruited into the army.

It is no surprise, then, that Sikh scholars are agreed that the Five K's "are the symbol of Sikh solidarity, unity and strength."[16] If Uberoi is right in suggesting that the *kirpan* should be viewed as being conjoined with the *kara*, then it follows that the *kirpan* is "a sword ritually constrained and thus made into the mark of every citizen's honour, not only of the soldier's vocation."[17] A sword that is "ritually constrained" is a sword that is bound to do only the work of justice, to be drawn on behalf of the oppressed and the weak, to be offered only in defense. The sword can be employed only when all other avenues have been explored and exhausted, and indeed failure to do so at that time would be tantamount to complicity in acts of evil and oppression. Though the sword was the natural adornment of the soldier, Guru Gobind, in designating the *kirpan* as one of the five distinctive symbols of the Khalsa, was clearly intending to convey that the men of the Khalsa would be much like soldiers in displaying bravery and fearlessness, but as their sword was to be the sword of baptism, they were also to exercise restraint. It is with the sword that the guru baptized the first five initiates: as the story goes, the guru asked for five men who would be willing to give their heads; eventually one man stepped forth and was taken into a tent, from which the guru emerged with a blood-stained sword; then another four men volunteered (no doubt with great hesitation), all seemingly dispatched in the same manner. But the guru then emerged from the tent with the five men and five decapitated goats.

Guru Gobind's father, let us also recall, had been martyred, and fear of persecution had led other Sikhs to lead lives of anonymity. While Guru Gobind was unwilling to let his people be martyred by Muslim rulers, he did not think they were to evade persecution by merging into the crowd. Thus the sword, as a characteristic mark of the Sikhs, was to render them intrepid, willing to forgo their lives of fear and anonymity for recognition by others, and place them on the path of self-recognition. As an eighteenth-century writer, Ratan Singh Bhangu, was to claim:

> The Guru reasoned and from thought he proceeded to action. His followers were to emerge as splendid warriors, their uncut hair bound in turbans; and as warriors all were to bear the name "Singh." This, the Guru knew, would be effective. He devised a form of baptism administered with the sword, one which would create a Khalsa staunch and unyielding. His followers would destroy the empire, each Sikh horseman believing himself to be a king. All weakness would be beaten out of them and each, having taken the baptism of the sword, would thereafter be firmly attached to the sword.[18]

As I have suggested, the attachment to the sword, or *kirpan,* must be perceived as attachment to an object that becomes an inalienable part of oneself, constitutive of a life of affirmation, honor, and self-respect. To forgo the *kirpan,* at least in the orthodox view, is to relinquish one's identity as a Sikh observant of the faith.[19]

Political Constructions of a Sacred Symbol

Though the story of the *kirpan,* from the time of Guru Gobind Singh's death to the early part of the twentieth century, when the *kirpan* must have first surfaced in North America, is too long for the confines of this study, a few remarks about the manner in which various governments of India in the twentieth century have sought to constrain the *kirpan*'s reach will contribute to an understanding of the contours of the present debate. By the late nineteenth century, Harjot Oberoi has argued, the Singh Sabhas, or Sikh associations, had systematized the strict adherence to the Five K's, along

Sikh Kirpans in California Schools

with other observances (such as visits to Sikh shrines and abstention from prohibited foods), as constituting a true and unambiguous Sikh identity.[20] *Kirpans* were to become quite visible in the 1920s, often described as the first phase of militant Sikh participation in the nationalist movement. The Central Sikh League had been inaugurated on 30 December 1919; by the following summer, a number of district Sikh Leagues had been set up. It is around this time, as one historian has written, that "the widespread adoption of Khalsa symbols denoting solidarity and militancy in the name of the faith" began to be observed. "Sikhs began in increasing numbers to wear black turbans (a symbol of militancy) and kirpans."[21] Agitation for the control of Sikh shrines, a movement that had started in 1914 but during the war had been relegated to the background, was once again revived. And in this the Akalis, a group that ascribed its origins to Guru Gobind Singh, were to play a large role. These Akalis, "carrying large kirpans," began to appear in public places during the summer of 1920.[22] The army was not spared of dissent either —and this was no small matter, as the Sikhs constituted a formidable presence in the army out of all proportion to their share of the population. As the Punjab government was to report in May 1920: "A young sepoy of the Depot of the 34th Pioneers at Sialkot appeared on parade with a large kirpan, which he refused on religious grounds to give up. He was sentenced by court martial to one year imprisonment for insubordination. . . . The Sikh League are interesting themselves in the case."[23]

While the movement for the liberation of *gurdwaras*— Sikh temples whose administration was in the hands of priests *(mahants)* considered to be excessively Hinduized and sometimes even pawns of the British—was to gain momentum, the government of the Punjab struggled to arrive at some policy that would enable it to prevent the public display of *kirpans,* and thus preserve its authority, without generating allegations of religious interference. It was clear that matters had come to a head: in December 1920, for example, Sikhs belonging to the newly constituted Shiromani Gurdwara Prabhandak Committee (SGPC), an organization committed to handing over management of the *gurdwaras* to strict followers of the faith, had forcibly occupied three *gurdwaras,* in each instance brandishing *kirpans* and axes. On numerous other occasions in 1921, Akalis "armed with axes and kirpans" captured Sikh shrines. And in a government report on the agitation published in 1922, reference was specifically made to the *kirpan* as a "Sikh religious emblem" that had "figured so prominently in Sikh agitation during the past few years." Less benignly, the author of the report noted that the "lethal nature of this weapon, which has grown in size until it is now indistinguishable from a sword," had occasioned complaints from other Indian communities who desired to know why the Sikhs were being granted special privileges.[24]

By February 1922, the Punjab government had decided that district officers were to disarm Akali militants. For fear of offending the religious sensibilities of Sikhs, the Akalis were not to be divested of their *kirpans,* though the government sought to curtail their length. The SGPC was opposed to any such measure, however, as the Sikh faith imposes no limits on the size of the *kirpan.* As though to underscore the sensitivity of the issue, a Sikh in one regiment went on a hunger strike on 7 February when he was forbidden from wearing a *kirpan* larger than allowed by the regulations.[25] The SGPC agreed only that misuse of the *kirpan* would entitle the government to take action, and it called upon the Sikhs in the army to observe regulations pertaining to the wearing of *kirpans* and black turbans.[26] The army staff, nonetheless, continued to maintain that the length of the *kirpan* be restricted to nine inches. It was at the behest of the army that the government of India wrote to the Punjab government to express its disapproval of the policy followed in the Punjab. The government of India, wrote one official, had acquiesced in the view that it was not opportune to enforce limitations on the size of the *kirpans* when negotiations between the Punjab government and SGPC on the questions of *gurdwara* management appeared to be making good progress. "They are not, however," he added, "clear as to the reasons which have led the local Government to authorise the wearing of swords and of kirpans indistinguishable from swords by Sikhs." Though the government of India recognized the wisdom of not instituting prosecutions, it thought that the Punjab government had practically authorized, "even though subject to conditions, the carrying of weapons prohibited by law." The government of India could not see how *kirpans* "practically indistinguishable from swords" were being "worn with impunity," and it noted that the "question of imposing a definite limitation on the size of Kirpans may require to be considered."[27]

The question of what to do with *kirpans,* however, was sidelined for the moment, and with the passage of the Sikh Gurdwaras Act of 1925 the grievances of the SGPC and Khalsa Sikhs appear to have been at least partly resolved. Indeed, between 1925 and 1928 most of the provinces had passed legislation exempting Sikhs carrying *kirpans* from the provisions of the Indian Arms Act of 1878, which expressly forbid Indians from bearing arms.[28] Subsequent to India's independence in 1947, the Sikhs were able to attain a further concession. Article 25 of the Constitution of India (1950), relating to the free exercise of religion, stated in its explanatory clause that the wearing and carrying of *kirpans* was "included in the profession of the Sikh religion."[29] This meant that Sikhs throughout India could now carry *kirpans* of unspecified length in public without having contravened the law; the constitution also appeared to be conceding that Sikh identity is distinct, as Sikhs alone were allowed the privilege of carrying *kirpans.* The second "explanation" following Article 25, however, stipulated that references to Hindus and their religious institutions were to be so construed as to include adherents of Sikhism, Buddhism, and Jainism.[30] If Sikh identity was being affirmed in the first explanatory clause, the second clause appeared to assimilate Sikhs into the Hindu fold. Such a provision was always liable to become the basis for an allegation that an attempt was being made to eliminate Sikhs, render Sikhism sterile and even effeminate, or that in Hindu India Sikhs were bound to be a repressed minority.

At a conference of the Akali Dal—the political party representing the interest of the Khalsa Sikhs if not the entire Sikh community—held in February 1981, Harchand Singh Longowal, the president of the conference, reminded the gathering that the "Sikh nation is unique in refusing to be absorbed in the Brahmanical traditions and modes of the Hindu nation" and that "Sikhs were still struggling for asserting our rightful claim to our identity and nationhood."[31] He also declared his intent to have certain demands, endorsed by the SGPC and forty-five in number, accepted by the government of India, and to this end negotiations between the SGPC and the government began later in the year. Among these demands, which complained of the government's refusal to grant "holy city" status to Amritsar, its failure to name any train the Golden Temple Express (after the Golden Temple in Amritsar), and its negligence in safeguarding the life and property of Sikhs throughout India and abroad, was the demand that Sikhs be allowed to carry the *kirpan* aboard civilian aircraft on domestic and international flights.[32] This demand surfaced in many speeches by Sikh leaders. It is reported that Jarnail Singh Bhindranwale, the leader of the violent secessionist movement, urged his followers to carry the *kirpan* aboard Indian Airlines and Air India flights with the following words: "If a Hindu can wear his sacred thread *(janeu),* which is his sign, why can't a Sikh carry his sword?"[33]

Certain demands were conceded, including the right of Sikhs to carry *kirpans* of stipulated length on domestic flights,[34] but substantial differences remained. Disaffection among militant Sikhs continued to spread. The story of the bloody aftermath—including a campaign of terror and assassination in which many Sikhs and Hindus were the victims, the gross violation of the rights of many Sikhs to their life and livelihood by Indian police and armed forces in their drive to eliminate the terrorists, the fortification of the Golden Temple by Sikh terrorists led by Bhindranwale, the storming of the Golden Temple by the Indian Army, the death of Indira Gandhi at the hand of two Sikh assassins, the carnage unleashed upon Sikhs in Delhi, and the continuing war of terror and secession before the eventual "pacification" of militant Sikhs in the early 1990s—has been told in numerous works.[35] But what is most pertinent is that, particularly during the spread of Sikh militancy under Bhindranwale's leadership, Sikhs themselves were prominent if not preeminent among the victims of Bhindranwale's campaign to eliminate his enemies. As Rajiv Kapur has observed, Bhindranwale had emerged, from the outset of his new responsibilities as the head of a small center of Sikh religious learning, "as a rigid champion of Sikh orthodoxy. He toured Sikh villages, exhorted his congregation not to discard Khalsa symbols and baptized hundreds. An essential feature of his preaching was that, in keeping with Sikh traditions, all Sikhs should bear weapons."[36] Bhindranwale urged his audience with the exhortation *"shastradhari howo"*—that is, to become the bearers of weapons—and as Veena Das has noted, the "most visible sign of the masculinity of the Sikh in this discourse is his sword." There was nothing that Bhindranwale more ardently desired than that Sikhs "shed their femininity." And this was to be achieved not only by wielding the sword but by emphatically repudiating Hinduism, construed as a feminine faith. Bhindranwale was to propound the idea that Sikhs had been a "race whose history is written in the blood of martyrs," and such a race of men could not conceivably be deemed to have accepted the designation of Mahatma Gandhi as the "father of the nation," a man whose very techniques of resistance were feminine. "Can those who are the sons of the valiant guru, whose symbol is the sword," Bhindranwale was to ask his audience, "ever accept a woman like [the] Mahatma as their father?"[37]

Bhindranwale and his followers targeted not merely those Sikh leaders who were opposed to his teachings, and such newspaper editors as had dared to raise their voices against him, but moderate Sikhs who had abandoned the symbols of their faith and thus relapsed into Hinduism, abjuring their masculinity (as the militants imagined) for a contemptible femininity and renouncing the strict tenets of their pure faith for the idolatry and softness of a pluralistic Sikhism quite comfortable with, if not indistinguishable from, Hinduism. This is the old fear that haunts every Sikh who is keen on maintaining boundaries that constantly invite transgression. Perhaps these symbols alone remained, nearly five hundred years after the birth of the faith, to differentiate Sikhs from Hindus—itself a rather desperate thought—and if these too, perchance, were not observed, then who could say who is a Sikh? As if in grim testimony of Bhindranwale's premonitions about the frail nature of Sikh identity, many Sikhs attempted to escape the holocaust unleashed upon them following the assassination of Indira Gandhi by shaving their beard and cutting their hair; others, not so lucky, were first shaved before being burned alive by the paid hooligans of party and local bosses.[38]

Inalienable Symbols in an Alien Land?

Conflicts that rage within a country are often echoed within the lives of emigrants settled abroad. The movement among Bhindranwale and other extremists, many of whom are no longer living, for a separate state called Khalistan was to receive substantial support from Sikhs settled overseas. Jagjit

Singh Chauhan, an advocate of armed violence against the Indian state, set up a sovereign state of Khalistan from his base in London and became its self-styled president. With the support of other wealthy or influential Sikhs, such as the Californian Didar Singh Bains, reputed to be the world's biggest peach farmer, Chauhan canvased among the substantial populations of Sikhs in the United States, Britain, Canada, and the former West Germany for support. The All-India Sikh Students' Federation, the militant youth wing of the Akali Dal, established chapters in the United States, Canada, and Britain, and branches of the Dal Khalsa, set up in India in 1978 "with the avowed object of demanding the creation of an independent sovereign Sikh State," were opened in Britain and West Germany in 1983.[39] The attack on the Golden Temple, as well as the violence unleashed upon Sikhs following the assassination of Indira Gandhi, were bound to embitter Sikhs overseas. "Many Sikhs in Yuba City," Bruce La Brack has written in his recent study of Sikhs in California, "and elsewhere outside of South Asia have now embraced the idea of Khalistan as the *only* alternative to the present impasse and are willing to support it ideologically and financially."[40] His study does not indicate the dissensions among Sikhs overseas, however, and there have been disagreements among the Sikh community in the matter of Sikh children carrying *kirpans* to school, a matter I shall leave for later.

Bruce La Brack further notes that the symbols of the faith were not strictly observed by Sikhs, if indeed at all, during the period from around 1900—when the Sikh presence first became noticeable on the West Coast of the United States and Canada—to the late 1950s. The Stockton *gurdwara*, for example, even allowed worshipers to enter the shrine with their shoes on and their heads uncovered.[41] But with the arrival of students and other new emigrants in the 1950s, and "a reawakening of concern for tradition in older resident Sikhs," the wearing of the Five K's seems to have gained some

Vinay Lal

acceptance. Though some newcomers were "persuaded to shave in conformity to what older Sikhs felt were American standards of dress and grooming," the "Sikh newcomers generally retained the beard and turban." A few of the older Sikhs themselves readopted the symbols of the faith, leading La Brack to conclude that "external orthodoxy was increasing."[42] La Brack makes no mention of the *kirpan*. Indeed he suggests, rather unpersuasively, that the substance of the debate over why some Sikhs readopted the five symbols is "not as important as . . . its presence."[43] But in the first few decades, when discrimination against Asians was rampant and Sikhs were in any case assimilated into the "Hindu" fold, perhaps Sikhs wisely wished to draw no further attention to themselves.[44] In the Punjab itself, during the 1950s, there was a movement for a Punjabi homeland, and there can be little doubt that the self-assurance of Sikhs overseas received a boost from the events back in India. Moreover, by the late 1950s and early 1960s, the Sikhs in California had made a considerable presence for themselves and some had reached positions of enormous affluence. The time was certainly ripe for asserting the faith. And along with unshorn hair, there is no more moving and visible symbol of the faith than the *kirpan*.

Acceptance of the *kirpan*, however, has been fraught with difficulties. Over the last few years, there has been a flurry of political and legal activity culminating in the legal decision in the Cheema case and the aborted attempt by the California Assembly to enact legislation that would permit Sikh children to carry *kirpans* to schools without the fear of inviting official sanctions. To recapitulate the circumstances of the Cheema case, three children of the Cheema family residing near Merced, California, in the Livingston Union School District, were baptized as Khalsa Sikhs during the school vacation in December 1993. When school reconvened in January, they returned wearing the five symbols of their faith, including the *kirpan*. The *kirpans* were worn under their clothes, as is common in

Sikh Kirpans in California Schools

the case of baptized Sikhs at work or school, and thus were not openly visible to others. One of the three children was, however, observed to be wearing a *kirpan* by his classmate. When the matter was brought to the attention of the school principal, the Cheema children were at once suspended from school. It was explained that, in having brought *kirpans* to school, the children had contravened district regulations as well as the California Penal Code, Section 626.10, which makes it a public offense to bring to school, with specified exemptions, any "dirk, dagger, ice pick, knife having a blade longer than 2½ inches," as well as numerous other specified objects.[45] The *kirpan*, the Cheema family was told, was to be considered a weapon within the meaning of the existing legislation.

When the school district refused to reconsider lifting the ban it had imposed on the Cheema children unless they were willing to leave their *kirpans* at home, the American Civil Liberties Union asked the district to reconsider its position, pointing out that in another school district the matter had been resolved "in a manner which preserved the rights of Sikhs to attend school while wearing their *kirpans*." A meeting of the school board was then convened—though as attorneys for the Cheemas were to point out, members of the board received a memorandum from the superintendent's office advising them to adhere to the policy of "no knives in school" in light of the school's "compelling interest" in furnishing "an environment which is perceived to be safe." It was proposed, as a "viable alternative," to allow the children to wear a "symbolic necklace replica" of a *kirpan*, though why the wearing of such a replica should have required the permission of school authorities remains a mystery. In the event, the board refused to entertain the position taken by the Cheema family, and indeed the Sikh adults who had come to this public meeting were themselves threatened with arrest for having arrived at the meeting wearing their own *kirpans*. The district was once again requested "to at least allow the Cheema children to return to school while the legality of defendants' actions was being litigated," but this request was rejected. The district court was then asked by the counsel for the Cheema family, Stephen Bomse and the ACLU, to issue an injunction preventing the school district from excluding Sikh students from attending school without violating their right to the free exercise of religion under the Religious Freedom Restoration Act of 1993. The district judge, Garland Burrell Jr., refused to issue such an injunction, but on appeal the U.S. Court of Appeals for the Ninth Circuit reversed and remanded the district court's decision.[46]

In considering the case presented by the plaintiffs in the court of appeals, a number of considerations come to the fore. First, as the plaintiffs argued, similar cases had arisen in other school districts—in the United States as well as Canada, which has a substantial Sikh population—where Khalsa Sikh students had been allowed to attend school while wearing *kirpans*. They noted that Sikh students in the Selma Unified School District in California had expressly been allowed to carry *kirpans*, and the superintendent of schools had stated: "I am unaware of any actual or threatened incidents of kirpan-related violence or other form of kirpan misuse, in this District or elsewhere" (BOA, p. 9). The official placed in charge of multicultural education in the Surrey School District in British Columbia had stated that schools in her district had "several thousand Sikh students," "many" of whom "attend wearing *kirpans*" without any problem. As she emphasized in a letter attached to her declaration in February 1994, "since the beginning of this century, baptized Sikhs have been attending public schools wearing kirpans. In this long period of time, there is no record of an association between kirpans and violence, and there is no record of kirpans being used inappropriately" (BOA, p. 10). The plaintiffs also argued that in Ontario the court ordered the school district to admit Sikh children wearing *kirpans*, as a study had shown that most other school districts in Canada follow a similar policy. And indeed the court went so far as to state that "there is no evidence that kirpans have sparked a violent incident in any school, no evidence that any other School Board in Canada bars kirpans, and no evidence of a student anywhere in Canada using a kirpan as a weapon" (BOA, p. 11). A like study in Calgary, commissioned by the school board, not only recommended that the school district "recognize the right of Khalsa Sikhs to wear Kirpans" but noted that in numerous districts Sikh children wearing *kirpans* had been accommodated without the necessity of having to institute a policy (BOA, p. 11).

The plaintiffs, then, had established that throughout California and Canada other school districts had been able to accommodate the religious beliefs and practices of Khalsa Sikhs without compromising the safety of other schoolchildren. Moreover, they had brought to the court's attention the inability of the Livingston Union School District to furnish a single instance of violence in schools, either in its own district or for that matter anywhere else, in which the *kirpan* had been used.[47] The plaintiffs then proceeded to provide further grounds for why an exemption ought to have been granted to Sikh children. Although the school authorities were inclined to view the *kirpan* as little better than a weapon, they had ignored the fact that the Cheema children, much like other baptized Sikhs, had been required to undergo "an intensive training course to become familiar with the obligations of the Khalsa." If they were required to wear the Five K's at all times, even while bathing and sleeping, they were also advised that the *kirpan* was not to be used as a weapon; it was to be removed from its sheath only for certain religious observances, certainly never as an offensive weapon to harm others; and the initiates were also "required to affirm their understanding of, and commitment to, these principles as a condition of initiation" (BOA, pp. 6–7). One expert in the Sikh religion had stated in his declaration that "every Khalsa Sikh is carefully schooled in the obligations concerning the kirpan just as they are schooled in their other religious duties" (BOA, pp. 11–12).

Perhaps more significantly, the school district had a mistaken conception of its duty to provide, equally to all children, an environment that was safe and conducive to learning. School boards are undoubtedly expected to set reasonable guidelines to ensure safety, but as the study commissioned in Calgary had concluded, a school district "is not expected to guarantee the absolute safety of students for of course this is impossible. Many items common and necessary to an educational setting can be used to inflict harm or damage if the will is there" (BOA, p. 11). If a weapon were to be construed merely as any object with the capacity of inflicting harm, then it stood to reason that such objects as are commonly allowed in schools—scissors, compasses, baseball bats—and can clearly be used as offensive weapons ought not to be allowed. While guns and brass knuckles, on the one hand, and acid in the laboratory and bread knives in the cafeteria, on the other hand, are all material things that might be used to inflict harm, the latter objects are allowed because they fulfill a necessary and legitimate function. *Kirpans* were to be construed as falling within the latter category: as religious symbols, they are indispensable to the life of Khalsa Sikhs (BOA, pp. 22–24). Moreover, whatever theoretical danger the *kirpan* posed, the risk had been further minimized by the concessions already agreed to by the Cheema family: while the blade length of three inches exceeded the legally permitted length of two and a half inches, the *kirpan* was much duller than a typical knife; furthermore, the family had agreed to having the *kirpans* sewed down "so tightly that even the adult members of the Livingston school board were unable to remove the kirpan from its sheath" (BOA, p. 25).[48]

Two conclusions followed. The obligation of the school

was only to provide all children with a safe environment; but in choosing to exclude Khalsa Sikh children carrying *kirpans*, the school district was seeking to turn the school into a "hermetically sealed" environment (BOA, p. 24). This is neither possible nor even reasonable. As the plaintiffs for the attorneys noted, even a child's home is only a "reasonably, not a perfectly, safe world." Parents often keep loaded guns in their home, for instance, "although we know to a certainty that some children accidentally will be injured or killed as a result" (BOA, p. 24). We do not, however, altogether ban guns. The district court, submitted the plaintiffs, had additionally erred in referring to the *kirpan*'s "inalienable" character as a "knife." The *kirpan*'s "inalienable" character, quite to the contrary, "is as a sacred symbol in the Sikh religion," and the fact that the *kirpan* could, in theory, be used to inflict injury did not alter its "inalienable" nature as a religious emblem. A baseball bat might well be construed as a piece of wood, or an object for hammering a nail into a piece of wood, but preeminently it remains a special kind of sporting implement used to hit a round ball. It can no doubt be used, and indeed it has been so used, to smash a person's skull or inflict some other grievous wound, but that does not alter its fundamental characteristic as a "baseball bat." Similarly, the essential characteristic of a *kirpan* is that it is a religious symbol of the faith. That is indeed its ontological status, and to construe it as a weapon is to do the *kirpan* injustice and to commit an act of epistemic violence.

The district, then, had failed to show that the Livingston Union School District is in some manner unique and that the experiences of school districts elsewhere cannot serve as a guide to the school authorities. The district had likewise failed to establish that there had previously been any difficulty in allowing Sikh children to wear *kirpans* at school and that something in the history of the school district, or indeed in the history of the Sikhs and their religion, warranted the belief that a *kirpan* represents a real threat as an object of violence. Nor had the district established that the *kirpan* has ever been employed as an offensive (or for that matter defensive) weapon in schools. Did "fear and discomfort" furnish adequate grounds for the argument that the state had a compelling interest in preventing the Cheema children from attending school? And if "fear and discomfort" are to satisfy the compelling interest standard, is there any "rational or evidentiary response" that could overcome such a defense (BOA, p. 21)? It is fair to question, noted the plaintiffs, "whether the District's policy is rooted as much in a concern for school safety as in hostility to its small Sikh minority" (BOA, p. 26).

Legal Pluralism in a Multicultural Society

In arguing their case on behalf of the Cheema family before the court of appeals, the attorneys for the plaintiffs and the American Civil Liberties Union resorted to the recently enacted Religious Freedom Restoration Act (RFRA) of 1993.[49] Justifying the introduction of this legislation, Congress noted that the framers of the Constitution had clearly intended to secure "the free exercise of religion as an unalienable right" and that the "establishment clause" clearly prohibited the state from engaging in any activity leading to the establishment of any religion. If the state was bound to observe neutrality in matters pertaining to religion, it was also bound to recognize that "laws 'neutral' toward religion may burden religious exercise as surely as laws intended to interfere with religious exercise" (Sec. 2.a.2). Where such neutrality appeared to hinder the free exercise of religious thought, the state was bound to show that it had "compelling justification" in refusing to grant an exemption from a certain law or regulation and, moreover, that the application of the burden of not granting an exemption "is the least restrictive means of furthering that compelling governmental interest" (Sec. 2.a.3;

Sikh Kirpans *in California Schools*

Sec. 3.b.1–2). In refusing to grant an exemption to its policy of prohibiting weapons from school grounds in order to accommodate the right to free exercise of religion of its Khalsa Sikh students, the state had perforce to demonstrate that it had a compelling interest in refusing an exemption and that the course pursued of banning the children from school was the "least restrictive means of furthering that compelling governmental interest."

The Religious Freedom Restoration Act, as Congress itself had determined, became necessary because the "compelling interest" standard had been massively weakened and compromised as a consequence of the Supreme Court's decision in the case of *Employment Division v. Smith*, 494 U.S. 872 (1990).[50] While a general consideration of this standard is well outside the parameters of this chapter, let us note that there are two broad versions of the right to the free exercise of religion. In the narrower view, "religious liberty consists of not being discriminated against" and "the law that applies to any religious minority will be the same as the law that applies to anybody else."[51] Religious freedom, therefore, consists in the right to equality. In the less restrictive view, religious freedom is not merely a right to nondiscrimination; it is a "liberty right"—a "substantive right not to be regulated with respect to certain matters that are very important to the individual." In this view the right to the free exercise of religion is "a right presumptively not to be regulated: the state should not burden a religious practice without a compelling reason."[52]

It was the less restrictive view of RFRA, which obligated the state to provide a compelling reason to prevent someone from the free exercise of religion, that the ACLU and the plaintiffs for the Cheema family invoked to have their position vindicated. In the Santeria animal sacrifice case,[53] where the City of Hialeah (Florida) had sought to curtail the free exercise of religion—in particular the sacrifice of chickens—by adherents of the old African faith of Santeria, on the grounds that the state had a compelling interest to prevent injury to animals, harm to children, infringement of zoning regulations, and unsanitary conditions, the Supreme Court made it known that the compelling interest standard was not to be "watered down."[54] It was the more stringent standard, restored by the Supreme Court in the Santeria case, that Congress sought to give effect to through RFRA; and it was the standards stipulated by RFRA that the plaintiffs for the Cheema family sought to have applied by the court of appeals in their case. Thus the plaintiffs had to show that they had a sincere religious belief; moreover, they had to establish that some government action substantially burdened or threatened the free exercise of their religion; finally, provided the first two conditions were met, it was incumbent upon the government to show that its action in preventing the children of the Cheema family from attending school was "in furtherance of a compelling governmental interest" and represented "the least restrictive means of furthering that compelling . . . interest" (BOA, p. 18).

There was never any question that the Sikhs have a sincere religious belief. On the second issue, the district court, while eventually refusing to issue an injunction that would have prevented the school district from excluding the Cheema children from their school, nonetheless conceded that "as a result of the District's no-knives policy, Plaintiffs must choose either to follow a fundamental precept of their religion and forfeit the opportunity of attending school, or forsake one of the precepts of their faith in order to attend school" (BOA, p. 10, n. 13). Such a choice, the court admitted, "effectively penalizes the free exercise of [their] constitutional liberties," and "this penalty constitutes a substantial burden on Plaintiffs' free exercise of their religion" (BOA, p. 10, n. 13). On the district court's own ruling, then, it only remained to determine whether the school district had a compelling interest in ensuring the safety of all children attending the school where the

Cheema children were enrolled, and whether the least restrictive means of ensuring such safety was to bar the Cheema children from attending school until such time as they were willing to keep their *kirpans* at home.

While the ACLU and the plaintiffs for the Cheema family were not unmindful of the fact that the school authorities are bound to provide an environment that is safe and conducive to learning, they did not think that any environment can be hermetically sealed. Although the plaintiffs' attorneys did not state so, it is apparent that they thought the school district was bound only to fulfill its obligation to an extent that can be considered reasonable; more pertinently, they were inclined to argue, the question is not whether the school authorities had a compelling interest in maintaining a safe environment, as this is scarcely to be doubted, but whether they had a compelling interest in denying an exemption to the district's policy of "no knives" in order to accommodate the free exercise rights of Khalsa Sikh children. In the famous case of *Wisconsin v. Yoder*,[55] noted the plaintiffs' attorneys, the Supreme Court had ruled that Wisconsin's compelling interest in ensuring compliance with its system of compulsory school education, while valid in the generality of cases, was not such that Wisconsin could not deny an exemption to Amish children whose parents, for religious reasons, could not keep their children in schools beyond the eighth grade (BOA, p. 20). If the school could not provide an exemption, was it not bound to show there were legitimate grounds for believing that the *kirpans* would be used to commit an act of violence on school grounds? The Livingston Union School District, as the plaintiffs' attorneys argued, had failed to provide any instance of an act of violence having been so committed, and it had just as evidently failed to consider that other school districts had successfully accommodated Khalsa Sikh children who wished to carry their *kirpans* to school alongside their obligation to provide a safe environment conducive to the educational process. The school authorities had evidently also failed to meet the test that their purported "compelling interest" could not be satisfied in a less restrictive fashion.

The failure of the Livingston Union School District to consider an exemption to its policy prohibiting knives and other weapons from school was rooted, submitted the plaintiffs' attorneys, in nothing but fear. But even the Supreme Court, they continued, has ruled that fear cannot serve as the substantive basis for denying exemptions to policies or regulations that are otherwise justifiable: if fears are not always groundless, they are not always well grounded either, and it is questionable whether apprehension of risk or danger, particularly in a case where all the evidence points to the absence of such danger, can be allowed to serve as the basis for certain policies that stand in opposition to fundamental rights guaranteed by the Constitution itself. Integration of neighborhoods and schools might never have been possible if the authorities had allowed themselves to be paralyzed by the fear of reprisals from white segregationists; and if authorities had succumbed to the near hysteria displayed by parents and school boards, children diagnosed with HIV (and, in fewer cases, AIDS itself) would have been barred from schools when there was no evidence to suggest there was legitimate cause for concern (BOA, pp. 27–28). In one AIDS-related case,[56] a court in Florida, while recognizing the "concern and fear . . . flowing from" the community, "particularly from the parents of school age children," had unequivocally stated that "the Court *may not* be guided by such community fear, parental pressure and the possibility of lawsuits. These obstacles, real as they may be, cannot be allowed to vitiate the rights [of the excluded students]" (BOA, p. 28; emphasis in the original). Pressing their case further, attorneys for the plaintiffs suggested that fear "can mask the basest forms of prejudice" and noted that the argument from fear requires no evidence. What can the protection of First Amendment rights mean when one is only allowed to exercise such rights as do not evoke someone's fear? "Freedoms that are protected only when there is no cost or risk to others," the court of appeals was reminded, "are scarcely freedoms at all" (BOA, p. 26).

The court of appeals, as mentioned earlier, reversed and remanded the district court's judgment. In ruling on a preliminary injunction, denied by the district court, which would have barred the school district from applying its no-knives policy to ban the possessions of *kirpans* at school, the court of appeals stated: "We weigh the likelihood of harm against the likelihood of success on the merits." The court of appeals noted that the school had made no offer of accommodation; nor had it shown that banning the children from school was the "least restrictive means of furthering [its] compelling governmental interest." The court of appeals did not think that the district court's view that some children might be frightened by the *kirpans*—or that others might think it unfair that some children were allowed knives while they were not—was anything more than speculation. "The district's concern that it treat all children the same is not a compelling interest," the court stated, "because accommodation sometimes requires exactly the opposite: accepting those who are different and recognizing that 'fairness' does not always mean everybody must be treated identically."[57] The district court was thus enjoined to direct the parties to submit to "an agreed plan of accommodation, which will protect the safety of the students and accommodate the religious requirements of the Cheema children."[58] Following an impasse, the district court ordered that the Cheema children were to be permitted to return to school with their *kirpans*, subject to certain conditions.[59]

While the court of appeals was deliberating the issue, a bill was pending before the California legislature to amend the California Penal Code (Sec. 626.20)—which bans weapons from school grounds—to exempt the carrying of a knife as part of any recognized religious practice.[60] On 24 August 1994, the Assembly voted 44–22, over objections by Republicans (many of whom are members of the National Rifle Association), to allow Sikh children to carry *kirpans* to school; later in the month, the Senate passed the bill on a unanimous 30–0 vote.[61] This bill did not, however, receive the assent of the governor of California: in his veto message Pete Wilson—while admitting that the bill addressed a "venerable religious practice" and the Sikhs had "an exceptional record as law-abiding citizens"—said he could not be a party to a piece of legislation that "authorize[s] the carrying of knives on school grounds" and would mean abandoning "public safety to the resourcefulness of a thousand school districts."[62] It is not unpredictable that Wilson, who has scarcely compiled a flattering record for protection of minority rights, should have vetoed the bill. The veto does not preclude school districts, acting on their own discretion, from granting exemptions for *kirpans* to their no-weapons policies. Indeed, in the school districts of Fremont, Yuba City, Live Oak, and Selma, Sikhs are allowed by virtue of explicit policy and administrative directive to carry *kirpans* to school, subject to certain conditions.[63]

The cultural politics of *kirpans* remains, despite the judicial activity and legislative record, somewhat elusive. No uniform administrative or legislative policy on *kirpans* in schools exists, and despite the decision by the court of appeals, some school districts will undoubtedly be encouraged by the governor's veto to persist with policies that would prevent *kirpan*-carrying Sikh children from attending school. After Wilson's veto, some Sikhs immediately announced that they would continue to pursue their cause. Ram Singh, one of the leaders of the Sikh community in Fremont, criticized the governor for obscuring the fact that it is a "religious freedom issue clear and simple. Wilson is trying to put a spin on it, making it a safety and crime issue so he can use it in his campaign."[64] Similarly, the author of the bill, Senator Bill Lockyer, has been quite strident in his criticism of the governor's veto, describing it as another instance of Wilson "pandering to anti-ethnic groups. Wilson caved in to the religious right wing, but when it comes to protecting the religious principles of others, he seems to be completely disinterested."[65] The supposition that Wilson was merely appeasing the white population shortly before the November 1994 elections is, if anything, kind to him, as it implies that Wilson would have, at any other time, assented to the legislation. Lockyer's criticism thus goes further: certain freedoms that are routinely claimed on behalf of Christians are seldom extended to minorities who practice other religions.

But neither Lockyer's support of the bill nor the ACLU's defense of the right of Sikh children to wear *kirpans* to schools hints at the division of opinion within the Sikh community itself, not to mention other members of the Indian communities in Northern California. One Sikh in Hayward stated quite candidly that entrusting a *kirpan* to a Sikh child is "like giving a baby a razor blade"; another Sikh said: "Someone gets mad and lashes out, and Sikhs get mad really fast."[66] Another Sikh in the same area thought it was "not a good idea to carry [*kirpans*] in schools. Maybe something may happen with the boys." Yet another Sikh did not think that God would be angry with the children if they failed to carry their *kirpans* to school: "I still love my religion. But we have to obey the rules and regulations of the country we are living in. The safety—and security—comes first, and everything else comes afterward."[67]

These remarks scarcely reveal, however, the intense anxieties that have been generated over the entire question of Sikh identity. And as I suggested earlier, the debate over the *kirpan* must also be located in relation to Sikh politics in India and the revival of the symbols of the faith, particularly among supporters of Sikh separatism and adherents of the idea of Khalistan. By the early nineteenth century, Khalsa Sikhs had evolved into a distinct community whose members were instructed to have no contact not only with Muslims but with various categories of reprobate Sikhs, including those who disputed the lineage of the Sikh gurus and "those who shaved their heads" and "did not wear a turban." In the early part of the twentieth century, "a ferocious onslaught" was launched against all Sikh men who dared to wear the dhoti, a garment associated with Hindus, or who had their ears pierced.[68] Similar attempts to construct boundaries—to keep the Sikh community "bound" rather than "fuzzy"—appear to characterize the thinking and practice of orthodox Sikhs today. As has now been well documented, clean-shaven and "naked-headed" Sikhs have been the victims of organized attacks by orthodox Sikhs, not just in India, but in the United States and Canada; conversely, in the last ten to fifteen years, the wearing of long hair and unkempt beards has become the most visible mark of one's membership in the brotherhood of the Khalsa, the Pure. Veena Das's observations once again come to mind: militant Sikh discourse is characterized by "use of rigorous dualisms to define self and other," and assertions of masculinity have become central in this discourse. The "emphasis on ties between *men* as the defining ties of community" is notable; what is iconic about this masculinity is both the brandishing of the sword *(kirpan)* and keeping one's hair *(kes)* long.[69] As Bhindranwale was to exhort Sikh males: "If you do not want beards then you should ask the women to become men and you become women. Or else ask nature that it should stop this growth on your faces."[70]

Didar Singh Bains, whom we encountered earlier as the world's biggest grower of peaches, is one of the most prominent supporters of the idea of Khalistan. Bains certainly appears to have heeded Bhindranwale's counsel: he first took to keeping his hair and beard long in the early 1980s and is now committed to proselytization: "People can't be half pregnant. I got baptized and my wife will one day too."[71] In her study, published in 1988, of one Sikh community in Northern California, Margaret Gibson noted that "a split had occurred within the . . . community well before this research commenced, ostensibly because of differences regarding the maintenance of the Five Ks and other traditional Sikh values and customs." She notes that more recent Sikh immigrants to the United States have been taking over the *gurdwaras,* "insisting that traditional ways be observed."[72] The same phenomenon can be observed in Canada. There the violence within Sikh communities is attributed to

> efforts by younger, more orthodox, more recently-arrived Sikhs to intimidate their fellow Sikhs who are more moderate, more relaxed and resettled in their adopted country. The main thrust has been to capture the existing gurdwaras and through them, order the recovering of the "naked heads," impose new discipline, control the temple funds—and then proceed toward uniting what traditionally has been a cavalierly disunited overseas Sikh expression.[73]

Thus among the older members of the Ross Street Gurdwara in Vancouver, a number of men were physically assaulted for being clean-shaven and "naked-headed."[74] Since *kirpans* are generally worn under the clothes, an oracular demonstration of militancy among Sikh adults through the brandishing of *kirpans* has not, in California, been an issue, but the whole phenomenon of the revival of the five symbols of the faith has undoubtedly played its part in generating the controversy over kirpans in school.

In the discourse on *kirpans* being undertaken by Keshadhari Sikhs in the United States, one claim is directed to members of the Sikh community—particularly to those Sikhs who are construed, by virtue of their failure to keep their hair long or to carry a *kirpan,* as having abandoned the faith. It is not unusual, though hardly reassuring, that Sikhism appears in the diaspora in an ossified and orthodox form. And though the idea of Khalistan has suffered an appreciable decline among Sikhs in India, the notion in the United States continues to have an extraordinary longevity.[75] The "purer" form of the faith is more easily observed in the diaspora than it is in the homeland, where the lived practices of the faith often accommodate themselves to the presence of other faiths sharing family resemblances. This pattern is easily observable in the case of Hinduism as well, and the practices of Hindu associations in the United States suggest that a "Hindu" is not only more easily defined abroad than at home but the parameters of what is allowed to pass for "Hinduism" are also more narrowly defined. Thus, in a Hindu temple in Northern California, access to the deity was restricted by the priest to "vegetarians" and some latitude allowed to those attired in "Hindu clothing." And not much later, the Federation of Hindu Associations calmly conferred its first "Hindu of the Year" award upon Bal Thackeray, the leader of the Shiv Sena in Bombay who has been charged with inciting hatred against the Muslims and organizing a pogrom, such as the "riots" of December 1992 and January 1993, against them.[76] This phenomenon—greater orthodoxy overseas than at home—cannot be considered with equanimity.

Yet the discourse on *kirpans* in the United States contains within it a second claim—one that is directed to members of the dominant white community. The politics of this claim must not be confused with the politics of the disputes within the Sikh faith. Whatever the politics of identity within the Sikh community, the presence of *kirpan*-carrying Sikh children in California's schools has clearly raised other anxieties about identity and cultural politics. To some observers it is inexplicable that so much heat should have been generated over the subject of *kirpans*—which apparently have so far never been used to inflict violence upon children—when schools have been afflicted with scores of other problems that seem insurmountable. Speaking to a reporter, one leader of the Sikh community in Fremont stated: "There are a lot of other problems in schools. Why aren't they focusing on them?"[77] The concern over *kirpans* appears to be most prevalent among those, such as conservative legislators and members of the National Rifle Association, who are otherwise keen supporters of a constitutional provision allowing ownership of guns among private citizens and have resolutely opposed legislation that would place restrictions upon the sale and purchase of guns in a country where murder takes the place of civil war and street crime takes the place of terrorism. It is noteworthy that in 1995 the Supreme Court, in its decision in the Lopez case, determined that Congress was not within its jurisdiction in instituting federal legislation banning the possession of guns near schools.[78] If this is the sentiment of the highest court of the land, one might well wonder why the carrying of *kirpans* to school by Sikh children has aroused such controversy and fear.

Significantly, too, the display of religious commitment by the Sikhs, in an age when there are countless other flirtations to amuse the youth, appears to have been one of the principal considerations for support rendered to Sikhs. Describing the *kirpan* as a "symbol of peace," a "symbol of forbearance," one lawmaker added: "I would pray to God my grandchildren should go to school with Sikh boys and girls who have the religious commitment the kirpan symbolizes."[79] Similarly, while admonishing the Livingston Union School District authorities for persisting with their ban on *kirpans,* one local newspaper entreated them to "recognize the fact that these are students of high moral commitment, something to be valued at a time when the enduring values are so lightly held by so many."[80]

The perception that Sikh children embody, in an age of frivolity and the demise of religion, the virtues of faith and discipline may be unduly generous to the Sikh community. It is even possible to argue that Sikh children who are carrying *kirpans* to school are the victims of a dispute that has arisen within the faith over the meaning of Sikhism and the nature of Sikh identity. As elsewhere, these children might be bearing the burden of conflicts and anxieties that adults are unable to resolve. There is also the more pressing consideration whether such a perception, such as that expressed by Christians who envy the Sikhs their resolute religious convictions, can serve as the foundation for a cultural pluralism. It is a telling fact that on the three occasions when the Livingston school board met to discuss the issue before it reached the courts, not a single non-Sikh family stepped forward in defense of the Cheema family.[81] The ACLU's successful intervention on behalf of the Cheema family, as well as the protection accorded to the free exercise of religion by the Constitution and, as it appeared then, the Religious Freedom Restoration Act, have aided yet again in obfuscating the limits to liberalism. It is quite clear that the decision of the court of appeals, which in any case allowed only an injunction to be issued to prevent the Livingston Union School District from excluding the Cheema family before the matter came to trial, could just as easily have gone the other way; and the more recent decision of the Supreme Court in 1997 to strike down RFRA as unconstitutional suggests the precariousness of legal victories won at the level of the lower courts. RFRA, in any case, merely restored the tighter criteria for state intervention that should never have been abjured in the first place.

The activism of the ACLU and like organizations preserves for minorities those liberties that are constantly being eroded by virtue of judicial conservatism and, more often, the fundamentally conservative ethos of an American pluralism that knows only how to incorporate diversity. When diversity makes demands, and speaks in the language of difference, as have the Sikhs whose children carry *kirpans* to school, the fabric of American multiculturalism is easily torn. It is no difficult matter to accommodate diversity when such "accommodation" ensures a supply of cheap labor, provides assurance that the myth of America as the beacon of freedom and the door of opportunity will persist, and in innumerable other ways continues to do the work of maintaining American hegemony. Where assimilation is the prevailing model, claims of diversity are more easily accommodated and diversity even becomes a matter of pride—an instance of the capacity of the nation-state and the people of America to tolerate others. This accommodation does not require an acknowledgment of the Other or recognition of a fundamental and irreconcilable difference.

Legal pluralism, though it momentarily triumphed in the Cheema case, ought not to constitute the limits of cultural pluralism: that has been made all the more clear by the erasure of the Religious Freedom Restoration Act from the statute books. The reliance on courts, or on administrative fiat, or on legislative remedies, must necessarily constitute part of the panoply of mechanisms available in a democracy for attaining justice, but these avenues for the redress of grievances do not necessarily make for a pluralistic society. The language of rights has entered the discourse of cultural minorities just as surely as it was stitched into the fabric of Western political thought in the Enlightenment. What has thereby been obscured is the possibility that in lieu of claiming rights, minorities might start thinking of insisting that states be subjected to the fulfillment of certain duties. Rights are claimed against the state, and this has the paradoxical effect of endowing states with agency just when they are being cajoled into disempowering themselves or giving credence to a more equitable mode of distributive justice.[82] The discourse of rights, which puts dominant communities in the position of deciding whether they shall be prepared to endow others with rights, does not compel them to consider their duties, and the interrogation of the Self, which is principally what cultural pluralism can aim at, is never achieved.

The law, it must also be clear, can attempt to provide for equitable conditions of justice, but it cannot produce affection, just as it cannot exorcise fear. The fear of the *kirpan* may well be the primal fear of symbols that are outside a culture's system of significations but hint at a politics of which one is dimly aware; and indeed a great deal in the politics of the *kirpan* is unreadable except to those who are well versed in the politics of Sikhism and the Indian nation-state. The fear of *kirpans,* to raise the specter of untranslatability, is the fear of being unable to understand the language being spoken by one's neighbors: it is the fear of being unable to render the unfamiliar familiar through an act of translation. In a curious fashion, the politics of *kirpans,* while raising important questions about the capacity of Americans to make way for cultural accommodation, also beckons to the politics of Sikhism in India and elsewhere in the diaspora. And thus, by constituting itself as a sovereign discourse, the discourse on *kirpans* marks its independence from American discourses of acculturation and the dominant social framework of understanding.

Thus the question of Sikh identity is central to the conflict over *kirpans* and yet, in some respects, marginal from the American standpoint. Nonetheless, the issue of *kirpans* in schools portends a great deal for understanding what might be the future of cultural pluralism in America. All communities will have to learn to live with a certain degree of *discomfort,* though this idea has not so far entered the discourse of cultural pluralism and multiculturalism. If the fear of the *kirpan* is also the fear of otherness, as I would submit, then perhaps we ought also to accept that otherness cannot always be assimilated and that living with otherness provides a salutary lesson in formulating a moral code of living. We can applaud diversity, but diversity is easily incorporated, as the American paradigm suggests. Diversity still hints at centripetality: the center must hold; difference points to centrifugality: the center radiates outward and dissolves.[83] The privilege of having others being attendant upon their worldview is one that Americans have yet to learn to disown. As the issue of *kirpans* in schools has shown, the true conditions for the survival of plurality will only emerge when the fabric of the accepted discourse of diversity begins to unravel.

Notes

I am extremely grateful to Stephen Bomse, of the law firm of Heller Ehrman White & McAuliffe, for allowing me to review his legal material. I would also like to express my appreciation of the assistance offered by Bill Lockyer, California state senator, and Cathy A. Catterson, clerk of the U.S. Court of Appeals for the Ninth Circuit, and their respective office staffs. My research assistant, Mark Mairot, provided invaluable help in contacting local school boards. This study was completed in early 1995 and was originally published as "Sikh Kirpans in California Schools: The Social Construction of Symbols, Legal Pluralism, and the Politics of Diversity," *Amerasia Journal* 22(1) (1996):57–89.

1. I have not used diacritical marks in this study. The word *"kirpan,"* like most other Indian words, whether in Sanskrit, Hindi, Hindustani, or Punjabi, is in italics.

2. Text of Governor Pete Wilson's veto message, 30 September 1994, on Senate Bill 89.

3. Among the conventional authorities in the field, one might enumerate the works of W. H. McLeod, *Guru Nanak and the Sikh Religion* (Oxford: Clarendon Press, 1968), *The Evolution of the Sikh Community* (Oxford: Clarendon Press, 1976), *Early Sikh Tradition* (Oxford: Clarendon Press, 1980), and *The Sikhs: History, Religion, and Society* (New York: Columbia University Press, 1989), as well as Khushwant Singh's two-volume *History of the Sikhs* (Princeton: Princeton University Press, 1963–1966). Some Sikh scholars have taken strong exception to the work of McLeod, which is sometimes construed as being disrespectful of the faith, while Khushwant Singh's unequivocal condemnation of the violence perpetrated by extremist Sikhs has not endeared him to the more

radical members of the community. For a more recent history, which dwells largely on the political life of Sikhs in the twentieth century, see Rajiv Kapur, *Sikh Separatism: The Politics of Faith* (Delhi: Vikas, 1987). The recent work of Harjot Oberoi, particularly his *Construction of Religious Boundaries: Culture, Identity, and Diversity in the Sikh Tradition* (Oxford: Oxford University Press; Chicago: University of Chicago Press, 1994), has been very influential, not to mention controversial. It is the benchmark against which all future studies of Sikhs and Sikhism before the twentieth century will be judged.

4. See Khushwant Singh, *The Sikhs* (London: Allen & Unwin, 1953), p. 25. The word "guru" is most accurately rendered as teacher or master, though in colloquial parlance it has many other usages; *pir* is a Muslim holy man. Numerous words are used to describe the Muslim population of South Asia; the word "Mussulman" is used most frequently in Hindustani.

5. See Brian Stock, *The Implications of Literacy* (Princeton: Princeton University Press, 1983), cited by Oberoi, *Construction of Religious Boundaries*, p. 49.

6. For an interesting account of the manner in which the five men were chosen see Kapur, *Sikh Separatism*, p. 5. "Punjab" is from the word *"panj"* (five), and Punjab is the land of five rivers. The numeral five would appear to have a special significance in Sikhism, for there are also five *takhats* (literally "thrones") or shrines of authority for Sikhs, mainly associated with the life of Guru Gobind Singh. Moreover, during the baptism of the Sikh child, which is presided over by five Sikh men known for their wisdom and devotion, the sanctified water *(amrit)* is placed on the head of the neophyte, and sprinkled in his eyes, five times, and five times he is given this *amrit* to drink. The *amrit* is itself prepared in an iron bowl where water and sugar crystals are stirred by a double-edged sword: all this is to the accompaniment of the recitation of five quatrains from the writings of Guru Gobind Singh. See Surinder Singh Johar, *Handbook on Sikhism* (Delhi: Vivek, 1977), pp. 105–129, and Oberoi, *Construction of Religious Boundaries*, p. 64.

7. This is scarcely to argue that observance of caste has been eliminated among the Sikhs. As noted by W. H. McLeod, *Who Is a Sikh? The Problem of Sikh Identity* (Oxford: Clarendon Press, 1989): "Whereas the doctrine of the Panth expressly condemns caste, a substantial majority of Sikhs observe certain significant features of caste in practice" (p. 110).

8. J. P. Singh Uberoi, "The Five Symbols of Sikhism," in Fauja Singh et al., *Sikhism* (Patiala: Punjabi University, 1969), p. 129. As can be imagined, I have, for the sake of brevity, given only the most crucial details.

9. Ibid., pp. 130–131.

10. Ibid., pp. 132–133.

11. Ibid., p. 123.

12. Cited by McLeod, *Who Is a Sikh?*, p. 98.

13. Uberoi, "The Five Symbols of Sikhism," p. 136.

14. John Malcolm, "Sketch of the Sikhs," *Asiatick Researches* 11 (1810):220, cited by McLeod, *Who Is a Sikh?*, p. 59. Malcolm did not explicitly mention the five symbols, but the "arms" must be a reference to the *kirpan* and the "steel" to the *kara*.

15. R. W. Falcon, *Handbook on the Sikhs for the Use of Regimental Officers* (Allahabad: Pioneer Press, 1896), p. 15, cited by Oberoi, *Construction of Religious Boundaries*, p. 362.

16. Johar, *Handbook on Sikhism*, p. 90.

17. Uberoi, "The Five Symbols of Sikhism," p. 132. Johar states, in his *Handbook on Sikhism*, that the adoption of the *kirpan* was a "declaration of sovereignty over oneself which non-acceptance of restriction on wearing of arms implies." He adds: "The deeper spiritual meaning of the Kirpan is that it is symbolic of the triumph of transcendental knowledge over ignorance and darkness. The sword, in the mind, cuts at the root of ignorance, evil and worldly attachment and destroys them utterly" (pp. 95–96). This is not an unlikely interpretation, except that Johar leaves it unsubstantiated, besides which it has too much of the tone of an *advaitist* outlook. The teachings attributed to Guru Gobind Singh, founder of the Khalsa, are really more reminiscent of the teachings of Guru Nanak.

18. Ratan Singh Bhangu, *Prachin Panth Prakas*, 4th ed., edited by Vir Singh (Amritsar, 1962), 16:32–36, cited by McLeod, *Who Is a Sikh?*, p. 27.

19. A militant in the Sikh secessionist movement of recent years tells an interesting story of the consequences he had to suffer upon being inadvertently parted from his sword. One hot summer day, while he was sleeping in his underwear, the sword that hung from a swordband on his left arm slipped off without stirring him from his deep sleep. Soon thereafter some of his comrades arrived at his home and were guided by his mother to where he lay asleep. They went back to her and said: "Look at this boy, he has been baptized and has taken a vow to keep the five articles of faith and now he has parted himself from his sword." Thereupon she replied, "All right, I'll bring a stick. You beat him with it and teach him to be loyal to his faith." For "this unconscious conduct" the militant was produced before "five Sikhs, a sort of court in [the Sikh] tradition" and given "religious punishment." See Cynthia Keppley Mahmood, *Fighting for Faith and Nation: Dialogues with Sikh Militants* (Philadelphia: University of Pennsylvania Press, 1996), p. 45.

20. Oberoi, *Construction of Religious Boundaries*, p. 25.

Vinay Lal

21. Kapur, *Sikh Separatism,* p. 92. Though turbans were not numbered among the five symbols of the Sikh faith, by the early part of the nineteenth century, and perhaps slightly earlier, they had become an inextricable part of Sikh identity. W. H. McLeod has written that the wearing of turbans, though lacking "formal sanction . . . during the nineteenth and twentieth centuries, has been accorded an increasing importance in the endless quest for self identification." The turban, he says, became part of the "*Khalsa* code of discipline." See McLeod, *Evolution of the Sikh Community,* p. 53. For a particularly good discussion of the turban, of the British hand in the creation of Sikh identity, and more generally of the conceptualization of clothes and uniforms during the Raj, see Bernard S. Cohn, "Cloth, Clothes, and Colonialism," in Annette B. Weiner and Jane Schneider eds., *Cloth and the Human Experience* (Washington, D.C.: Smithsonian, 1989), pp. 304–309.

22. Kapur, *Sikh Separatism,* pp. 92–93; see also Singh, *The Sikhs,* pp. 102–117.

23. Kapur, *Sikh Separatism,* p. 92. The Punjab government's report is to be found in the Fortnightly Report, 31 May 1920, in file 95 (Deposit), Home (Political) Proceedings, Government of India [henceforth Home Political, GOI], in National Archives of India [henceforth NAI], New Delhi.

24. *The Akali Dal and Shiromani Gurdwara Prabhandak Committee, 1921–22* (Simla: Government Printing, Punjab, 1922), pp. 2, 4, and 16; copy in NAI: Home Political, GOI, file 459/II/1922.

25. NAI: Home Political, GOI, file 459/II/1922, p. 38, "Brief note on trouble in four Indian units during February 1922."

26. Kapur, *Sikh Separatism,* pp. 141–143.

27. NAI: Home Political, GOI, file 459/II/1922, letters from S. P. O'Donnell, secretary, Home Department, GOI, to chief secretary, Punjab Government, 16 and 29 March 1922.

28. "Exemptions of Kirpan from Restrictions Under the Arms Act," *Panjab Past and Present* 7(1) (April 1993):162–172.

29. Constitution of India, Article 25, "Explanation I."

30. This is, however, an exceedingly loose interpretation of the constitution, and I have stated it in the form that some Sikhs had accepted. Article 25 reads as follows:

1. Subject to public order, morality and health and to the other provisions of this Part, all persons are equally entitled to freedom of conscience and the right freely to profess, practise and propagate religion.

2. Nothing in this article shall affect the operation of any existing law or prevent the State from making any law—

   a. regulating or restricting any economic, financial, political or other secular activity which may be associated with religious practice;

b. providing for social welfare and reform or the throwing open of Hindu religious institutions of a public character to all classes and sections of Hindus.

Explanation I: The wearing and carrying of kirpans shall be deemed to be included in the profession of the Sikh religion.

Explanation II: In subclause (b) of clause (2), the reference to Hindus shall be construed as including a reference to persons professing the Sikh, Jain, or Buddhist religion, and the reference to Hindu religious institutions shall be construed accordingly.

Clearly Explanation II cannot be read as a general endorsement of the view that Sikhs, Jains, and Buddhists were to be construed as Hindus, and indeed legal experts are agreed that the expanded definition is applicable for the purpose of clause 2(b). This intervention was inspired by the attempt to keep Hindu temples open to the untouchables or harijans (as they were then called)—for example, harijans who had converted to Buddhism, but who still wished to avail themselves of the right to worship at a Hindu temple, would for that purpose be considered Hindus and thus be entitled to worship at that temple. According to D. V. Chitaley and S. Appu Rao, *The Constitution of India with Exhaustive, Analytical and Critical Commentaries,* 2nd ed. (Bombay: All India Reporter, 1970), 2:471: "Explanation II applies only for the purpose of cl. (2) (b), and the expanded definition of Hindus in Explanation II cannot be relied upon for other purposes." It is also important to note that, according to legal opinion, Explanation I envisions that a Sikh may legally carry only one *kirpan,* this *kirpan* to be—in concordance with the articles of Sikh faith—of unspecified length and shape. A *kirpan* is to be allowed to Sikhs as an emblem of their faith, and one *kirpan* suffices as such an emblem. Moreover, "the Explanation only applies to the particular kirpan which is actually used as a religious emblem, but not to a stock of kirpans out of which one may be used as an emblem." Additional *kirpans,* like any other weapon, may be worn upon the procurement of a license. See Chitaley and Rao, *Constitution of India,* 2:471, and Durga Das Basu, *Commentary on the Constitution of India,* 6th ed. (Calcutta: S. C. Sarkar & Sons, 1978), D: 232.

31. Cited by Kapur, *Sikh Separatism,* pp. 220–221.

32. For a list of the demands see Government of India, *White Paper on the Punjab Agitation* (New Delhi: Government of India Press, 1984), pp. 61–65.

33. See Veena Das, "Time, Self, and Community: Features of the Sikh Militant Discourse," *Contributions to Indian Sociology* (new series) 26(2) (July–December 1992): 252.

Vinay Lal

34. *White Paper on the Punjab Agitation*, pp. 9–10. The *kirpan* could be no longer than nine inches, and its blade length was not to exceed six inches. It was explained that Sikhs would not be allowed to carry *kirpans* on international flights, as Air India was bound by international regulations and conventions about the carrying of weapons.

35. For two quasi-scholarly accounts of the events of 1980–1984 see Kuldip Nayar and Khushwant Singh, *Tragedy of the Punjab: Operation Bluestar and After* (New Delhi: Vision Books, 1984), and Mark Tully and Satish Jacob, *Amritsar: Mrs. Gandhi's Last Battle* (London: Jonathan Cape, 1985). See also the cryptic account by Rahul Kuldip Bedi, "Politics of a Pogrom," in Arun Shourie et al., *The Assassination and After* (New Delhi: Roli Books, 1985), pp. 51–76. For a short but graphic account of the massacre of Sikhs in Delhi following the announcement of Indira Gandhi's assassination see People's Union for Democratic Rights (PUDR) and People's Union for Civil Liberties (PUCL), *Who Are the Guilty? Report of a Joint Inquiry into the Causes and Impact of the Riots in Delhi from 31 October to 10 November* (Delhi, 1984). It cannot be emphasized enough that the characterization of the carnage of 1–4 November as "Hindu-Sikh riots" is almost wholly inappropriate. The Sikhs were massacred; there was no retaliation. Nor was this preeminently an instance of communalism, for as the PUCL/PUDR report established, the killings were orchestrated by political bosses. For more recent events, from 1984 to 1990, see Man Singh Deora, ed., *Aftermath of Operation Bluestar*, 2 vols. (New Delhi: Anmol, 1992). I have used the word "pacification" deliberately, for the ease with which brutal suppression came to be embodied as "pacification" in the English language is rather remarkable. See George Orwell, "The Politics of the English Language," in *A Collection of Essays* (New York: Doubleday Anchor, 1957).

36. Kapur, *Sikh Separatism*, p. 226.

37. Das, "Time, Self, and Community," pp. 251–252. On Gandhi's femininity, and his attempted feminization of Indian politics, there is nothing more brilliant than Ashis Nandy's work: "Final Encounter: The Politics of the Assassination of Gandhi," in his *At the Edge of Psychology: Essays in Politics and Culture* (Delhi: Oxford University Press, 1980; paperback ed., 1990), pp. 70–98, and *The Intimate Enemy: Loss and Recovery of Self Under Colonialism* (Delhi: Oxford University Press, 1983), especially pp. 48–54. A more sympathetic picture of Bhindranwale emerges in Pritam Singh, "Two Facets of Revivalism: A Defence," in Gopal Singh, ed., *Punjab Today* (New Delhi: Intellectual Publishing House, 1987), pp. 169–170, and in the accounts tendered by Sikh militants in Mahmood, *Fighting for Faith and Nation,* especially pp. 50–72.

38. There is a poignancy in the story of the two men, Sukhjinder Singh and Harjinder Singh, who carried out the assassination of General Vai-

dya, leader of the Indian armed forces that stormed the Golden Temple in Operation Bluestar and thereby desecrated the venerable shrine. In order to gain membership into Vaidya's golf club, they shaved their beards and cut their hair; and if this should appear inexplicable, considering the orthodox fidelity to the Khalsa symbols, it is worthwhile considering the comment of one Sikh militant that if Sikh men are unable to offer their hair in the guru's service, how could they conceivably offer their heads? See Mahmood, *Fighting for Faith and Nation,* p. 155.

39. Government of India, *White Paper on the Punjab Agitation,* p. 38; for the activities of Chauhan, Dal Khalsa, and others, see pp. 35–40.

40. Bruce La Brack, *The Sikhs of Northern California 1904–1975* (New York: AMS Press, 1988), p. 452.

41. Bruce La Brack, "California's 'Punjabi Century': Changing Punjabi/Sikh Identities," in Pritam Singh and Shinder S. Thandi, eds., *Globalisation and the Region: Explorations in Punjabi Identity* (Coventry: Association for Punjab Studies, 1996), p. 373.

42. La Brack, *The Sikhs of Northern California,* pp. 239 and 243–244.

43. Ibid., p. 244.

44. For a brief but lively account of the racism directed against Indians in the United States in the first few decades of the twentieth century see Ronald Takaki, *Strangers from a Different Shore* (Boston: Little, Brown, 1989), and a short monograph by Roger Daniels, *History of Indian Immigration to the United States: An Interpretive Essay* (New York: Asia Society, 1986).

45. California Penal Code, Sec. 626.10(a).

46. This narrative rests largely on the "Brief of Appellants" filed in the Court of Appeals for the Ninth Circuit in the case, No. 94–16097, of *Rajinder Singh Cheema, et al., Plaintiffs/Appellants, v. Harold H. Thompson, et al., Defendants/Appellees,* pp. 1–13. This brief will hereafter be cited as "BOA." I also consulted newspapers, particularly the *San Jose Mercury News,* the *Oakland Tribune,* and the *San Francisco Chronicle.*

47. Although I am told that there have in fact been incidents of violence in schools in which the *kirpan* was used, I have seen no documentary evidence in substantiation of this claim. In any event, such evidence, were it forthcoming, makes no difference to the tenor of my arguments.

48. As the BOA notes, some Sikhs consider stitching the handle of the *kirpan* to the cloth strap to be unacceptable. But this was not an issue the court had to face, as the Cheemas had agreed to this limitation as a condition for wearing a *kirpan* at school (BOA, p. 7, n. 3; see also BOA, p. 12, n. 7).

49. Religious Freedom Restoration Act of 1993, 42 USC 2000bb; Public Law 103–141 (H.R. 1308), 16 November 1993.

50. This case is summarized in Douglas Laycock, "Free Exercise and the Religious Freedom Restoration Act," *Fordham Law Review* 62(4) (February 1994): 886–888.

51. Ibid., p. 885.

52. Ibid.

53. *Church of the Lukumi Babulu Aye, Inc. v. City of Hialeah*, 113 S. Ct. 2217 (1993).

54. See Laycock, "Free Exercise," pp. 889–892, and BOA, p. 15.

55. *Wisconsin v. Yoder*, 406 U.S. 205 (1972).

56. *Ray v. School Dist. of DeSoto County*, 666 F. Supp. 1524 (M.D. Fla. 1987).

57. Judgment of the court in *Rajinder Singh Cheema, et al., v. Harold H. Thompson, et al.*, No. 94–16097, U.S. Court of Appeals for the Ninth Circuit.

58. Judgment of the court in *Rajinder Singh Cheema, et al., v. Harold H. Thompson, et al.*, No. Civ. F-94-5360 GEB, U.S. District Court for the Eastern District of California.

59. These conditions had previously been agreed to by the Cheemas, though not by the school. The Cheemas agreed that the *kirpan* would be about six and a half to seven inches in length, inclusive of the blade, of a dull type, which was to be three to three and a half inches; the *kirpan* was to be sewn tightly to its sheath and was to be worn under the clothes so as not to be readily visible. The school had not agreed to these adjustments proposed by the family. In addition, the Cheema family agreed that a designated official would have the right to make reasonable inspections and that the right to wear a *kirpan* would be suspended if any of the foregoing conditions were violated. And, finally, it was agreed that the school would take "reasonable steps to prevent any harassment, intimidation or provocation of the Cheema children by any employee or student in the District." See ibid.

60. California Senate Bill 89, 1993–1994 Reg. Sess. 626.10 (g) (1993).

61. Yasmin Anwar, "Assembly Takes Up Religious Knife Debate," *Oakland Tribune* (24 August 1994):A9–10; Greg Lucas, "Bill Allows Sikh Daggers on Campus," *San Francisco Chronicle* (25 August 1994); and "Senate OKs Bill Allowing Sikh Ceremonial Daggers," *San Jose Mercury News* (31 August 1994). In an earlier vote in the Assembly, the bill was defeated 34–14, but as only forty-eight of the eighty lawmakers had shown up, the vote was rescheduled. As an editorial in the *Oakland Tribune* (24 August 1994) stated: "The usual small parade of know-nothings, with troglodyte right-wing Republican Ross Johnson of Fullerton out front, led the charge against the bill." Johnson, charged the newspaper, "raised the specter of knife fights on school grounds," while Republican Assemblywoman Paula Boland claimed that anyone could

wear a kirpan and claim immunity from sanctions on religious grounds, though the bill specifically rules out that eventuality" ("Assembly Tramples Religious Freedom," p. A12).

62. Text of Governor Pete Wilson's veto message, 30 September 1994, on Senate Bill 89. See also Greg Lucas, "Wilson Veto for Knives at School," *San Francisco Chronicle* (1 October 1994):A19.

63. Personal written communication from Lee Brittenham, superintendent of schools, Yuba City Unified School District, 24 January 1995, and from William Walker, director of pupil services, Fremont Unified School District, 8 February 1995.

64. Suzanne Tay-Kelley, "Wilson Veto of Kirpan Bill has Mixed Sikh Reaction," *Oakland Tribune* (2 October 1994).

65. Ibid.

66. Yasmin Anwar, "Sikhs on Pins and Needles Over Daggers," *Oakland Tribune* (26 April 1994): A1 and A6.

67. Tay-Kelley, "Wilson Veto of Kirpan Bill."

68. See Oberoi, *Construction of Religious Boundaries,* pp. 68–69 and 345.

69. Das, "Time, Self, and Community," p. 257.

70. Quoted in ibid., p. 252.

71. See Warren Una, *Sikhs Abroad: Attitudes and Activities of Sikhs Settled in the USA and Canada* (Calcutta: Statesman, 1985), pp. 19–20.

72. Margaret A. Gibson, *Accommodation Without Assimilation: Sikh Immigrants in an American High School* (Ithaca: Cornell University Press, 1988), p. 49. She appears to think that the real struggle is over the *gurdwaras* (pp. 49–50), and thus the "ostensible" fight over the symbols, but curiously she sees the two issues as somehow separate.

73. Una, *Sikhs Abroad,* pp. 33–34.

74. Ibid., pp. 8, 10, 26, and photographs between pp. 18 and 19.

75. See Batuk Vora, "Guns Fall Silent in Punjab, But Khalistan Lingers on in US," *India-West* (10 June 1994):53 and 60.

76. Viji Sundaram, "Diet, Dress Code Enrage Hindu Worshippers," *India-West* (31 March 1995):A1, 12, 16; for the news item on the "Hindu of the Year" award see *India-West* (9 June 1995).

77. Jennifer Bjorhus, "School's Knife Ban Angers Sikhs," *San Francisco Chronicle* (1 August 1994):A12.

78. "Excerpts of Justices' Opinions on Ban on Weapons Near Schools," *New York Times* (27 April 1995):A16.

79. Greg Lucas, "Bill Allows Sikh Daggers on Campus," *San Francisco Chronicle* (25 August 1994).

80. "Abandon the Issue: No Point in Livingston Pursuing the School Knife Ban," editorial in *Modesto Bee* (8 September 1994):A8.

Vinay Lal

81. Bjorhus, "School's Knife Ban Angers Sikhs," p. A12.

82. For an extended consideration of this issue see Vinay Lal, "The Imperialism of Human Rights," *Focus on Law Studies* 8(1) (Fall 1992):5ff.

83. Arjun Appadurai, in "Patriotism and Its Futures," *Public Culture* 5 (1993):411–429, suggests quite brilliantly why the idea of immigration, which represents centripetal forces, now appears less attractive than the idea of diasporas, which are generated by centrifugal forces.

Chapter 4

Journey to the Far West:
Chinese Buddhism in America

I R E N E   L I N

Although a number of interesting studies have appeared on Chinese religions in America, the direct application of Western schemes and labels to the study of Chinese religions in the United States is problematic. Situating new and unfamiliar religious groups in today's categorical schemes leads to a biased understanding of the new. Stark and Bainbridge's elaboration of the church, sect, and cult typology, for example, based on a continuum of tension between religious groups and the sociocultural environment, requires a Christian understanding of religious organizational splintering and formation.[1] But in contemporary Chinese religious culture there is no centralized ecclesiastical authority to establish orthodoxy or orthopraxy and no hierarchical structures equivalent to the Western typology of church, sect, and cult.[2] Religious authority and acceptance in the society are often gained through the spiritual attainment of the group's founder as manifested by supernatural powers of blessing, healing, or protecting its members. Furthermore, the offering of social services or conversion of believers through the founder's charisma adds legitimacy. Chinese culture does not view religious traditions and religious groups as mutually exclusive. A person can belong to different religious organizations simultaneously and appeal to one or another or even many. Religious authority is diffused among a great number of decentralized and independent religious groups—some small, some large. Given these classification issues, scholarship on Chinese religions can be roughly grouped into three types. The first covers research on indigenous Chinese religions transplanted to the United States by the earliest Chinese immigrants between 1854 and 1883 as well as the Chinese temples of Northern California built by these immigrants. The second focuses on Chinese Buddhism in the larger context of Buddhist traditions in America. The third comprises short descriptions of selected Chinese Buddhist organizations in America, primarily found in encyclopedias of American religions.[3]

The study of Buddhism in the United States is based largely on European American encounters with Buddhism.[4] This literature has been dominated by studies on Zen, Tibetan Buddhism, Theravada traditions, and a Japanese new religion, Soka Gakkai/Nichiren Shoshu. (The Soka Gakkai separated from the Nichiren Shoshu priesthood in 1991.) This selective emphasis reflects Buddhist traditions that have attracted European American interest.[5] As a prime example of this bias, Charles Prebish uses the term "American Buddhism" to describe the struggle of a foreign religious tradition to acculturate and accommodate to the American mindset.[6] Despite his focus on the acculturation process of American Buddhism over three time periods, Prebish neglects the Buddhism of Asian Americans. To bring their experience into his framework, one would need to develop new labels and expand the perimeter of the term "acculturation of Buddhism" to account for the Buddhist experiences of the Asian Americans. Similarly, Emma McCloy Layman examines Buddhism in America from the vantage point of European Americans:

"Buddhism in America does not really have an American style, but appears as an Oriental anachronism in a Western society. Some of the values . . . are consonant with those of the Judeo-Christian tradition. . . . The ideology and practices of Buddhism are in conflict with the dominant values of our technological, materialistic, and secular society."[7]

The paucity of studies on the Buddhism of Asian Americans extends to a general ignorance about Chinese religions in America. Chinese religions are no longer represented solely by "joss houses," not merely characterized by ancestor worship in private homes, and not adequately defined by the European American encounters with them. Rather, the religious experience of Chinese Americans must take into account the perspective of Chinese Americans themselves. Recognizing such a need, this study begins the larger project by supplying the institutional picture of specific communities of Chinese Americans gathering for communal worship. From 1965 to 1990, the Chinese American population increased about four and a half times, driven primarily by immigration. The heterogeneity characterizing Chinese immigration since 1965, mainly a result of the quota system under the 1965 amendments to the Immigration and Nationality Act of 1952 and subsequent series of amendments to the 1952 act,[8] resulted in a proliferation of Chinese religious organizations in the United States. Chinese Buddhist organizations founded after 1965, an important subset of Chinese American religious organizations, have not received adequate attention in the Asian American or religious studies literature.[9] Here I wish to look at the issues relevant to an understanding of Chinese Buddhist organizations through a case study of Hsi Lai Ssu (Hsi Lai means "coming to the west," which connotes "the Buddha dharma coming west,"[10] and Ssu means "temple")— otherwise known as the International Buddhist Progress Society, a Chinese Buddhist organization in Hacienda Heights, ten miles east of Monterey Park, in Southern California.[11] Hsi

Irene Lin

Lai originated as a Taiwan-based, ethnic Chinese, Buddhist organization with a predominantly middle- and upper-class membership. This study explores how Hsi Lai functions to retrieve, preserve, and create a post-1965 Chinese American identity while at the same time bridging the realities and multiple characteristics of a large and heterogeneous Chinese American population—race, ethnicity, nationality, class, gender, and religion.[12]

Hsi Lai Temple

Hsi Lai Temple in Southern California is the largest overseas branch of the Fo Kuang Shan (Buddha's Light Mountain) in Taiwan.[13] Fo Kuang Shan was founded in 1967 by Master Hsing-yün, the forty-eighth patriarch of the Lin-chi school of Ch'an Buddhism. Hsing-yün, born in 1926 in China, became a novice monk at the age of twelve and was fully ordained three years later. Subsequently he attended the Ch'i-hsia Vinaya School and the Chiao-shan Buddhist College. The master left China for Taiwan in 1949 and is perceived to have personally revitalized Buddhism in Taiwan. Hsing-yün was the first monk in Taiwan to utilize television and radio programs to propagate Buddhism and the first to use public forums to give large-scale public lectures on Buddhism.[14]

For Hsing-yün, the revitalization of Buddhism "lies in its people, wealth, spirituality, and undertaking." His methods for pursuing such an end are through "humanization," "modernization," and "internationalization" in the form of Buddhist cultural, educational, social, and medical programs. Fo Kuang Shan has evolved into the largest Buddhist center in Taiwan and has many branches throughout Taiwan and the world. In the United States, aside from the Hsi Lai Temple, there are many branch temples in cities including San Francisco, San Diego, Austin, Dallas, Denver, and New York, along with numerous local chapters throughout the country. Prior to the construction of the Hsi Lai Temple, Fo Kuang Shan's first temple in the United States was an old church in Maywood, California, called the Pai-t'a Ssu (White Pagoda Temple), which became too small to accommodate the needs of its members.[15]

Hsi Lai Temple was built in 1988 and occupies over twenty acres. Construction costs exceeded $30 million, financed by donations primarily from Taiwan, though substantial donations were also received from the United States, Malaysia, and Hong Kong. The completion of the temple was delayed for two and a half years because of opposition from the community, composed of many conservative, affluent, and retired European Americans who had a wide range of concerns and fears.[16] Nearby residents claimed, for example, that the temple would be "oversized for a neighborhood of single-family homes, that it would jam surrounding streets with traffic, and that it would be a jarringly inappropriate cultural presence." Other concerns resulted from the community's misunderstanding of Buddhism and Chinese culture: concerns about noise from chanting of sutras, gongs, and firecrackers; the "adverse influence" on the youth resulting from the unfamiliar clothing of Buddhist monks and nuns; the unfounded fear of animal sacrifices on the temple site (and thus the fear for neighborhood dogs because "the Chinese all eat dog meat"); and the worry that the children might be entrapped by the new "religious cult."[17]

Six public hearings and over one hundred meetings took place before the Hacienda Heights city council finally granted the permit for construction of Hsi Lai Temple. Hsi Lai had to accommodate the objections of residents by changing the color of the temple to a less conspicuous one; lowering the height of its buildings; forgoing the installation of an eighty-foot golden statue of the Buddha near the front entrance; taking measures to lessen the chances of fire from the use of incense; limiting parking space to prevent too many people from going to the temple at once and causing traffic problems; and erecting a wall on a section of freeway to prevent potential traffic hazards posed by the view of the temple. Despite such opposition from the community before the construction period, for the opening day ceremony the temple received congratulatory letters from U.S. Congressman Matthew Martinez, California Secretary of State March Fong Yu, other state officials, and prominent Buddhist leaders from thirty countries.

Hsi Lai's stated goal is threefold: to offer a spiritual and cultural center for the United States; to provide Westerners a place for learning about the dharma; and to facilitate the exchange of culture between East and West. When its policy requiring Hsi Lai members to conform to a unified standard of behavior set by Fo Kuang Shan conflicts with its policy of blending Buddhism with the local culture, the latter often takes precedence over the former.[18] All monks and nuns at Hsi Lai wear amber-colored robes, for example, whereas at Fo Kuang Shan such robes are reserved for those of higher rank and lower-ranked monks and nuns wear black robes. The reason for such a change at Hsi Lai is that amber is more pleasing to the American eye than black.

Organization

As an organization Hsi Lai Temple consists of three elements: the temple, the Buddhist sangha (monastic order), and the Buddha Light International Association (BLIA). The temple provides not only a place of worship but also a forum for lectures, discussions, classes, communal rituals, and other Buddhist services and activities. Communal practices and other activities are conducted in Mandarin Chinese, with simultaneous English translation on most occasions, provided mainly for 1.5 (childhood immigrant) and second-generation Chinese Americans. Furthermore, to accommodate the needs of its members, classes on Buddhism are offered in Mandarin, Cantonese, and English. Religious activities are offered on most weekday evenings and all day on weekends. Group activities are designed in accordance with varying levels of interest and understanding of Buddhism.[19] The massive physical structure of the temple includes the Bodhisattva Hall, the Buddha Hall, V.I.P. suites, reception rooms, classrooms, a gift shop, auditoriums, a museum, a memorial pagoda, a library, administrative offices, and living quarters for the monks and nuns.[20] The parking lot, which can accommodate two hundred cars, is often insufficient to satisfy the parking needs during major holidays such as Chinese New Year.

The second element is the monastic order. The temple is administered by monks and nuns hand-picked and sent from Fo Kuang Shan: in 1988 the number of monks and nuns reached fifty. After the passage of the Immigration Act of 1990, allowing for religious workers to immigrate to the United States under the fourth preference and to enter the United States as nonimmigrants under R visas, the number of monks and nuns doubled. The organizational hierarchy of Hsi Lai Temple is subsumed under that of Fo Kuang Shan. The Religious Affairs Committee is the leading governing unit of the main monastery, subsidiary and associate monasteries, and all other organizations and units.[21]

The third element of the religious organization is the lay Buddha Light International Association, established by Fo Kuang Shan in fifty-one countries, with membership reaching 1 million, predominantly Chinese and overseas Chinese. The goal of BLIA is to ensure that "Buddhism moves from the monastic to the laity, from temple to society, from self-realization to helping others, from quietude to action, from disciple to teacher, from Taiwan to the world."[22] BLIA allows the laity to take an active role in propagating the dharma and shaping "contemporary Buddhism";[23] BLIA sponsors and organizes all activities inside and outside temple premises that are not part of the regularly scheduled rituals, practices, and religious services of the temple. BLIA, which claims to be the fourth largest social organization in the world,[24] applied for United Nations membership as a nongovernmental organization in February 1994. In the United States, it consists of twenty-two chapters, nineteen subchapters, and five organizing communities. The establishment of a local chapter typically starts with a Hsi Lai member inviting friends in her local community to her home for an informal discussion of the dharma. After several meetings, when the number of people attending reaches one hundred, formal lectures on the dharma are set up and group practices such as dharma discussion, meditation, and liturgy take place at members' houses on a rotating schedule. With permission from Hsi Lai Temple, a local BLIA is established, accompanied by election of local chapter officers and solicitation of donations from group members. The local chapter then organizes large-scale Buddhist activities in its community—inviting monks and nuns from Hsi Lai Temple to talk on the dharma, for example. At the end of such talks, attendees can officially "take refuge" and become lay disciples of Master Hsing-yün through ordination ceremonies. It is by becoming a lay disciple of Master Hsing-yün that one becomes an official member of the Hsi Lai Temple.[25]

Social Functions

Apart from being a religious organization, Hsi Lai Temple serves as a community center helping Chinese immigrants cope with American society. During the initial stages of the establishment of Hsi Lai Temple, the abbess in charge at the time, Venerable Tzu-chuang, under the instruction of Master Hsing-yün, emphasized free practical services for the overseas Chinese community: locating relatives and friends, helping immigrants find jobs by providing channels for networking, and organizing seminars to educate immigrants about American laws, customs, the educational system, and the job market.[26] Over the years Hsi Lai Temple has expanded these services in conjunction with its propagation of the dharma. Its services as an overseas Chinese center now include free transportation to and from the airport, free meals, and a place to stay for those in need.

To preserve, strengthen, or even create the Chinese identity of its members, Hsi Lai Temple offers Mandarin, Taiwanese, and Cantonese classes, mainly to 1.5 and second-generation Chinese Americans. Special classes on Chinese culture are offered, as well, including Chinese art, folk dance, music, cooking, and tai-chi, classes that help overseas Chinese to keep in touch with their ancestral roots. The vice-president of the BLIA's Los Angeles chapter, a Chinese American, has said: "BLIA has soothed the hardships of the loss of roots due to living in a foreign country, developing the limitless treasures within our hearts, uniting the hearts of all Chinese globally." At present the members of Hsi Lai Temple are predominantly Chinese, though increasing numbers of Buddhists of other races and nationality are joining.[27]

The temple has also taken on certain functions of an embassy. Due to the lack of diplomatic relations between Taiwan and the United States, the de facto Taiwanese embassy, representing the government of Taiwan, is called the Coordination Council for North American Affairs (CCNAA). In offering its premises as the reception hall for the CCNAA, The temple has thus itself become a de facto embassy—seeking, for example, to help bridge tensions between the People's Republic of China and Taiwan by hosting representatives of both governments.[28] It maintains good relations with political figures both in the United States and abroad. Top American officials (for example, Vice-President Albert Gore) have visited Hsi Lai Temple, and Taiwanese government officials have made the temple a must stop on visits to the West Coast.

The temple also acts as a social relief center: providing aid to neighboring communities, donating money and books to local schools, offering conference rooms free of charge for educational and cultural group gatherings, and helping to preserve the environment through reforestation, recycling, and community cleanup programs. BLIA sponsors soup kitchens for the homeless and presents food baskets and gift certificates to low-income families. Moreover, BLIA provides relief in times of natural disasters in the People's Republic of China and the United States and also sends aid to Third World countries through local BLIA chapters.

Hsi Lai Temple opens its doors to visitors as a cultural center, as well, by fostering cross-cultural understanding. It regularly sponsors group visits to the temple: as many as two thousand people visit Hsi Lai each month, of whom two-thirds are European American and the remainder are mostly Chinese, with a few from other Asian countries. Individual visitors to the temple are predominantly Chinese Americans.[29] On the one hand, the temple offers Chinese language and cultural classes and sponsors Chinese cultural activities introducing traditional and contemporary art forms to the community; on the other hand, the temple offers cross-cultural training programs such as Japanese and Spanish-language classes, Western dessert making, social dancing, and aerobics. In addition, Hsi Lai performs Buddhist religious and cultural activities in the community at large—for example, Hsing-yün has performed a blessing service before the California State Senate. To foster better understanding of American culture for Chinese Americans, Hsi Lai Temple also offers activities celebrating American holidays such as Halloween and Thanksgiving. Furthermore, to familiarize its members with non-Buddhist religious holidays and celebrations, articles on various traditions are regularly featured in the temple's newsletter, *Hsi Lai News*.

Hsi Lai Temple proclaims itself to be the home for all its members. The family atmosphere is sustained through numerous services and activities. The temple maintains a large kitchen and dining facilities, for example, serving three buffet-style vegetarian meals every day to the clergy and laity. Most of the members who live nearby eat daily at the temple. Furthermore, Hsi Lai provides living quarters in houses it owns, adjacent to the temple grounds, to members who wish to stay there as the need arises, especially those who live far from the temple.[30] The emphasis is on individual Buddhist families coming "home" for reunion with the large extended family. BLIA believes that families should spend more time together and accordingly sponsors regular activities that emphasize family involvement, such as parent–children sporting events, concerts, plays, and art shows.[31] Moreover, to accommodate the needs of two-income families, Hsi Lai Temple provides child care and elderly care.

At the request of parents, children's classes are offered after school and on weekends as a supplement to regular schooling. In the summer of 1994, Hsi Lai University opened on the premises of the temple, with authorization from the California superintendent of public instruction, as a degree-granting school of theology. The university offers bachelor's and master's degrees in Buddhist studies. Construction of an East Coast campus on 470 acres in New York state is being planned. Chinese parents concerned about the liberal atmosphere of American universities can send their children to school in a more conservative environment.[32] Hsi Lai University tries to bridge the gap between Buddhist theology and religious studies by having religious studies scholars on the faculty. It also offers its conference rooms and libraries for use by religious studies scholars not affiliated with the university.[33] Moreover, it sends qualified monks and nuns to pursue graduate degrees in religious studies at top-ranked universities. BLIA sponsors adult and community education programs, by regularly offering seminars and lectures to increase the lay understanding of Buddhism, and provides lectures in local colleges, high schools, city halls, stadiums, jails, and senior centers. In addition to sponsoring conferences, meetings, and exchange programs between Buddhists of different traditions, BLIA also promotes interchange between Buddhist and non-Buddhist traditions—for instance, Master Hsing-yün has received visits from the Dalai Lama and ambassadors from the Vatican.

To make Buddhist teachings and Fo Kuang ideals easily accessible, Fo Kuang Shan operates its own publishing house and audio-video production center. It has produced over four hundred Buddhist publications and audio and video materials in Chinese, English, and Korean, distributed in twenty countries. Moreover, Hsi Lai University Press was established in 1994 with the initial objective of publishing Master Hsing-yün's works in English.[34] Periodicals are published in Chinese and English by the different Fo Kuang organizations, as well, in order to update members on Fo Kuang events and propagate Buddhist teachings. These periodicals include *Awaken the World, Universal Gate, Hsi Lai News,* and *Buddha's Light Century.* Hsi Lai also uses other media to propagate its teachings to a broader audience: BLIA regularly sponsors programs on local radio stations and broadcasting networks, for example, and Hsi Lai Temple contributes dharma talk-shows to a local Chinese television channel.

The Meanings of Hsi Lai

Hsi Lai Temple provides the context for overseas Chinese to reinforce and reinvent Chinese identity through religion, ethnicity, nationality, culture, family, and education. In response to a modern industrial society characterized by pluralism, religion becomes subject to the forces of fashion—what Peter Berger calls the dynamics of "consumer preference."[35] Competing for people's time and interest, Hsi Lai's Buddhism has been "designed, produced, and marketed" with the needs of its members and potential members in mind. At the current stage of the temple's development, its target is mainly the overseas Chinese.

Journey to the Far West

Building a "Plausibility Superstructure"

If Hsi Lai Temple is to maintain its meaning in a religiously pluralistic and ethnically diverse society, a social base, or what Berger calls a "plausibility structure," is necessary.[36] In most modern settings, however, a religious group seeking to maintain itself in pluralistic competition with other religious groups has a new social engineering problem: rather than enlisting the society as a whole for the purpose of social confirmation, the problem now is constructing and maintaining a subsociety that serves as the plausibility structure for the demonopolized religious system.[37] In the case of Hsi Lai, where Chinese Buddhists are geographically separated by the Pacific Ocean from the main social group that serves as its basis of plausibility, the significance of the plausibility structure becomes especially important. Because the worldview of the Chinese Buddhists is not shared by the American public at large, Hsi Lai Temple needs to establish a subsocietal plausibility base to maintain their belief system. To avoid little fragmented universes of meaning, Hsi Lai Temple has created a broad social base that provides a holistic universe of meaning. In its effort to provide an entire worldview for the Chinese American Buddhists, Hsi Lai has created a "plausibility superstructure" that incorporates numerous substructures—a religious organization, an ethnic community, a de facto embassy, a social relief center, a cultural center, and a school. Through religion, these substructures serve diverse roles in creating and maintaining different aspects of the Chinese American identity.

For members, Hsi Lai Temple's supersocial base for maintaining and reinforcing its distinctive system of meaning enables the simultaneous fulfillment of religious, cultural, communitarian, national, familial, and educational needs. For nonmember Chinese Americans, the temple with its religious rituals and practice, cultural events and activities, ethnic community, de facto embassy, and traditional and holiday celebrations are available to all. The association through activities, in various forms, creates opportunities for nonmembers to become socialized into the Fo Kuang worldview in varying degrees. This worldview is described in a booklet, *How to Be a Fo Kuang Buddhist,* requiring members to place the monastery, the community, Buddhist undertakings, and Buddhism above the self.[38] Hsi Lai Temple's creative incorporation of numerous identities avoids compartmentalization (separation of secular versus sacred spheres) and solid boundaries in order to accommodate the heterogeneous needs of the Chinese Americans.

At the weakest level of association are tourists, followed by those who come to participate in cultural festivities or to take advantage of the temple's cultural training courses—those who view Hsi Lai as an overseas Chinese community center. Then there are the politicians and celebrities who come to Hsi Lai Temple for social or political reasons—those who view Hsi Lai as a large charitable organization or a de facto representative of the Taiwanese government. Alternatively there are those who send their children to attend classes or the university—those who view Hsi Lai as a provider of education. There are Buddhists who have not taken refuge under Master Hsing-yün and visit the temple only on important Buddhist holidays—those who view Hsi Lai Temple as one religious organization among many. Among those who have taken refuge as disciples of Master Hsing-yün, involvement and association with the temple also vary. Some volunteer their services; others contribute money; still others participate in key rituals and services or some combination thereof. There are disciples who participate in all religious functions as individuals, and there are others who involve their entire family in all activities and events, whether religious or not, truly identifying with Hsi Lai as "home," thus constituting the core members of the temple.

Hsi Lai's Role in the New Ethnicity

There is no single Chinese identity in the United States or, indeed, throughout the world of the Chinese diaspora. Following the tendency of the Chinese people and Chinese culture, which have been "constantly amalgamating, restructuring, reinventing and reinterpreting themselves," overseas Chinese have been constructing their own cultural identities in non-Chinese environments.[39] The term "Chinese American" is both a political label and a symbolic identity.[40] The old concept of ethnicity based on the assumption of "bio-cultural-territorial isolate frame of reference" is no longer applicable to the overseas Chinese in diaspora who have come to the United States from different parts of the world.[41] More applicable to these overseas Chinese is the concept of new ethnicity—"an affective/symbolic and behavioral strategy frame of reference, which is contingent upon the larger social environmental context."[42] "New ethnicity" represents an effort by ethnic minorities to balance the need for a sense of belonging with the desire to "alter the established distribution of power, privilege and prestige so as to gain economic, political, and cultural rights/advantages."[43]

Hsi Lai Temple provides the context for post-1965 Chinese Americans to construct their identity—an identity characterized by heterogeneity, hybridity, multiplicity, fluidity, and situation.[44] This identity is made up of numerous subidentities, including race, ethnicity, culture, nationality, class, gender, and religion, which may be selectively chosen and combined or sometimes ascribed by the community at large. Hsi Lai is a multicultural resource for these Chinese Americans. It is a cultural carrier in preserving traditional Chinese culture; a cultural broker in bridging Chinese subculture and American culture; a cultural entrepreneur in helping to define a new Chinese American identity.[45] Through Hsi Lai's offering of a wide range of educational programs and activities, the content of Chinese and American identities is being creatively selected and incorporated. While Chinese identity can be

Irene Lin

affirmed, American identity can be strengthened. Thus identity becomes inclusive and not exclusive. Through cultural training classes and activities—retrieving and recreating Chinese national and traditional culture in addition to introducing non-Chinese cultures—Chinese Americans who participate can identify with their nation and tradition while at the same time becoming international and transcending the limits of such culture.[46] An added layer of identity is provided by Hsi Lai: that of Chinese Buddhists, in particular, Fo Kuang Buddhists. The construction of a new ethnicity, one that can be manipulated situationally, may suit the lives of today's Chinese Americans, who can choose to be ethnically visible or invisible depending on whether such identity is deemed beneficial. Whether Hsi Lai will be used as a means for mobilizing its members to further their political, social, or economic interests remains to be seen.[47]

Revitalization

Because religious systems may compensate for the loss of native culture, immigrant communities often reinscribe aspects of older traditions in their new context. In the case of post-1965 Chinese Americans with nostalgia for Chinese roots, Hsi Lai Temple provides an instance of religion reviving and constructing Chinese culture and identity. Furthermore, Hsi Lai demonstrates how Buddhism has been revitalized to accommodate the needs of modern industrial society and adapt to a culturally pluralistic environment.[48]

Hsi Lai Temple strives to make Buddhism relevant to modern society. It repackages tradition to fit the modern context through its choice of organizational structure, its design of activities for members, potential members, and the community, and its use of modern mass media and technology. Traditional Buddhist ways are changed by "coming out of the forest and entering into society" and by serving the community through "involvement in families, nations, and the world."[49] Past images of Buddhism are transformed from "passivity to activity," from "pessimism to optimism," from "aversion to the world to engagement in the society and love of existence," and from the practice of asceticism to practice in a quiet, wealthy, and comfortable environment.[50]

Hsi Lai's emphasis on this-worldly orientation, as opposed to the traditional otherworldly orientation, is manifested in its goal to create a Buddhist Pure Land (paradise) here on earth. Master Hsing-yün advocates the ideal of "placing wealth among the devotees." He sees to it that modern facilities are built so that Buddhist devotees can practice in a surrounding replete with wealth and comfort. In tangible ways, Fo Kuang Shan can be viewed as the eastern Pure Land and Hsi Lai Temple the western Pure Land—sacred, prosperous, and serene. Through BLIA and its effective mass media, the local is transcended, globalized, and unified. In the *Buddha's Light* newsletter, Fo Kuang Shan is introduced as a Buddhist sacred place to which believers can make pilgrimages.[51]

Another illustration of Hsi Lai Temple's this-worldly orientation is its development of a Buddhism for daily life, represented by the BLIA. By keeping old ways alive while teaching new ways, and by providing a stable source of meaning and belonging, this megatemple represents a sheltering canopy of legitimation for the Chinese Americans' new identities by reference to their tradition.[52] Traditional functions of the temple, such as offering talks on the dharma and providing a place for religious practice, are expanded to accommodate the needs of the communities—for example, in performing ceremonies for anniversaries, birthdays, weddings, and commemorations.

Panethnicity and Buddhist Organizations

For post-1965 Chinese immigrants who are multicultural, multilingual, and from different socioeconomic backgrounds, "Asian American panethnicity" in terms of a consciousness of shared culture, language, and religion is still a foreign concept. Yen Le Espiritu's referent for Asian American panethnicity is based on the institutionalization of Asian American consciousness, reflecting an efficient mobilization of diverse people based on common political, social, and economic interests or experience.[53] To the extent that religion and culture are intertwined, the boundaries between different Asian and Asian American cultures may not be so fluid. Post-1965 Chinese immigrants do not share the same worldview and experiences as American-born or American-raised Asians. The impact of pan-Asian identity, however, may increase as the immigrant children come of age.

Hsi Lai Temple, with its predominance of post-1965 Chinese immigrants, has not yet showed signs of becoming an Asian panethnic Buddhist organization. Despite the overwhelming majority of members of Chinese origin, currently there is a slow but steady increase of European American members. Hsi Lai strongly encourages this European American membership—for example, *Hsi Lai News* regularly features profiles of new European American members.[54] The implications of this phenomenon—merging the boundaries between Chinese Americans and European Americans but not between Chinese Americans and other Asian Americans—in a religious community suggests more questions than this study can entertain.

Hsi Lai is beginning to reach out to other Asian American groups by participating in cross-ethnic Asian Buddhist activities. On 3 April 1994, for instance, Hsi Lai participated in a Hanamatsuri (flower festival) celebration sponsored by the Buddhist Sangha Council of Southern California and the Japanese Buddhist Association. Seven Buddhist organizations representing Chinese, Vietnamese, Japanese, Korean, Tibetan, and Sri Lankan traditions came together to participate in the celebration. In another instance, on 21 August 1994, Hsi Lai invited monks from other Chinese, Sri Lankan, Thai, and Tibetan temples and monasteries to participate in its Sangha (monastic order) Day.[55] Such gatherings may represent the initial stages of panethnicity. The next step for Hsi Lai is to extend its membership to people of different Asian ethnic backgrounds. If Asian American panethnicity is characterized by political identification for the purpose of mobilizing diverse people to further their common interests, what role, if any, can religion play in defining the content of "Asian American panethnic" consciousness? This question is an interesting topic for further research.

Hsi Lai is also attempting to expand the borders of its present status as a Chinese Mahayana Buddhist organization to become a pan-Buddhist organization. Master Hsing-yün states that "no distinction will be made in regards to area, country, and race"; thus BLIA will preach Buddhism with a view of the whole world as one.[56] For the inauguration of the BLIA's international headquarters and the first general membership conference, held from 17 to 22 May 1992, Hsi Lai Temple invited over four thousand delegates from all five continents, bringing together Buddhists from the Southern (Theravada) and Northern (Mahayana) traditions, as well as the exoteric (Sutric) and esoteric (Tantric) schools. Moreover, Hsi Lai signed an agreement with the abbot of Wat Phra Dhammakaya Temple in Thailand, representing the Theravada tradition, for the purpose of cooperating on projects and exchanging monastic and lay personnel. BLIA chapters worldwide regularly sponsor conferences and meetings among Buddhists of different traditions.[57]

There seems to be gap between the ideal of Buddhism as a nonethnic social truth—especially as articulated by Master Hsing-yün—and the reality of Hsi Lai as a Buddhist organization creating a form of Buddhism and a Buddhist community relevant to the needs of its predominantly Chinese American members. Despite the temple's efforts to encourage European Americans to join the organization, they remain a novelty. Though European American members are introduced in the *Hsi Lai News,* new Chinese American members do not receive such attention.

Irene Lin

Much of Hsi Lai Temple's success can be attributed to its ability to retain cultural continuity with Taiwan while at the same time modifying its social base in accommodation to American culture. By providing a wide range of activities and a network of internal connections, it stimulates its members to a high level of commitment and involvement.[58] Another factor in its success is its ability to attract and maintain members of different ages and economic backgrounds. Master Hsing-yün particularly stresses the importance of making Buddhism attractive to youth—and Hsi Lai provides structures and activities for primary socialization into its unique worldview by reaching out to entire families with children, not just individuals. Moreover, it facilitates secondary socialization through its structure and programs.[59] Finally, by providing a community accepted by the American public at large and the world at large, as well as a home to the Chinese American Buddhists through its plausibility superstructure, it makes its members feel at ease with their unique identity and worldview and at the same time makes it easier for them to confirm the reality of their world.

This case study of Hsi Lai Temple highlights a dimension of Buddhism in America that has been largely overlooked: the Buddhism of Asian Americans. Even though Buddhism represents both a religious and a cultural option for European Americans and Asian Americans, historically their experiences of Buddhism have developed differently. Thus the unique experiences of Asian Americans with Buddhism must be examined from their perspective. As illustrated by Hsi Lai, religion plays an important role in retrieving, preserving, reviving, and creating cultural identities for Chinese Americans, especially among recent immigrants. The construction of a new ethnicity, as a survival tactic, results from the Chinese Americans' effort to preserve their tradition while assim-

153

ilating or accommodating to the dominant culture. Therefore, the study of Asian American religious organizations in general is at the intersection of religious studies, comparative ethnic studies, and Asian American studies and methodologies from these fields should be employed jointly to account for ethnic Asian religious phenomena. But rather than adopting wholesale the methodologies employed in the study of Judeo-Christian religions, we should employ new approaches for non-European Americans and non-Judeo-Christian phenomena.

Furthermore, the categories and labels used to study post-1965 Asian American religious organizations will probably change with the fluid development of these groups. Hsi Lai is moving gradually from a predominantly ethnic Chinese Buddhist community to a mixed Buddhist community attracting nonethnic Chinese members. To the extent that the children of its Chinese immigrant members come of age or "Asian-American panethnic" or "panethnic" members become a reality, Hsi Lai may adapt its teachings, practices, and organization to accommodate the needs of these nonethnic Chinese minorities and European Americans. How Hsi Lai chooses to balance the interests of its ethnic Chinese members against those of nonethnic Chinese members will play a significant role in determining its future.[60]

Notes

I would like to thank Carl Bielefeldt, Rudy Busto, Bernard Faure, John Kieschnic, and Venerable Yifa of Hsi Lai Temple for their help and constructive criticism.

1. Whereas the "church" is defined as an established religious body in the society, both sect and cult are "deviant" religious bodies in increasing relative tension with their surrounding sociocultural context. A "cult" in this model is defined as a movement with no previous ties to another established religious body, originating in the host society through innovation, or imported from another society. In this typology,

if members of an imported cult are primarily an immigrant ethnic population, then the cult is regarded as an ethnic church. See Rodney Stark and William Sims Bainbridge, *The Future of Religion: Secularization, Revival, and Cult Formation* (Berkeley: University of California Press, 1985), pp. 25 and 189. The suitability of applying Western labels such as "cult" to Chinese religions also needs to be examined. Upon the transformation from a religious organization that is based on ethnic population to one that seeks to recruit converts from the population at large in the United States, Chinese religions, according to this scheme, leave the domain of ethnic religions and enter the field of "alternative religions." The change may trigger the labeling of "new religious movements" as alternatives to mainstream American religions, that is, those that are "not normatively Judeo-Christian." See Robert S. Ellwood Jr., *Religious and Spiritual Groups in Modern America* (Englewood Cliffs, N.J.: Prentice-Hall, 1973), p. 2. The term "cult," however, is inappropriate on at least three grounds. First, given its pejorative connotation, it generates fear and suspicion. Second, it is supposed to refer to "new" religious groups in society, but transplanted Chinese religions are hardly new and may belong to long-established traditions in their country of origin. Third, "cult" is a catchall term that does not allow for adequate distinction among different types of "nonmainline American religions." Given these problems in applying Western schemes and labels, a more fitting terminology is desirable for studying Chinese religions in the United States. For discussions on new religious movements see David G. Bromley and Phillip E. Hammond, eds., *The Future of New Religious Movements* (Macon, Ga.: Mercer University Press, 1987); Jacob Needleman and George Baker, eds., *Understanding the New Religions* (New York: Seabury Press, 1978); Geoffery K. Nelson, *Cults, New Religions, and Religious Creativity* (London: Routledge & Kegan Paul, 1987). Charles S. Prebish, in *American Buddhism* (North Scituate, Mass.: Duxbury Press, 1979), pp. 173–174, discusses the interpretation of the term "new religion" as "new in the sense of group, which has arisen in America within the last one hundred fifty years and are still extant" and as "unusual or exotic."

2. Other models have been applied to the Asian religions in the United States. Peter W. Williams, in *America's Religions: Traditions and Cultures* (New York: Macmillan, 1990), p. 417, uses the categories of ethnic religions, export religions, and cults or new religions to describe Asian religions in the United States. Catherine L. Albanese, in *America: Religions and Religion* (Belmont, Calif.: Wadsworth, 1992), p. 318, employs the categories of church, meditation, evangelical, and ethnic Buddhism to characterize different Buddhist groups in the United

States. See also Jan Nattier, "Visible and Invisible: Jan Nattier on the Politics of Representation in Buddhist America," *Tricycle: The Buddhist Review* 5 (1995):42–49, who posits the typology of elite, evangelical, and ethnic Buddhism. These categories reflect similar biases of Western perspectives.

3. Indigenization is the process through which foreign-born religion changes through contact with native religion and culture. See Kiyomi Morioka, "Gairai shukyo no dochakuka o meguru gaineteki seiri" (A conceptual examination of the indigenization of foreign-born religions), *Shicho* 107 (1972):52–57. See also Carlyle C. Haaland, "Shinto and Indigenous Chinese Religion," C. H. Lippy and P. W. Williams, eds., *Encyclopedia of American Religious Experience* (New York: Scribner's, 1988), pp. 669–709. L. Eve Armentrout Ma, "Chinese Traditional Religion in North America and Hawaii," in *Chinese America: History and Perspectives* (San Francisco: Chinese Historical Society of America, 1988), pp. 131–147, is primarily a study of the religious practice of traditional or popular Chinese religion, which combines Buddhism, Taoism, elements of Confucianism, and local cults. Ma states that many recent immigrants still practice this Chinese traditional religion. See also Mariann Kaye Wells, *Chinese Temples in California* (Berkeley: University of California Press, 1962), p. 108; Peter Harvey, *An Introduction to Buddhism: Teachings, History, and Practices* (Cambridge: Cambridge University Press, 1990); Emma McCloy Layman, *Buddhism in America* (Chicago: Nelson-Hall, 1976); Charles S. Prebish, "Buddhism," C. H. Lippy and P. W. Williams, eds., *Encyclopedia of American Religious Experience* (New York: Scribner's, 1988); and Rick Fields, *How the Swans Came to the Lake: A Narrative History of Buddhism in America* (Boston: Shambhala, 1992). The only Chinese Buddhist organization presented is the Sino-American Buddhist Association in Northern California. (In 1984, the name of the organization was changed to Dharma Realm Buddhist Association.) See Gordon Melton, *The Encyclopedia of American Religions* (Wilmington: N.C.: McGrath, 1978), pp. 424–430.

4. See *Tricycle: The Buddhist Review*, Fall 1994, special section on "Dharma, Diversity, and Race." According to Bell Hooks, "Waking Up to Racism," pp. 42–44, many Buddhists of color in the U.S. do not have visibility. Victor Sogen Hori, in "Sweet and Sour Buddhism," pp. 48–52, states that Westerners in the United States have projected their cultural attitudes onto Buddhism. In "Confessions of a White Buddhist," pp. 54–56, Rick Fields says that American Buddhism is being defined by the whites in their own image. Addie Foye, "Buddhists in America: A Short, Biased View," p. 57, comments on the division of Buddhism into Asian American Buddhism and European American Buddhism, which leads to the invisibility of African American Buddhists.

Irene Lin

5. For example, the Dharma Realm Buddhist Association, formerly known as the Sino-American Buddhist Association, is often portrayed as representative of the Chinese Buddhist organizations. Its association with Ch'an/Zen and its large European American following have attracted the attention of scholars.

6. See Prebish, "Buddhism."

7. Layman, *Buddhism in America*, p. 279.

8. Bill Ong Hing, *Making and Remaking Asian America Through Immigration Policy, 1850–1990* (Stanford: Stanford University Press, 1993), p. 81. The 1965 amendments abolish the 1924 discriminatory national origins provision, which was retained in the Immigration and Nationality Act of 1952, favoring immigrants of Western European origins. The subsequent series of amendments of the 1952 act in 1990, collectively referred to as the Immigration Act of 1990, provides for an overall increase in worldwide immigration. The 1990 act increases the allocation for both family-related and employee-related immigration and further creates a separate basis by which "diversity" immigrants (nationals of countries previously underrepresented since 1965 due to visa issuance), can enter the United States. Amendments of the 1952 act that are directed toward the increase of Chinese immigrants entering the United States are as follows: the 1981 amendment creates a separate quota of 20,000 for Taiwan, which Taiwan previously shared with China and Hong Kong. In 1987, the annual quota for Hong Kong was increased from 600 to 5,000, then to 10,000 from 1990 to 1993, and subsequently to 20,000. Furthermore, thousands of students were admitted from Taiwan, Hong Kong, Southeast Asian countries, and the People's Republic of China. See INA §201–203. Aside from the Chinese immigrants from China, Hong Kong, and Taiwan, ethnic Chinese immigrants who entered the United States are composed of refugees from Vietnam, Laos, and Cambodia who were admitted to the United States since 1975 and the overseas Chinese in Southeast Asian and Latin American countries facing anti-Chinese discrimination and political unrest. This latter group came to the United States for a more stable investment environment and better educational opportunities for their children. See L. Ling-chi Wang, "Roots and the Changing Identity of the Chinese in the United States," in Tu Wei-ming, *The Living Tree: The Changing Meaning of Being Chinese Today* (Stanford: Stanford University Press, 1994), p. 196. See also INA §207. As an unintended consequence, however, the amendments to the 1952 act polarize the Chinese immigrants into two categories: professionals and service workers. Peter Kwong, in *The New Chinatown* (New York: Hill & Wang, 1987), p. 22, calls these two categories the "Uptown Chinese," made up of the professionals who do not settle in Chinatowns, and the "Downtown Chinese," made up of man-

ual and service workers who tend to live in Chinatowns with their sponsoring relatives of similar humble origin from rural areas of southern
China. In addition to differences in place of birth and socioeconomic
class, the Chinese Americans differ in their native dialect and place of
origin—China, Hong Kong, Taiwan, Southeast Asia, and Latin America—according to Hing, pp. 86–87.

9. One motivation for focusing on this subset is that Chinese American Buddhists are characterized by the superposition of two culturally
differentiating factors: non-European heritage and non-Judeo-Christian
belief. The combination of these two factors engenders unique experiences that warrant separate study and present distinctive methodological challenges. Examples of Chinese Buddhist organizations that have
arisen since the late 1960s include the Hsi Lai Temple, True Buddha
School, Dharma Realm Buddhist Association (previously known as the
Sino-American Buddhist Association), and Buddhist Tzu-Chi Association of America.

10. Since Hsi Lai Temple uses the Wade-Giles system, Chinese terms
related to the temple will be transliterated using that system instead of
pinyin. See Heinrich Dumoulin's *Zen Buddhism: A History —India and
China* (New York: Macmillan, 1988), for the legend of Bodhidharma,
the twenty-eighth Indian patriarch and first patriarch of Ch'an in China.
Bodhidharma is said to have come to China from the west (India),
bringing the "seal of the Buddha mind" from the motherland to China.
Hsi Lai can alternatively be read as "coming from the west," depicting
the dharma having come from the west and now returning to the west.

11. See Timothy Fong's *The First Suburban Chinatown: The
Remaking of Monterey Park, California* (Philadelphia: Temple University Press, 1994). Religious organizations should be distinguished from
religious consciousness. As used here, a religious organization is a community gathered for common worship and furtherance of a religious
belief. Religious consciousness, on the other hand, is an awareness of or
interest in a religious belief, with differing intensity, which may entail
private or common worship. Thus private forms of worship are not
within the scope of this study. Much of Chinese traditional religion in
the United States represents what Carlyle Haaland calls an "invisible
institution," whose rituals are conducted in private. See also Williams,
America's Religions, p. 419.

12. A basic assumption here is that religion can help to construct
Chinese American identity by maintaining and constructing Chinese
culture at the periphery. This notion of periphery is twofold: geographically, Chinese culture is being constructed in the United States, far from
China; culturally, it is being constructed by Chinese Americans, away

from the American mainstream. According to Tu Wei-ming, "Cultural China," pp. 1–34, "cultural China" is being shaped by the periphery instead of the center by the Chinese in diaspora.

13. The main sources for this case study are books, newsletters, journals, booklets, and flyers published by Hsi Lai Temple, a related organization, or an unrelated third party commissioned by Hsi Lai. Most of the information regarding the detailed operation of the temple, its founder, and its history is published in Chinese, whereas information on its activities and objectives is available in both Chinese and English. This study also relies on personal observations of the rituals and activities in addition to conversations with members of the monastic order and laity at Hsi Lai. Most of the members of the order at Hsi Lai have a good command of at least two languages: Mandarin, Taiwanese, English, or Japanese. Many of the monks/nuns in higher administrative ranks studied at graduate schools primarily in Japan and secondarily in the United States.

14. Hsing-yün, *Perfectly Willing* (Hacienda Heights, Calif.: Hsi Lai University Press, 1994).

15. Hsing-yün wrote articles that called for reform of the practice of Buddhism, spoke out against governmental interference in religion, and suggested the establishment of laws assuring equal treatment of all religions in Taiwan. See Hsing-yün, *Perfectly Willing*, pp. 5 and 134–135. In the Chinese version of the text, the two terms *"jen-chien"* (translated as "humanitarian" or "humanistic") and *"sheng-huo"* (daily life) are subsumed in the English translation into "humanization." In this context I think Hsing-yün is trying to convey that Buddhism is being made relevant to daily life, or socially engaged; see Hsing-yün, *How to Be a Fo Kuang Buddhist* (Hacienda Heights, Calif.: International Buddhist Progress Society, 1987); Fo Kuang Shan has branches in the United States, Canada, Argentina, Paraguay, Brazil, Costa Rica, Japan, Hong Kong, India, Malaysia, the Philippines, Australia, England, Switzerland, Germany, France, and Russia; see Fu Chi-ying, *Chuan deng: Hsing-yün ta shih chuan* (Handing down the light: The biography of Venerable Master Hsing-yün) (Taipei: Commonwealth, 1995), p. 254.

16. Hsing-yün brought back five blocks of bricks from India, holy sand from the Ganges, and mud from Fo Kuang Shan, which were all deposited into the foundation of Hsi Lai Temple—illustrating that "although the source of the pulse of Dharma is far, the flow of the Dharma reaches far"; see Fu, Chuan deng, p. 252. In November 1988, *Life* magazine published a picture of Hsi Lai naming it the largest temple in the western hemisphere. In the following year, *Reader's Digest* had an article on Hsi Lai. See *Los Angeles Times* (10 January 1988).

Journey to the Far West

17. *Los Angeles Times* (10 January 1988); Fu, *Chuang deng*, p. 254.

18. Fu, *Chuang deng*, p. 252; see Hsing-yün, *How to Be a Fo Kuang Buddhist;* Hsing-yün, *Perfectly Willing*, p. 4.

19. Communal practices and activities include talks, classes, meditation retreats, short-term monastic retreats, Five Precepts retreats, and Amitabha Buddha seven-day chanting retreats. The short-term monastic retreat provides the participants with firsthand experience of monastic life for five days. The Five Precepts are not to kill, not to steal, not to lie, not to engage in improper sexual conduct, and not to use intoxicants. Aside from the general activities open to all, there are special activities for the Fo Kuang Women and Fo Kuang Youth associations. Hsi Lai Temple also regularly offers separate Buddhist camps and retreats to accommodate the different needs of its members: college students, children, teenagers, retired people, teachers, and mothers/housewives.

20. The Bodhisattva Hall houses images of Samantabhadra (representing great practice), Ksitigarbha (representing benevolence), Maitreya (Future Buddha), Avalokitesvara (representing great compassion), and Mañjusri (representing great wisdom). The Buddha Hall has images of Bhaisajyaguru (Medicine Buddha), Sakyamuni Buddha (the historical Buddha), and Amitabha Buddha (Buddha of Eternal Light).

21. The average age of the monks and nuns is thirty. The nuns outnumber the monks at Hsi Lai; see Fo Kuang Shan, *Our Report*, p. 44. The Religious Affairs Committee, made up of thirteen members and seven alternates, elected by secret ballot, serves a term of six years. The abbot of Fo Kuang Shan, elected by the committee members, acts as the chair of the committee and spends a maximum of two terms in office. The Religious Affairs Committee consists of the Veterans Council, Domestic Supervisory Council, International Supervisory Council, Education Council, Culture Council, Fo Kuang Shan Culture and Educational Foundation, Fo Kuang Pure Land Cultural and Educational Foundation, University Education Organizing Committee, Buddha Light International Association Development Committee, International Buddhist Progress Society, Religious Affairs Advancement Committee, and Cultivation Center. See Fo Kuang Shan, *Our Report*, pp. 43–44.

22. Fu, Chuang deng, pp. 275 and 270. Master Hsing-yün has retired from the position of abbot of Fo Kuang Shan and become actively involved with the BLIA. BLIA claims that the benefits of joining its organization include meeting fellow members and having many friends, increasing wisdom in home fellowship meetings, skill training programs, assistance in job hunting, increasing business contacts, getting personal advice, participating in Buddhist study clubs, being hosted by fellow members while traveling around the world, assistance in funeral, mar-

Irene Lin

riage, and other events, and "sanctifying the spirit" by participating in countless activities. See Hsing-yün, *The Buddha Light International Association: Who Are We?* (Hacienda Heights, Calif.: BLIA Headquarters, 1994), p. 5.

23. BLIA, 1995.

24. According to BLIA, the other three organizations are the Rotary Club, the Lion's Club, and the United Way. See Fu, *Chuang deng*, p. 279. On the inauguration day of the BLIA International Headquarters and the First General Membership Conference at Hsi Lai Temple, former president of the United States George Bush and president of Taiwan Li Teng-huei sent letters of congratulations.

25. Hsing-yün, *Who Are We?*, p. 20. These figures regarding number of chapters and so on are valid as of January 1994. The information on how to set up a BLIA chapter is from the *Fo Kuang Shih Chi* (Buddha's Light Newsletter), 1 February 1993. Prominent members of the Chinese community are asked upon their visit to the temple to set up a BLIA chapter in their community and become the head of the local chapter; after taking refuge in the Buddha, the Dharma, and the Sangha (the monastic order), the participants become newly initiated Buddhists.

26. Fo Kuang Shan, *Our Report*, p. 39.

27. Hsing-yün, *Who Are We?*, p. 13; Fu, *Chuang deng*, pp. 274–275. According to the Hsi Lai News, during the January 1994 precept retreat, of the four hundred devotees that came from different parts of the United States and Canada, seventy-five were "Western Buddhists."

28. Fu, *Chuang deng*, p. 253.

29. The figures for individual visitors to the temple were not available at the time of the study; group visitors include Buddhist and non-Buddhist religious groups, politicians, students, and military personnel.

30. Only lunch is open to visitors of the temple; a donation of $5 is required. Occasions for staying in the houses owned by Hsi Lai include late evening ceremonial rituals, weeklong retreats, or celebrations of buddhas' or bodhisattvas' birthdays or enlightenment days.

31. Some of these events include performances by the different Hsi Lai organizations, such as the Hsi Lai Women's Association, Hsi Lai Youth Association, Buddha's Light Symphony Orchestra, and Buddha's Light choirs. To accommodate the concerns of many parents that "the modern world presents children with a precarious environment for growing up," BLIA regularly sponsors a "safe, fun, and productive environment" in which children and youth can enjoy themselves while learning new skills and meeting new friends. During summer and winter vacations, BLIA sponsors retreat camps. During the course of the year, BLIA provides competitions in music, art, public speaking, and writing.

In addition, BLIA youth groups visit sister youth groups in other communities, offering participants a chance to learn new cultures and customs and make new friends.

32. Fo Kuang Shan, *Our Report,* p. 26; In Taiwan, Fo Kuang Shan operates successful preschool, kindergarten, elementary, junior high, high school, college, and graduate programs on its premises. Its reputation for turning out well-disciplined and well-educated students in Taiwan led Chinese parents in the United States to ask that Hsi Lai Temple provide a similar educational environment in the United States. The opening of Hsi Lai University is a step toward accommodating this request.

33. Hsi Lai has sponsored domestic and international academic conferences such as the International Buddhist Conference, the World Sutric and Tantric Buddhist Conference, the International Buddhist Academic Conference, and the Buddhist Youth Academic Conference. See Hsing-yün, *Who Are We?*, p. 11.

34. The Fo Kuang publications include Buddhist sutras, commentaries, histories, philosophy, liturgical texts, reference materials, and a collection of Master Hsing-yun's lectures and writings. Reference materials include the Fo Kuang Tripitaka, a four-volume Fo Kuang dictionary of Buddhist terms, and a table of important dates and events in Buddhist history. At present Hsi Lai is creating a CD-ROM version of the Buddhist Tripitaka. Audio and video tapes featuring sermons, sutras, publications, songs, music, and televised programs are available in Mandarin, Taiwanese, Cantonese, Hakka, and English. In 1995, over 250,000 audio and 35,000 video tapes were in circulation. See Fo Kuang Shan, *Our Report,* p. 8; Hsing-yün, *Who Are We?*

35. For the concept of religion as a consumer product and thus subject to consumer preference see Peter Berger, *The Heretical Imperative: Contemporary Possibilities of Religious Affirmation* (New York: Harper & Row, 1982). See Sara Bershtel and Allen Graubard, *Saving Remnants: Feeling Jewish in America* (New York: Free Press, 1992) for a discussion for how synagogues in the United States appeal to the current social and cultural tastes of their clientele and more generally how Jewish Americans are choosing their identities, freely creating and incorporating pieces of tradition, including varying degrees and elements of religious and ethnic identities.

36. See Peter Berger, *The Sacred Canopy: Elements of a Sociological Theory of Religion* (New York: Doubleday, 1967), p. 45. Berger asserts that worlds are socially constructed and socially maintained. Thus a religion requires a plausibility structure within which the reality, as defined by the religious tradition, is taken for granted and within which succes-

sive generations of individuals are socialized in a way that the world, as defined by the religious tradition, will be real to them; p. 46.

37. Ibid., p. 49. Compare this to religious monopolies of the past: "When an entire society served as the plausibility structure for a religiously legitimated world, all important social processes within it served to confirm and reconfirm the reality of this world"; ibid., p. 48.

38. Hsing-yün, *How to Be a Fo Kuang Buddhist.*

39. David Yen-ho Wu, "The Construction of Chinese and Non-Chinese Identities," in Tu Wei-ming, ed., *The Living Tree: The Changing Meaning of Being Chinese Today* (Stanford: Stanford University Press, 1994), p. 151.

40. "The term 'Asian American' was adopted in order to allow a presumed ethnicity to achieve political identity and group solidarity"; Paul Wong, "The Emergence of the Asian American Movement," *Bridge* 2 (1972):32–39.

41. Evelyn Kallen, *The Western Samoan Kinship Bridge: A Study in Migration, Social Change and New Ethnicity* (Leiden: Brill, 1982), p. 30. The concept of old ethnicity refers to "any arbitrary classification of human populations utilizing the bio-cultural criterion of (actual or assumed) common ancestry in conjunction with the geo-cultural criterion of (common) ancestral territory and socio-cultural criterion of (common) ancestral heritage (culture and social institutions)"; ibid., p. 29.

42. Ibid., p. 30.

43. Ibid. The concept of new ethnicity has developed "as a symbolic system which can be manipulated situationally so as to enable individuals and/or groups to maintain and revitalize their sense of ethnic belonging (roots) in context where this is valued and deemed advantageous, and to remain ethnically invisible when other interests and identities (occupation, political affiliation and so forth) come to the fore"; ibid., p. 31.

44. See Lisa Lowe, "Heterogeneity, Hybridity, Multiplicity: Marking Asian American Difference," *Diaspora* 1 (1991), for the application of the concepts of heterogeneity, hybridity, and multiplicity to the characterization of Asian American culture.

45. See Bernard Wong, "Elites and Ethnic Boundary Maintenance: A Study of the Roles of Elites in Chinatown, New York City," *Urban Anthropology* 6(1) (1977):1–22, for a discussion of these concepts.

46. Shigeo H. Kanda argues in "Recovering Cultural Symbols: A Case for Buddhism in the Japanese American Communities," *Journal of the American Academy of Religion* 14 (4 suppl.) (1978):445–475, that religious institutions (especially Buddhist churches in America) play a key role in sustaining, interpreting, and transmitting cultural symbols and

values. He argues that Buddhism, more than Christianity, is an important receptacle for Japanese American tradition because of its bicultural and ethnic character. Kanda calls for the recovery of cultural symbols and sees Buddhist symbols as capable of grafting on meanings from other cultural traditions. In contrast to Kanda's view, the concept of new ethnicity involves constructing cultural identities, not just recovering cultural symbols and grafting meanings onto existing symbols. It also entails creating new cultural and religious symbols to reflect the heterogeneous needs of ethnic minorities in a new social context.

47. See Albanese, *America: Religions and Religion,* pp. 43–47, for a discussion of how the traditional Native American religions have served as vehicles for maintaining Native American identity and encouraging political action.

48. For comparative studies see Robert N. Bellah, "Epilogue," in *Religion and Progress in Modern Asia* (New York: Free Press, 1965), pp. 168–229. Bellah argues that Japan faces four prospects of modernization: conversion to Christianity, reformism, pure traditionalism, and neotraditionalism. See Charles H. Hambrick, "Tradition and Modernity in the New Religious Movements of Japan," *Japanese Journal of Religious Studies* 1(2–3) (1974):217–253. In his analysis of tradition and modernity in new Japanese religious movements, he argues that they adapt a traditional myth-symbol system to a modern situation, assuming the role of folk "neotraditionalism."

49. Hsing-yün, *Perfectly Willing,* p. 3. The forest refers to the old Buddhist ideal of the wandering renunciate of the forests versus a newer ideal of settled monastics in the villages. See Reginald A. Ray, *Buddhist Saints in India: A Study of Buddhist Values and Orientations* (Oxford: Oxford University Press, 1994).

50. Hsing-yün, *Who Are We?,* p. 3; Hsing-yün, *Perfectly Willing,* pp. 132–136.

51. Yung Kai, ed., "Buddhist Sacred Places of the World (3)," *Buddha's Light Newsletter* (October 1992): 1–6. This characterization of Fo Kuang Shan as a sacred place can be extended to Hsi Lai due to its claim to be a Pure Land on earth and a site housing a bone relic of the historical Sakyamuni Buddha.

52. Compare Hsi Lai as a "megatemple " to Calvary Chapel, an evangelical "megachurch" in Santa Ana, California, that also provides a broad network and activities for its members. See Randall Balmer, *Mine Eyes Have Seen the Glory: A Journey into the Evangelical Subculture in America* (New York: Oxford University Press, 1993), pp. 12–30.

53. Yen Le Espiritu, *Asian American Panethnicity: Bridging Institutions and Identities* (Philadelphia: Temple University Press, 1992). Com-

Irene Lin

pare Espiritu—who distinguishes between the institutionalization of the panethnic consciousness as a political resource and panethnic consciousness in terms of common culture, language, and religion—with William Wei, *The Asian American Movement* (Philadelphia: Temple University Press, 1993), who does not make such a distinction but instead speaks of the existence of Asian American consciousness from the presence of the Asian American movement.

54. Despite the profile of an African American member in the March–April 1994 issue of *Hsi Lai News,* there are few African Americans at Hsi Lai.

55. May Lui, "Age-Old Alms-Round Reenacted on Sangha Day," *Hsi Lai News* (September–October 1994): 1.

56. Hsing-yün, *Who Are We?,* p. 7.

57. The three major forms of Buddhism are Theravada (popular in Southeast Asia), Mahayana (dominant in China and Japan), and Vajrayana (notable in Tibet and Japan). Vajrayana is often seen as simply a part of Mahayana. Chinese Buddhist organizations are primarily Mahayana and secondarily Vajrayana. See Albanese, *America: Religions and Religion;* Hsing-yün, *Who Are We?,* p. 7; Fo Kuang Shan, *Our Report,* p. 41.

58. Hsi Lai's activities present an effective mobilization of laity and resources. Because of the proliferation of construction projects, activities, and rituals sponsored by Hsi Lai Temple requiring massive capital and labor, the members who support Hsi Lai are generally from the middle or upper middle class, with a significant number from the upper class. These members have the money and time for all the frequent and diverse Hsi Lai events. Hsi Lai Temple recently added an Eighteen Arhats (Buddhist Saints) Garden and a Kuan-shih-yin (Bodhisattva of Compassion) Garden; members and potential members are given the option of participating in rituals by mailing in a donation in order for their names to be read during the ceremonies. In this way, those who cannot come to the temple can equally receive blessings. According to the abbess, Venerable I-kung, although construction of Hsi Lai was financed primarily by donations from Taiwanese supporters, the temple's current operating expenses are covered by donations from U.S. supporters.

59. "Primary socialization is the first socialization an individual undergoes in childhood, through which he becomes a member of society." See Peter Berger and Thomas Luckmann, *The Social Construction of Reality: A Treatise in the Sociology of Knowledge* (New York: Anchor Books, 1966), p. 130. "Secondary socialization is any subsequent process that inducts an already socialized individual into new sectors of the objective world of his society"; ibid.

60. In studying Chinese religious groups in the United States, one would like to know if the phenomenon of bridging traditional and modern aspects of religion and culture is occurring in wider Buddhist and non-Buddhist contexts. Especially promising is the comparative study of traditional Chinese religions in Asia and Chinese American religions. The comparative study of Chinese American religions and Japanese new religions, both in Japan and the United States, would enable us to draw parallels and note discontinuities. Such a study can, of course, be extended to ethnic minority religions in general and other nonmainstream religions.

Irene Lin

PART II _____

Searching for Self and Soul _____

This part of the book moves the discussion into the contemporary setting and asks how religion has informed the search for meaning that accompanies identity formation. In Chapter 5, on the role of religion among college students, Rudy Busto of Stanford University inquires why so many Asian American students have gravitated to evangelical Protestant Christian student organizations. Busto's analysis suggests that notions of the model minority myth and upward social mobility offer clues to why these groups are flourishing. In Chapter 6 Heinz Insu Fenkl tracks student responses to the shaman who visited his class at Vassar College, but the experience also triggers Fenkl's own layered experiences with shamanism. The child of a German father and Korean mother, Fenkl sees in the ritual a sense of being caught between categories of culture, language, blood, nationality, and place of origin.

In Chapter 7, participant observation is central to Jung Ha Kim's study of a Korean American congregation in the U.S. South and the roles that women play in an immigrant church. Although women comprise the majority of the church population, they are often overlooked even in studies that focus on race/ethnicity (read Korean American males) and gender (read white American women). Chapter 8, by Protestant theologian Sang Hyun Lee, examines the concepts of pilgrimage and home. Lee compares the marginal status of Asian Americans with Jesus' standing during his day and, from that liminal space, argues for a creativity and energy that pushes creation toward home.

Chapter 5

The Gospel according to the Model Minority?:
Hazarding an Interpretation of Asian American
Evangelical College Students

R U D Y   V .   B U S T O

Then he poured out to God the anguish in his heart: the sorrow for
his sin, the rebellion against his parents, the arrogance of his philo-
sophic mind . . . his desire to run his own life. He yielded his mind
and heart to Jesus the Truth and the Life. Then he prayed the Lord's
Prayer as best as he could remember it. "Come to me," Jesus said,
"and I will give you rest." Bob believed that would happen. And it
did. And more too. Joy.

—*James W. Sire,* Chris Chrisman Goes to College

In James Sire's fictional account of freshman year at Hansom
State University, Bob Wong, a Chinese American student from
Mendocino, California, is "born again" after a year of intensive prayer and prodding by his evangelical Christian friends.
Born in Taiwan and raised in the United States, Bob Wong is
caught between the Chinese Buddhist culture of his immigrant parents and his desire to "be rid of his Chinese roots."
An avowed atheist when he arrives at Hansom State, by the
end of freshman year Bob's newfound Christian faith presents
him with one final challenge: facing his parents. "What to say?
He knew he had to somehow begin to see them as his parents,

to 'honor' them, to show this in a way they with their Chinese and Buddhist heritage would recognize. How was he to do this? He didn't know."

Lots of questions for Bob Wong. Sire's story intersperses the details of Chris Chrisman and his friends' freshman year with discussions of the philosophical traps of relativism, individualism, and pluralism awaiting evangelical students in the college classroom. It comes as no surprise that Sire includes an Asian American character in his plot, as Asian American students in the 1990s have become central players in American evangelical Christianity. His characterization of Bob Wong—hardworking, philosophically tenacious, and troubled by his Asianness—hints at larger issues about Asian American identity in the context of evangelical Christianity. This chapter rephrases Bob Wong's question, "What to say?" about Asian American college students and evangelical Christianity.

With a long history and numerous traditions, evangelical Christianity is one of the fastest-growing religious/social movements in the United States.[1] Depending on sources and definitions, evangelical Protestants comprise upward of 20 percent of the nation's population, or somewhere between 30 and 50 million believers.[2] As part of the late-twentieth-century American spiritual reawakening since the 1970s, large numbers of Asian American college students are turning to a personal relationship with Jesus Christ through the encouragement and support of national and local prayer and Bible study organizations. On college campuses, evangelical "parachurch" organizations like Campus Crusade for Christ (CCC), The Navigators, and InterVarsity Christian Fellowship (IVCF) continue to draw large numbers of students to their weekly Bible studies, prayer meetings, and social events. This vigorous—some would say aggressive—Protestant Christianity is very much at home on the college campus. In fact, evangelicalism and university students have shared a long history together in the United States, especially after World War II in the Youth for Christ movement that spawned a generation of influential evangelical leaders.[3]

The current perception that large numbers of Asian American college students are evangelical and participate in parachurch organizations remains for the most part anecdotal. It is curious that Asian American studies, focused so centrally on community studies and historical retrieval, has ignored the phenomenon of evangelical Christianity in Asian America. The lack of empirical data, interpretations, or even acknowledgment of evangelicalism among Asian American college students is glaring.[4] In comparison, our scholarly understanding of religion in African American, Chicano/Latino, and Native American communities is more advanced.[5] This essay is a preliminary charting of this largely unknown terrain and a call for systematic research and analysis of religious affiliation, beliefs, and practices in Asian American communities. Without the luxury of plentiful data or even a substantive body of writing on the subject of evangelical Christianity in Asian American communities, I will describe what I perceive to be salient problems, point out contextual issues, and hazard an interpretation how and why Asian Americans are becoming increasingly associated with evangelical Christianity on the college campus.

The 1970s: Convergence in the Watershed Years

In the United States, parachurch organizations have operated at full speed on college campuses since the 1940s. The rapid growth of evangelical campus organizations in the 1970s was fueled by the personal spiritual vacuums left in the wake of cultural upheaval late in the 1960s and a generation of post-1960s university students in search of meaning and values. For many students, campus Christian organizations introduced the ideology and lifestyle of evangelical Christianity packaged in the culture of youth and articulated by college-educated leaders. Other students were drawn to the countercultural aspects of evangelical Christianity in the Jesus movement and the growth of youth-centered local churches. The late 1970s witnessed a wider acceptance of evangelical Christianity in the country—exemplified by the election of an openly evangelical president in 1976—and an emergent evangelical identity and political movement in full swing by the early 1980s.[6]

The 1970s also witnessed a dramatic increased presence of Asian Americans on college campuses. Asian American undergraduates almost tripled in number between 1976 and 1986 (from 150,000 to 488,000).[7] Because of this rapid growth, the 1970s saw a concomitant increase in Asian American involvement with both the large national parachurch organizations and local ethnic-specific "Bible studies" and "fellowships." In response to an increasingly diverse college population, Inter-Varsity, for example, developed a series of "ABC" (Asian, Black, and Chicano) conferences beginning in 1976 and experienced a membership boom in the 1980s producing a significant number of Asian American IVCF student leaders. Similarly, Campus Crusade for Christ launched an Intercultural Ministry in the mid-1970s.[8] Alongside the large national organizations, there are numerous local Bible studies and fellowships that are ethnic in nature and sponsored by local churches. The Asian American Christian Fellowship (AACF) at Stanford, for example, grew out of a 1973 campus Bible study group sponsored by the Japanese Evangelical Missionary Society ministry at California State University–Los Angeles.[9]

One should not, however, overstate the success of these ministries in the United States. The aggressive evangelism that took place in Asia after World War II was responsible for Christianizing an emigrant Korean and Chinese population. Campus Crusade for Christ's 1974 "Explo '74" weeklong evangelistic and missions training event in Seoul, for example, witnessed what was then the largest Christian gathering in

Korean history (exceeding 1.3 million participants). With "almost all Protestant churches in South Korea, numbering some 12,000 congregations represented," Explo '74 helps to explain the "miracle of the masses"—that is, the dramatic growth in Korean Christianity from 3 million believers in 1974 to 7 million in 1978.[10] A good percentage of Korean American evangelical students in the 1990s, then, would appear to be the harvest of Campus Crusade's farsighted sowing as Korean immigration to the United States rapidly increased in the decades following.

In Karl Fung's account of the impact of recently arrived overseas-born Chinese in his San Diego church community during the 1970s, he reveals that they were markedly conservative theologically and eventually divided the traditionally liberal American-born Chinese Methodist congregation. These conservative evangelical immigrants from Hong Kong and Taiwan, Fung observes, came out of a history of intense conservative Christian foreign mission work and were strongly attached to the "absolute authority and clear direction" of evangelicalism in the wake of massive social upheaval after the communist takeover of China in 1949.[11] Taken together the Korean and Taiwanese demographic shifts—toward an Asian American population primarily foreign-born, upper and middle class, and already familiar with evangelicalism—account for the Northeast Asian flavor to Asian American evangelicalism.[12]

Asian Americans and Parachurch Organizations

In 1991 the *New York Times* reported that among the "dozens of surprises" discovered in the National Survey of Religious Identification (NSRI) was the finding that Asian Americans overwhelmingly identified themselves as "Christian." The surprise, of course, is that contrary to popular assumptions and stereotypes, Asian Americans as a group do not self-identify as members or practitioners of "Asian" religions. In fact, the NSRI indicates that among Asian American respondents, 33.6 percent affiliated with Protestant denominations, 27.1 percent indicated Roman Catholic, 19.1 percent cited "no religion," and only 7.8 percent reported Buddhist or Hindu affiliation. (The real surprise here is how accurately James Sire characterized Bob Wong as part of the 19.1 percent religious "nones"!)[13]

Christianity is not a newcomer to Asian American communities. Any account of Korean history, for example, would be incomprehensible without acknowledging Christianity's essential role in the formation of the modern state or the centrality of the church institution in Korean American agitation for Korean independence. Similarly, the historical presence of Baptists, the Salvation Army, Presbyterian social work, and the YMCA in Chinese American history extends this long relationship between Asians and various types of Protestant Christianity back through the nineteenth century. Roman Catholicism, of course, has a centuries-old involvement in China, India, Vietnam, and the Philippines. Modern evangelicalism, in fact, arises out of the muscular Victorian Protestantism that accompanied American imperialism to Asia at the turn of the century.[14]

The perception that Asian American students are currently disproportionately involved in InterVarsity and Campus Crusade for Christ appears to be well founded. *Christianity Today* reports that InterVarsity's seventeenth triennial conference on missions, "Urbana '93," noticed a "fundamental change in the makeup of the delegates" with nearly two-fifths of the seventeen thousand or so attendees ethnic minorities. Asian Americans represented more than 25 percent of the conferees, and Korean Americans accounted "for nearly one out of ten attendees." Faith Kim, a longtime Korean American IVCF member, recalled that she was unable to find another Korean American delegate at Urbana '68 and interpreted the dramatic increase in 1993 as "the grace of God."[15]

Rudy V. Busto

In local campus chapters, Asian American participation appears to corroborate these dramatic numbers. In 1991, Asian Americans reportedly made up approximately 65 percent of the three hundred student members in the UC–Berkeley IVCF chapter. As a national organization, InterVarsity's large number of Asian Americans in its ministry hints at equally high numbers in similar organizations but may obscure the many Bible study groups operating alongside the large fellowships.[16] Relations between the large, multiethnic national ministries and the smaller Bible study groups appear to be supportive, with friendly competition and coalition work reinforcing a common ideology. It is not uncommon for Asian Americans to participate in both the big parachurch groups and the smaller ethnic fellowships. Mirroring the success of large non-race-specific parachurch organizations, for instance, the local chapters of the Asian American Christian Fellowship (AACF) "have grown to involve several thousand students on a number of strategic campuses throughout the USA." As a "nondenominational" Christian ministry, the AACF affirms itself as "a movement to impact the university and collegiate community, primarily those who are Asian Americans, with the life changing message of Jesus Christ."[17] Similarly, across the country the MIT branch of the Berkland Baptist Church ministry promotes itself as "a mostly Korean congregation of college students, graduates, and Korean adults. We also have members from China, Japan, Indonesia, and even California! Our main focus [is] to minister to English-Speaking second-generation Asian-American students, to train them up as disciples of Christ." Founded in 1981 by Korean ministers, Paul and Rebekah Kim, the Northern California ministry now boasts a presence on six East Coast campuses under the name Asian Baptist Student Koinonia (ABSK), as well as sister churches in Los Angeles, Seoul, and Taegu.[18]

One of the most puzzling aspects of these Asian American fellowships is the relationship between Asian American ethnicity and the ideology of evangelical Christianity that relegates ethnic difference to secondary importance. Or as evangelical author Ada Lum writes: "God is far more interested in what is happening to us inside. Are we becoming more like Jesus Christ his Son? That is what counts in the end (Romans 8:29)."[19] The Harvard-Radcliffe Asian American Christian Fellowship (HRAACF), for example, positions itself as a "sister fellowship" of the non-ethnic-specific Harvard-Radcliffe Christian Fellowship, "both of which draw upon the resources of InterVarsity Christian Fellowship." It is unclear from the HRAACF website how their evangelical universalist vision of drawing "people both individually and corporately into a deeper relationship with Jesus Christ through the transforming power of God's love and grace" is built around a particularized mission of "a dynamic community of faith in Christ embodying *the relevance of the gospel to Asian Americans*" (emphasis added). In fact, a sampling of Asian American evangelical fellowship websites reveals mission statements targeting Asian and Asian American students for outreach and membership while simultaneously affirming a non-race-specific evangelical identity.[20]

This elision of ethnic specificity also appears in the documents of the Chinese Christian Fellowship at Stanford (CCFS), an interdenominational group whose purpose is "to minister to Stanford students of Chinese ethnicity regardless of origin" and whose members are drawn from Hong Kong, mainland China, Taiwan, Singapore, Thailand, and the United States. To overcome the obstacles of national origin and language, CCFS offers its "coworkers" Bible studies in Cantonese, English, and Mandarin. Although the preliminary description of the organization is decidedly "Chinese," CCFS replicates an evangelical ideology that curbs an emphasis on the particularities of racial identity and is virtually indistinguishable from any other evangelical organization in its core desire to "search for the relevance of God in the world today by investigating the Bible and sharing our joys and challenges with each other." In the CCFS website pages, racial affiliation

Rudy V. Busto

(having overcome the obstacles of the diaspora) disappears. In matters of faith, coworker status is determined by one's relationship to Jesus, not Chinese descent.[21]

Asian American parachurch groups flourish as distinctly ethnic organizations, but with a theological twist. Because evangelicalism creates a new identity through conversion, the relationship between ethnicity and "born again" faith is unclear. At the level of organizations, Asian American Christian fellowships follow a set of beliefs and practice common to any evangelical parachurch group. For the individual believer, however, the connections between Asian American identity and evangelicalism may be confusing. For nonbelievers, evangelical Christianity may be seen as a threat to ethnic identity and a step toward an unwelcome form of assimilation. Preliminary student opinion on the subject indicates that there is no consensus among Asian Americans on either the appeal of evangelicalism or its fit with Asian American identities and Asian cultures. One Asian American student in Michigan, for instance, probably represents the position taken by many students suspicious of Christianity's association with Western imperialism: "Being a white religion . . . for me, the problem is knowing history and how Christianity spread and how it spread not always in a nice way. It makes me wonder how truthful it is and how much it is a white man's imperialistic tendencies upon other nations."[22]

Asian American evangelicals, on the other hand, report that being a Christian does not mean rejecting Asian American identity or Asian cultures. One IVCF Chinese American staff worker involved with InterVarsity since the early 1970s explained that she came to a deeper understanding of herself as Asian American through the Pacific Alliance of Chinese Evangelicals and an IVCF discipleship training program that took her to Singapore.[23] Other students find that evangelical Christianity reinforces "Asian" values of family, work, and education:

Many Confucian ideals are similar to Christian ideals—like honoring your parents, living a moral, virtuous life, and working hard. . . . There are definitely teachings from Buddhism that are very Christian . . . not harming anyone, trying to live a good life. . . . Asian culture has it embedded that you are supposed to give respect to older people. . . . My parents used to say bow to your grandmother when she comes. I might have just done it but I tended to be rebellious. But now I know from the Bible that that's a very Biblical thing. Now it's not just for cultural reasons, but for Bible reasons I want to follow that part of Korean culture.[24]

God's Whiz Kids? Spiritualizing Racial Politics

It is useful to consider how the "model minority" stereotype provides a context for understanding the relationship between Asian American students and evangelical Christianity. The contestation (panic?) over the numerical presence of Asians on college campuses, and the perception that Asian Americans are overrepresented in evangelical organizations, may be more than coincidence. My suspicion is that campus Christian organizations, besides offering a supportive and familial structure for Asian American students, reinforce an upwardly mobile middle-class ethic consonant with the model minority image —an image, Takaki reminds us, that results in Asian American students feeling pressured to conform to the picture of success and caving in to the denial of individual diversity. This stereotype has also fostered anti-Asian sentiment on college campuses prompted by fear of large numbers of Asian American students and the competition they supposedly represent.[25] As a standard of excellence for other minority groups to attain, the model minority image has trapped Asian American students inside a set of performance expectations. Evangelical Christianity simply reinforces this "whiz kid" stereotype with its strong moral code and work ethic. Not only that,

Rudy V. Busto

but Asian American evangelicals also appear to be stereotyped as God's whiz kids—exemplars of evangelical piety and action to which other evangelicals should aspire.[26]

In their portrayal of Asian Americans, evangelical Christians and organizations have embraced a religious version of the model minority by promoting Asian American evangelicals as "spiritual giants" and aggressive evangelizers. One writer, for example, views Korean American evangelical students through such a lens. In his description of Korean American youth ministers, he not only confirms their whiz kid status but employs them to chastise white believers and offers them up as morally superior members of the Asian American population:

> Middle-class Koreans, for example, have taken up residence in and around the major cities of the nation. Churches have been established, bringing to America the memory of the Christian values forged by war and revival. Second generation Korean-Americans have struggled with issues of identity, such as whether they will conform to the customs preferred by their parents or dress and behave like their American peers. To help survive the struggle many Korean churches have employed youth ministers who are attempting to mold a style of youth ministry which avoids the shallowness of American youth ministry, while not becoming enslaved to the materialism so endemic to the upwardly mobile emigrants. These youth workers, along with their Chinese and Indian counterparts, may prove to be the key to the future of youth ministry in America.[27]

As American evangelicalism adopts the model minority image of Asian Americans, the large numbers of Asian American students active in parachurch organizations only add plausibility. Like James Sire's depiction of Bob Wong, it is clear that at least some sectors of evangelical Christianity perpetuate supposed Asian values of filial piety, obedience, and hard work as complementing traditional Protestant values. Inter-

Varsity historians have already adopted this view and record that after the 1970s Asian Americans have become leaders in the triumphant propagation of evangelicalism across the nation's campuses.[28]

A Retreat into Evangelicalism?

Asian Americans are indeed overrepresented in campus evangelical parachurch groups. Moreover, a distinctly post-1965 Korean and Taiwanese immigration pattern appears to flavor the character of these organizations. According to Hammond and Hunter, evangelical students at secular colleges maintain strong faith positions at the cost of personal stigma and constant challenges to their "minority" viewpoint. This minority status of one's convictions fosters a "fortress mentality" as the price for defending an evangelical worldview.[29] For Asian American evangelical students, the "double whammy" effect of race and religion may in fact be very uncomfortable. As a result, evangelical parachurch groups may become safe havens against both racial antagonism and secular systems of thought. Espiritu's elaboration of how Asian American groups remove themselves from negative associations with stigmatized or problematic Asian groups through ethnic disidentification is potentially useful here, but there are no data to support such a strategy by Asian American evangelicals. Certainly the universalist message of evangelical Christianity bolsters a type of "built-in" disidentification from nonevangelicals in general ("the world") prompting an alternative identity based not on race/ethnicity, but on faith.[30]

Taking the theological call for Christians to be apart from the world (as in I John 2:15)—or more generally, "chosen" one step further—it may be helpful to think about Asian American evangelicals as part of a larger Christian people or "incipient ethnicity." Conceptualizing evangelical Christianity as ethnicity may account for the curious disappearance of

Rudy V. Busto

Asianness in the discourse and practices of Bible study groups organized, paradoxically, by and for specific Asian groups. Evangelicalism as a common religious ideology and culture shared by a diversity of students in large parachurch organizations seems to function like ethnicity in protecting otherwise stigmatized brothers and sisters from outside political tempests and negative stereotypes. Moreover, Asian Americans benefit where evangelicalism overlaps and coincides with dominant American culture rendering them less foreign.[31]

If religious affiliation mirrors the conditions and needs of ethnic believers (as Nattier suggests accounts for the large numbers of African Americans participating in "evangelical" Nichiren Buddhism),[32] expectations about Asian American students may lead at least some of them to seek refuge in evangelical fellowships. I am not arguing here that evangelicalism operates as a new or alternative ethnicity for Asian American students. But thinking about Asian American evangelical Christianity in the language of ethnicity helps to illuminate the relationship between ethnic association and religious affiliation.[33]

More Questions than Answers

It is clear that evangelical Christianity will continue to attract large numbers of Asian American college students because it provides well-structured and nurturing communities that help them survive the anxieties, alienation, and liminality of the college experience. Until well-documented evidence is available, we can only speculate why some Asian Americans, specifically Korean and Chinese American students, are more involved in evangelicalism than Chicanos, Native Americans, African Americans, or even Filipinos and South Asians.[34]

In an odd way, a comparison between Asian American evangelicals and the growing phenomenon of Christian athletes on campus may prove fruitful. The pressures placed on

Asian Americans to excel academically may be compared to the college athlete's obligations to winning or at least performing well. Negative stereotyping has also forced Asian Americans and athletes to share the spotlight of admissions controversies over questions of quotas and admissibility.[35]

A larger question that remains unexplored is the relationship between evangelical ideology, identity politics, and especially gender issues. On the increasingly racialized college campus where Asian American students are imaged as competitive, overrepresented, and culturally monolithic, evangelical organizations appear to function in contradictory ways: for evangelicals they are havens from the inescapable tempests over race issues; but from a nonevangelical viewpoint they are exclusionist, cliquish, conformist clubs that do nothing to refute stereotypes.[36]

Clearly there is a need for empirical research on Asian Americans (in their diversity) and their involvement with evangelical Christianity. As I have attempted to demonstrate, the larger contextual debates and contestation over Asian Americans in higher education, assimilation, and stereotyping must be taken into account when interpreting religion in Asian American communities. The caricatures of Asian Americans in evangelical writing have already proved the point.[37] At this stage in our understanding of evangelical Christianity in Asian American communities we remain, like Bob Wong, with many unanswered questions.

Notes

I would like to thank Judy Yung, Russell Jeung, Larry Padua, Belinda Fu, Liane Nomura, Irene Lin, David Yoo, Diana Akiyama, and students in my Asian American/Pacific Islander Religious Traditions Seminar, Winter 1995–1996, for their observations and critical comments.

1. An example of what evangelical faith entails is found in the MIT Korean Christian Fellowship's (MITKCF) statement of purpose: "The purpose of MITKCF is to establish, assist, and encourage students who

Rudy V. Busto

attest the Lord Jesus Christ as God Incarnate and have these major objectives: To lead others to a personal faith in Christ as Lord and Savior. To help Christians grow toward maturity as disciples of Christ through the study of the Bible, through prayer, and through Christian fellowship. To present the call of God to the world mission of the Church, and to help students and faculty discover God's role for them." [Online] World Wide Web: http://www.mit.edu:8001/activities/ mitkckf/purpose.html (September 1995).

2. Barry A. Kosmin and Seymour P. Lachman, *One Nation Under God: Religion in Contemporary American Society* (New York: Harmony Books, 1993), p. 197.

3. Joel Carpenter, "From Fundamentalism to the New Evangelical Coalition," in George Marsden, ed., *Evangelicalism and Modern America* (Grand Rapids: Eerdmans, 1984), pp. 3–16.

4. Note, for example, the absence of religion as a topic for discussion in the November/December 1989 special issue on Asian/Pacific American students in *Change: The Magazine of Higher Learning*.

5. One need only think of anthropology's focus on Native American worldviews, the centrality of the church institution in African American history, and more recently the boom in Chicano/Latino theology and Chicana expressive cultural production. The study of Asian American religious traditions has been eclipsed by the much broader study of Asian religions by European Americans.

6. For background on the long history of evangelical student ministries see Pete Lowman, *The Day of His Power: A History of the International Fellowship of Evangelical Students* (Leicester, England: InterVarsity Press, 1983); Richard Quebedeaux, *I Found It! The Story of Bill Bright and Campus Crusade* (San Francisco: Harper & Row, 1979); Robert Wilder, *The SVM—Its Origin and Early Years* (New York: Student Volunteer Movement, 1935); Wade Clark Roof, *A Generation of Seekers: The Spiritual Journeys of the Baby Boom Generation* (San Francisco: HarperCollins, 1993), pp. 101–103. See also Randall Balmer's discussion of Calvary Chapel in *Mine Eyes Have Seen the Glory: A Journey into the Evangelical Subculture of America* (New York: Oxford University Press, 1989), pp. 12–30.

7. Jayjia Hsia and Marsha Hirano-Nakanishi, "The Demographics of Diversity: Asian Americans and Higher Education," *Change: The Magazine of Higher Learning* (November–December 1989): 20.

8. Keith Hunt and Gladys Hunt, *For Christ and the University: The Story of InterVarsity Christian Fellowship of the U.S.A /1940–1990* (Downers Grove, Ill.: InterVarsity Press, 1991), pp. 353 and 301; Quebedeaux, *I Found It!*, p. 160.

9. "Background of AACF," Asian American Christian Fellowship Homepage [Online] World Wide Web: http://www.leland.stanford.edu/group/aafc/background.html (September 1995).

10. Quebedeaux, *I Found It!*, p. 40.

11. Karl Fung, *The Dragon Pilgrims: A Historical Study of a Chinese-American Church* (San Diego: Providence Press, 1989), pp. III–II2. A recent study notes: "Many of the new immigrants have been aligned with the United States and its military in [actual and potential] conflicts, and their political ideology, at least on arrival, is to the right of center." See Paul Ong, Edna Bonacich, and Lucie Cheng, eds., *The New Asian Immigration in Los Angeles and Global Restructuring* (Philadelphia: Temple University Press, 1994), p. 29.

12. Hsia and Hirano-Nakanishi, "Demographics of Diversity," p. 23, record that by 1980 the proportion of foreign-born Asian Americans had jumped to 62 percent.

13. Ari Goldman, "Portrait of Religion in U.S. Holds Dozens of Surprises," *New York Times* (10 April 1991): A11. Kosmin and Lachman, *One Nation Under God*, pp. 147–154, emphasize that Asian immigrants represent a self-selection process resulting in a Christian bias. They note that 61 percent of their Asian American respondents identified themselves as either Protestant or Roman Catholic and that "since the baptized elements of Asian societies and those who attended Christian mission schools tend to be most Westernized," Asian Christian immigrants outnumber non-Christian Asian immigrants.

14. For examples of this relationship see Artemio Guillermo, ed., *Churches Aflame: Asian Americans and United Methodism* (Nashville: Abingdon, 1991); Brian Masaru Hayashi, *"For the Sake of Our Brethren": Assimilation, Nationalism, and Protestantism Among the Japanese of Los Angeles, 1895–1942* (Stanford: Stanford University Press, 1995); Check-Hung Yee, *For My Kinsmen's Sake: A Salvation Army Officer's Quarter Century of Service in San Francisco Chinatown* (Rancho Palos Verdes: Salvation Army Western Territory, ca. 1986).

15. John W. Kennedy, "Urbana '93: Mission Force Looking More Asian in Future," *Christianity Today* (7 February 1994):48–49.

16. Hunt and Hunt, *For Christ and the University*, p. 319. IVCF claims that in the 1989–1990 academic year, minorities constituted 25 percent of its overall membership; see (Tammy Blackard, "Race Relations: Campus Ministries Respond to Racism," *Christianity Today* (27 May 1991):62–63. Without a survey or archival research, however, the dynamics or even approximate numbers of Asian American evangelicals on campus (as well as which campuses) are unknown.

17. "Background of AACF."

Rudy V. Busto

18. "Berkland Baptist Church," Asian Baptist Student Koinonia (MIT) [Online] World Wide Web: http://www.mit.edu: 8001/activities/kbsk/bbc.east.html (September 1995).

19. Ada Lum, *A Hitchhiker's Guide to Missions* (Downers Grove, Ill.: InterVarsity Press, 1984), p. 139.

20. "General Information," Harvard-Radcliffe Asian American Christian Fellowship [Online] World Wide Web: http://www. hcs.harvard.edu/~hraacf/about.hraacf.html (September 1995).

21. "CCFS Constitution," Chinese Christian Fellowship at Stanford [Online] World Wide Web: http://www.leland.stanford.edu:80/group/ccfs/constitution.html (September 1995).

22. Sunny Hyon, "The Gospel According to Asian Americans: Perspectives on Religion, Culture and Asian American Community," *Symphony of Voices: An Asian/Pacific American Women's Journal* 2 (Spring 1992):40.

23. Hunt and Hunt, *For Christ and the University*, pp. 318–319.

24. Hyon, "Gospel According to Asian Americans," pp. 40–41.

25. Ron Takaki, *Strangers from a Different Shore: A History of Asian Americans* (New York: Penguin, 1989), p. 479.

26. The University of Texas at Austin's Chinese Campus Christian Fellowship spells out this sober and puritanical faith in their general description: "We strive to obey God's command to be holy and Christlike. . . . We do not cheat. We are Temples of the Holy Spirit and we honor God with our bodies by not getting drunk, high on drugs, or abusing our bodies. We turn away from worldly passions, material extravagance, and selfish ambition. We give God our lives, money, and time. . . . We honor our parents, governments, and we obey all laws that do not conflict with God's laws. We work together with other Christians . . . to share the gospel, nurture, exhort, and encourage believers, oppose evil and guard against error." From the "General Description of ACCCF," Austin Chinese Campus Christian Fellowship [Online] World Wide Web: http://www.utexas.edu/aaacf/#description.html (November 1995).

27. Mark Senter III, *The Coming Revolution in Youth Ministry and Its Radical Impact on the Church* (Wheaton, Ill.: Victor Books, 1992), p. 173. See also David Claerbaut, *Urban Ministry* (Grand Rapids: Zondervan, 1992), pp. 146–148.

28. As the national parachurch organizations are forced to acknowledge racial tensions brought on by multiethnic campus demographics, these tensions are characterized as a black/white issue. Campus Crusade admits that there is racism among its members, noting "a tendency for Christians to cluster together and ignore racism . . . we cover it up by

The Gospel according to the Model Minority?

saying, 'We're all Christians' " (Blackard, "Race Relations," pp. 62–63). Asian Americans, predictably, serve as "good" models of evangelical leaders and disciples who are able to overcome obstacles of race in their faith. InterVarsity historians are careful to note that Asians and Asian Americans have been involved with InterVarsity ministries since 1947 (Hunt and Hunt, *For Christ and the University,* p. 299). See also Ralph Reed's careful manipulation of Asian Christians in relationship to race issues in his politically conservative *Politically Incorrect: The Emerging Faith Factor in American Politics* (Dallas: Word, 1994), p. 235ff.

29. Phillip E. Hammond and James D. Hunter, "On Maintaining Plausibility: The Worldview of Evangelical College Students," *Scientific Study of Religion* 22 (Summer 1984):221–238.

30. Yen Le Espiritu, *Asian American Panethnicity: Bridging Institutions and Identities* (Philadelphia: Temple University Press, 1992), pp. 20–23 and 124–135.

31. Scholars have long contemplated the role of religion in the construction of ethnicity. Rejecting a "hard" definition of ethnicity as necessarily biological or generational, religious affiliation seems to fulfill a number of "soft" criteria for ethnicity based on shared culture. Given the primordial qualities both religion and ethnicity share, it may be worth considering how close Balmer's characterization of American evangelicalism as a "subculture" skims along the edge of ethnicity. See Thomas O'Dea, "Mormonism and the Avoidance of Sectarian Stagnation: A Study of Church, Sect, and Incipient Nationality," *American Journal of Sociology* 60 (1954):285–293; Armand L. Mauss, *The Angel and the Beehive: The Mormon Struggle with Assimilation* (Urbana: University of Illinois Press, 1994). Mauss (p. 63) notes that the *Harvard Encyclopedia of American Ethnic Groups* includes religious groups among its entries. Another possibility is that evangelicalism serves as a type of "circuitous assimilation" through the creation of parallel institutions within ethnic groups. See Yusuf Dadabhay, "Circuitous Assimilation Among Rural Hindustanis in California," *Social Forces* 33 (1954):138–141.

32. Jan Nattier, "Visible and Invisible: Jan Nattier on the Politics of Representation in Buddhist America," *Tricycle: The Buddhist Review* (Fall 1995):42–49.

33. It is, however, tempting to consider Kitagawa's explanation that "much as the ancient Hebrew community came into being as the congregation *(qahal)* of various tribal groups, the Christian community from the beginning understood itself as the *ekklesia* (the Greek term for *qahal*) of various peoples *(ethnai)*." See Joseph Mitsuo Kitagawa, *The Christian Tradition: Beyond Its European Captivity* (Philadelphia: Trinity International Press, 1994), p. 4.

Rudy V. Busto

34. African Americans tend to form their own campus religious communities apart from larger interdenominational organizations. Larry Padua suggests that Filipino Americans are uninterested in these organizations because of their long association with American culture and their status as "little brown brothers" with nothing to prove with respect to their patriotism or willingness to assimilate (personal communication, 21 October 1995).

35. It is curious that athletes and Asian Americans are stereotyped in exactly opposite ways regarding physical and academic abilities. See D. Stanley Eitzen and George H. Sage, "Sport and Religion," in Charles S. Prebish, ed., *Religion and Sport: The Meeting of Sacred and Profane* (Westport, Conn.: Greenwood Press, 1993), pp. 79–117; Dana Y. Takagi, *The Retreat from Race: Asian-American Admissions and Racial Politics* (New Brunswick: Rutgers University Press, 1992), pp. 177–181.

36. Non-Asian students on the Stanford campus told me they associate IVCF and CCC with Asian American students. Among activist, progressive nonevangelical Asian American students, the tendency for evangelical students to shy away from campus politics is regarded as complacent and assimilationist.

37. See, for example, James and Lillian Breckenridge, *What Color Is Your God? Muticultural Education in the Church* (Wheaton, Ill.: Victor Books/SP Publications, 1995), especially the chapters "Examining Asian-American Cultures" and "Select Asian Groups"; see also Leonard Tamura, "The Asian-American Man: The Model Minority?" in *We Stand Together: Reconciling Men of Different Color* (Chicago: Moody Press, 1995), pp. 61–78.

Chapter 6

Reflections on Shamanism

HEINZ INSU FENKL

By quitting one's own country and dwelling in foreign lands one should acquire practical knowledge of non-attachment.

—from *The Precepts of the Gurus*

The world turns in cycles and epicycles, and usually we are brought back to the things closest to our hearts and spirits only at the end of a long journey. Things avoided or let go eventually come back not only to haunt us, but to complete us in unexpected ways, and it is when our heads meet our tails that we finally form that unifying shape known as Ouroboros, the Hermetic symbol of the circle made by a serpent.

In the spring semester of 1996 I was team-teaching a course, called "Asian/American Folk Traditions," which examined deeply resonant Asian traditions like Yoga, Taoism, Buddhism, and shamanism and then traced the threads of their influences into the American "new age." The course was really about consciousness and religion. My colleague, Larry Mamiya, brought to it his religion background; I contributed an eclectic range of information I had studied throughout my unfinished graduate career in cultural anthropology; by the end of the course we had touched on a remarkable array of topics ranging from Kundalini Yoga to quantum physics.[1]

We had many visiting lecturers—not all of whom were well received or exceptionally meaningful for the students.[2] But among them was Christina Stack, an American practitioner of "core shamanism,"[3] who left a lasting impression. After she left, the students would describe her as "wolflike," "totally self-assured," "disturbingly powerful." Even those who did not experience anything remarkable during the shamanic journey she conducted would agree that she had a certain resonant strength of character.

Stack had come with rattles and a large round skin drum of the Siberian/Inuit type. She had lit candles and incense in the darkened multipurpose room, and after a brief lecture on the nature of core shamanism she had taken us all on several "drum journeys" into the underworld. For some, the journeys were merely relaxing; but for others the experience was so intense that they had to be "brought down" individually after the ceremony. Some students retained incredibly vivid memories of their journeys; others reported an influence in their dreams for weeks afterwards. To me it was no accident— perhaps I should call it a "synchronicity"—that Christina Stack practices a form of shamanism that has very strong parallels with the Siberian tradition, the same tradition that predominates in Korea.[4]

I must admit that my own journey during that ceremony, as we lay on the rug in the dark multipurpose room, our eyes covered with strips of black cloth, was not as immediately intense as those of some of my students. In the midst of my visualizations of spiraling down that dark tunnel into the lower world, I found myself remembering simultaneously a ceremony I had attended in 1985 and one, from my childhood, for a boy who was killed by a taxi. When the shaman whistled, I recalled the sound of the reed flutes. And when her drumming resonated at some particular cadence, I recalled the beat of the hourglass *changu* drums and the up-and-down leaping dance of the Korean *manshin*. I suppose what I experienced then was a disjunction between memory and reality—or, rather, an unexpected *conjunction* of momentary reality with multiple layers of memory displaced in time.

□ □ □

It's a hot summer afternoon in 1985,[5] and on the altar sits a boiled cow's head, with rolled 1,000-won bills—offerings to the spirits—protruding from its ears and nostrils; the head is slowly leaking its juices onto the small table that supports it, and a swarm of fat flies is buzzing around rather lazily. The *manshin*,[6] in her black military hat and her bright red-blue-green silk costume, pulls the money out of the cow's orifices to chuckles of amusement. She then shoos the flies away, lifts the massive head with a grunt of effort, and skewers it—with a sickening crunching sound that makes everyone wince— onto a short-shafted trident. Now she lifts the heavy head again, with the shaft protruding from underneath like a ridiculously thin neck, and slowly lowers it onto a pile of coarse salt on top of a cutting board. If the head balances, the spirits are pleased; if it does not, more offerings will be needed. With all the participants gathered anxiously around, she rocks the head back and forth on top of the salt, adjusting the shaft this way and that, letting her assistant hold onto the oddly tranquil-looking head as she packs the salt underneath. There's no way the head can stand on that shaft—it must weigh fifty pounds; it would be like trying to balance a bowling ball on a chopstick—but then, at the signal, they let go, their fingers hovering scant millimeters from the cow's head and the trident shaft, and, unbelievably, it stands. It's so solidly balanced that the shaman smacks the trident shaft with her folded fan and the head does not waver. It seems as if it's been hammered right through the cutting board into the floor. Auspicious!

Heinz Insu Fenkl

And now, with the cow's head back on the altar, the *man-shin* is dancing frenetically on the floor in front of it, waving brilliant colored banners—yellow, green, blue, red—for her flag-divining ceremony. She flourishes the silk flags so quickly she leaves afterimages in the air, and then rolls them up together so their colors cannot be distinguished from the rods that protrude at the top. My wife, Anne, selects a flag to have her fortune told. But it's an inauspicious color. She does it again, and again it's inauspicious. Anne wants to petition the spirits, but something must be done first; the shaman announces that Anne will have to be exorcised of the bad influences that are hovering around her.

The *mansin* leads her by the hand and makes her squat down in front of the entrance to the house. She drapes the flags over Anne's head and makes her hold the short-shafted spear and trident—still dripping with the juices from the boiled cow's head—across her abdomen. While Anne is crouching there, disoriented and confused, head down and face hidden, the *mansin* calls out for the bad spirits to be gone and with a large butcher knife she violently cuts and thrusts at the air around Anne's head, barely missing her each time.[7]

Finally, the *mansin* fills her mouth from a dipper full of fresh water and sprays Anne's face three times. After tossing some food out toward the gate of the house to attract the spirits away from Anne, she declares the exorcism finished. And as promised, Anne chooses an auspicious flag in her very next attempt.[8] The audience cheers, and their cacophony, combined with the afterimages of the flag behind my closed eyes, takes me momentarily back to another shamanic ceremony I saw when I was a child. I am six years old, and a boy in the neighborhood has died after being hit by a Corona taxi.

□ □ □

I had known the boy and played with him, but it had never occurred to me—though I certainly knew about death by

Reflections on Shamanism

then—that this boy would always be gone. Forever. I was puzzled by the fact that in my memory the images of him were as vivid as the images I had of people who were alive. Now that the boy was dead, there was a disjunction between reality and memory, a disjunction of which I could not make sense. I had recently lost a pet bird, but there were other, living, birds that looked enough like the dead one to remind me that it was only one of many. With people I had somehow come to believe that each was an individual—we did not look enough alike to be substituted for one another, and so the death of one person was a permanent thing, the loss of something irreplaceable.

Shortly after the boy's death, there was a great racket in the neighborhood, and it wasn't long before we realized that it originated from his house. His mother had hired a *mudang* to perform a ceremony to ensure that his spirit would pass into the next world and not linger in this world to trouble the living. From the crack of dawn we heard a cacophony of hand gongs, reed flutes, and drums along with singing and chanting. I endured the noise with great curiosity all day, and sometime in the afternoon I followed my aunt and mother to see what was going on.

I am not sure I had ever experienced a religious state of consciousness before that day. But late that afternoon, as the shamanic ceremony came to a close, I saw something that resonates with me now as my first memory of religious *affect*— that feeling of awe which verges on terror but simultaneously provides a sense of profound and peaceful connection to the cosmos.[9] I know now that toward the end of the shamanic ceremony, the music and the shaman's dancing had put me in an altered state of consciousness along with many other participants and audience members. The shaman, in her bright and multicolored outfit, finally snapped her fan shut and stepped up to the very end of a long, narrow sheet of canvas that several people were holding up between them. (I remember it being as thick as sailcloth, but it was probably thinner.) The people stood like a gauntlet with the canvas stretched between them so that it hung, suspended in their hands, like a long, pale road. And, in fact, this was representative of the road the deceased spirit was to take into the next world. At the end of the ceremony, the shaman struck the very end of the canvas with her closed fan and the cloth ripped—with surprising force and speed—from one end to the other, with a loud tearing sound, so that its two halves spread out like the wings of a giant egret. The dead boy's spirit had moved on.

That tearing sound sent a shiver through my body. I remember feeling that it was I, and not the boy's spirit, that went down that path. At that moment I felt entirely disembodied, and yet connected to everything and everyone there in the courtyard of the dead boy's house. The sounds, the colors, the odors, the textures—they were all so unusually vivid that when I remembered this incident later, or recall it now, some of the images are so clear I can still stop them and dwell on them as if they were single frames of a film.

□   □   □

I have had my share of shamanic dreams and met my guardian animals in inexplicable circumstances, but I do not consider myself a shaman. I have practiced Zen and Yoga and have found that the mystical states all converge with one another though they are ascribed different ultimate meanings by each tradition.

The balancing of the cow's head and the ripping canvas path, I know, are just parlor tricks. I've balanced salt shakers on edge in the very same way, and I know the canvas had been cut beforehand to tear more easily. But these are not the meaningful aspects of the shaman's rituals—they're a consensual distraction and entertainment for the purpose of creating shared meanings. The tricks are cultural placebos that allow

Reflections on Shamanism

the real treatments to work.[10] Shamanism is really about synthesis, about the bringing together of things that might otherwise appear to be disparate: the world of the living and the world of the dead; the past, present, and future; the individual and the community; humans and animals; the person and the cosmos—and in every case, the synthesis creates a form of healing.

I think I am particularly moved by the power of the shaman because my own background was so full of displacement, disjuncture, and liminality even before my birth.[11] My father's life was a series of geographical displacements. He was displaced during his childhood when the Germans annexed the Sudetenland. He was born in a town near Prague, but then moved to a town in southern Germany near Munich with the other displaced Sudeten Germans—people who were outsiders while they were Czech and ironically became outsiders once again when they were absorbed into Germany. My father was a Hitler Youth, and when Germany fell, he was in a military academy digging tank traps. Had he been a few years older, he would have been in one of the youthful SS units that served as Germany's last line of defense against the Russians. After the end of the war, he served in the Labor Service, which was a German contingent in black uniforms working under the U.S. Army during the reconstruction. In 1952, he came to the United States and worked for the Maryknoll fathers on a dairy farm before he joined the U.S. Army and was sent to Korea where he met my mother in the late 1950s.

My mother's life was full of displacements, too, even before she married my father and was forced to move with him every time his duty station changed. During the Korean War, she didn't want to hide out in the hills with the other women of her village, so she dressed as a boy and traveled around the country. Her family was not divided by the war since their clan of Lees was localized around Sambongni. But because she was the youngest of ten children, she was shuttled from relative to relative after the death of her parents, when the family land was parceled out among the sons. The major displacements in her life were also isolations—she had to move to Washington state, then Germany, then to various other army bases in the United States, to follow my father after their marriage.

After my father's second tour of duty in Vietnam the army had sent him up to the Joint Security Area to be the sergeant of the honor guard at Panmunjom (in Korea's demilitarized zone).[12] On his visits home he talked about applying to be stationed in the states when his time in Korea was up because he wanted me and my sisters to be raised properly, away from what he called the barbarism and the pagan ceremonies he saw in our house. He wanted us to be going to church, saying confession, being confirmed as good Catholics, though he himself certainly was not one. He had seen the Virgin Mary during a malaria fever in Vietnam, and since then he was concerned about our spiritual welfare. It wasn't enough that we had all been baptized—since the Virgin Mary had come to him, perhaps he felt that he owed it to her to take us all to church and worship her son.

It was 1971 and I was eleven—a smart boy angry at my father and his religion. I had read the Bible by then, but I had no sense of how each bit of the Jesus story was supposed to teach a lesson. What I remembered was that Christ had knocked over the table of the moneychangers, he had let a prostitute anoint his feet, he had saved the life of an adulteress by pointing out the hypocrisy of her accusers, he had healed the sick and exorcised the possessed, and then his people had let the Romans nail him to a cross. I imagined Christ in dusty robes and dirty sandals walking through the desert, but in church there was the priest in a gold-trimmed, pure white cassock telling men—whose job it was to kill other men—that they should be Good Samaritans and build their houses on stone. The priest made the Jesus stories into riddles, but he was not a clever storyteller and his ploys did not fool me, even at that age. I thought perhaps he could not say what he really meant because he was an army priest saying mass in a chapel used by the Protestants, an enemy of his religion; the Protestants would call him an idol worshiper even when they shared the same God and prayed to the same murdered son. I understood the way each Buddhist temple up in the Korean hills had a separate shrine dedicated to the old man of the mountain, how even Buddhists often prayed to nature spirits and honored their ancestors, how Korean Christians often lapsed and called upon a *mudang* to perform healings, how everyone would give alms to the mendicants tapping their hollow wooden knockers—but the American religion I could not understand.

I went to a Korean Catholic church once to see if their priest was more logical or told better stories about Jesus, whose stories were, after all, very beautiful. But there I saw Christ's dead body on the cross, blood dripping from his crown of thorns and the nails through his palms and feet, a red gash under his ribs and tears of pain and abandonment dripping from his eyes. And the sarcastic banner above him— INRI: Jesus of Nazareth, King of Jews—the gross insult of the Romans. I wondered: How could these Catholics worship under this thing? Their savior abandoned by his father and left to die alone between two thieves? How could they line up under his body and eat the white disks that were supposed to be his flesh, sip the red wine that was supposed to be his blood, and go away healed? How could I worship this man with the unbearable agony in his eyes or the father who sent him to earth to be tortured to death? I could make myself pray to the Madonna, the mother of Christ, whose name as the great Virgin was the same as the name of the prostitute. I could understand that if the Father and the Son and the Holy Ghost were separate and yet one, then the mother of God could also be both the mother and lover of his son. But I also understood that my father's religion was one whose miracles were old; they were in the stories of the healing, the walking on water, the multiplying fishes and loaves; there were no miracles now. My father's priest could not lead the souls of the restless dead into the otherworld or heal the man whose arm was paralyzed by his ancestors because he had beaten his wife once too often. He could not bring luck to a family whose house was full of tragedy or bring children to a barren woman. My father's religion wallowed in stories and pictures of tragedy and suffering, but it could not heal what happened every day outside the gates of the U.S. Army post. And so, even at that age, I could not worship his God or the murdered son. I believed in ghosts and ancestors and portentous dreams of serpents and dragons because those were the things I could touch in my world.

My family left Korea, for the final time, in 1972. Following my father's new duty stations, we moved to Fort Benning, Georgia, then Baumholder, Germany, then to Fort Bliss, Texas, and finally to Fort Ord, California, in 1976. While we were in Europe, I had visited several cathedrals, including Notre Dame in Paris, but in none of them did the awe I felt (which I interpreted as an aesthetic response) compare to that simultaneous sense of dislocation and connection I had experienced in the shamanic ceremony in Korea. Even seeing the odd assortments of prostheses, crutches, and canes at a church near my German grandmother's town of Waldkraiburg—all evidence of the healings that had gone on there—did not produce in me that "primal" religious feeling.

Before I graduated from high school, I had read Freud, Nietzsche, Jung, and Hesse. In college I continued my readings: Hans Kung, Thomas Merton, D. T. Suzuki, Alan Watts, Mircea Eliade, Lao-Tzu, Chuang-Tzu, Einstein, more Freud, more Jung. Having had meaningful contact with Vassar's nondenominational Chapel Board group and their charismatic leader,[13] I found myself attracted to Zen; I consorted, for a time, with the Christian Fellowship. But the meanings I was searching for never converged. I was in too much turmoil over the complex personal and political issues surrounding my emerging consciousness of my liminal identity, and I was growing through the last phases of my adolescence, finally emerging from the long shadow of my father after he finally passed away, in 1982, from an Agent Orange–related cancer.

It took my return to Korea on a Fulbright in 1984 and then an immersion in anthropology and psychology as a graduate student to close the circle for me. I studied the anthropology of religion, but also the transpersonal psychology of Castaneda and his mythic Yaqui shaman, Don Juan.[14] I researched the topic of lucid dreaming,[15] and later the issue of negation in the dreaming of Australian Aborigines. And finally, having left my graduate career behind, I found myself applying all the eclectic knowledge I had gathered to teach an American Culture course purposely misnamed to attract students interested in Asian studies.

□ □ □

So in the spring of 1996, as I lay on the floor of the dark multipurpose room imagining that tunnel spiraling into the underworld, I found myself displaced in time with epicycles of memory playing out in ways more complex than I could have imagined. Later, I must admit I was rather envious of the students who had had the intense experiences—I, too, wanted to emerge in the underworld with that hallucinatory shamanic clarity and meet my spirit animals; I, too, wanted to leave this mundane reality and then return having learned some valuable lesson or being healed of some spiritual malady. It was only much later, after I had the leisure to reflect on what I had experienced, that I realized I had indeed gone through a shamanic process that day. Those flashes of interlinked memory that had taken me back to two different times, joined forward and backward with each other and to the moment that had evoked them—they were a shamanic synthesis of things and persons long separated. The six-year-old child at the house of a dead boy, the twenty-five-year-old student back in his transformed homeland, the thirty-six-year-old professor teaching at his alma mater—I had thought their differences nearly irresolvable, with only the happenstance of chronology linking them into the same person. And yet their paths had crossed and recrossed that afternoon in a way that made sense of all their engagement not only with the shamanic cere-monies in which they found themselves, but with each other. Again and again, I have thought myself to be forever caught in that problematic state between categories of culture, language, blood, nationality, and place of origin. Ironically, it was by dwelling in the state between displacements and disjunctures that I arrived at a realization of underlying wholeness. On the floor, with my eyes closed, with the drumming so rhythmic it seemed to be the oscillation of my own consciousness, I had known all of this effortlessly and intuitively in the way of the shaman.

> *Too many steps have been taken returning to the root*
> *and the source.*
> *Better to have been blind and deaf from the beginning!*
> *—Kakuan*[16]

Notes

Many thanks to Russell Leong for his patience, his quick feedback, and his insightful critiques of early drafts of this essay. Thanks also to Laurel Kendall, who helped arrange the shamanic ritual for the Fulbright Summer Seminar in 1995; to Yongsu's Mother, who performed the *chaesu kut;* and to Christina Stack, who performed the shamanic ritual at Vassar College in the spring of 1996.

The epigraph is from W. Y. Evans-Wentz, *Tibetan Yoga and Secret Doctrines* (London: Oxford University Press, 1965), pp. 71–72; see especially n. 1 on p. 72.

1. For example, the course covered Hinduism and Yoga, Chinese Taoism and Qi Gong, Zen Buddhism and kung fu, Tibetan Buddhism and the Bardo, and American spiritualism and chiropractic. Some of the less conventional topics included near-death experience, out-of-body

experience, and remote viewing (all of which were addressed, though in different terminology, by a Qi Gong master).

2. Madison Smartt Bell, author of *All Souls' Rising* (New York: Pantheon, 1996), talked at length about Julian Jaynes's theory of the origins of consciousness and the breakdown of the bicameral mind as well as his experiences with voodoo while researching his Haiti novels. William Linacre lectured on American chiropractic and during his demonstration surprised us by telling us how it emerged from the spiritualist tradition. Martial artist Larry Tan presented a demonstration on kung fu and discussed his own quest for identity. Tianhui Liu demonstrated Qi Gong and discussed its transmission to her via ancestors.

3. Christina Stack is a former student of Michael Harner. See Michael Harner, *The Way of the Shaman* (New York: Harper & Row, 1980), for a definition of core shamanism. The classic work on shamanism is Mircea Eliade, *Shamanism: Archaic Techniques of Ecstasy,* trans. Willard R. Trask (Princeton: Princeton University Press, 1964).

4. Archaeological evidence indicates the presence of shamanistic rituals as early as the Bronze Age; see Jung Young Lee, *Korean Shamanistic Rituals* (New York: Mouton, 1981), pp. 2–3. But if one does not distinguish between shamanism and animism (of which it is a development), then the shamanic tradition is arguably part of the most fundamental religious consciousness. See Laurel Kendall, *Shamans, Housewives, and Other Restless Spirits* (Honolulu: University of Hawai'i Press, 1985), for a concise background on Korean shamanism, particularly as a woman's tradition.

5. That summer Anne B. Dalton (then coordinator of the Fulbright Summer Seminar on Korean History and Culture) and I made arrangements for a formal shamanic ceremony with the help of Laurel Kendall, one of the leading researchers on Korean shamanism. Since Kendall had just finished her book, she introduced us to Yongsu's Mother, the shaman she had studied with during her fieldwork. After some debate we decided to hold a *chaesu kut* for Fred Carriere (then director of the Korean-American Educational Commission) and for the sake of the Fulbright Summer Seminar in general. A *chaesu kut* is a shamanic ritual for good luck or good fortune.

6. *"Manshin"* literally means "ten thousand spirits" in Korean. It is the term by which shamans, also called *mudang,* generally refer to themselves. The term is somewhat more respectful than *mudang,* which often has derogatory connotations in general use.

7. I had no idea what Anne was feeling then. Later she told me the experience was terribly frightening—that she had felt disembodied or "split off" in the way sufferers of profound trauma feel detached from

their bodies. I was probably assuming, at the time, that she shared some of my amusement and ethnographer's interest. But in retrospect I realize that I too was in an oddly abstracted state—partly from attempting to be participant and facilitator at the same time, partly from my own emotional resonances with that earlier *kut* in my past (not to mention the visceral fear of an accident).

8. While all nineteen participants of the summer seminar attended the *kut,* eight of the ten men left early to wait in the bus. The two men who stayed for the duration of the performance were both from the South; one of them was the only black participant of the seminar. In later evaluations of the event, the women were overwhelmingly positive (some said it was the most important aspect of the seminar) whereas the men (with those two exceptions) thought the *kut* was a waste of time and money.

9. Freud calls this "the oceanic feeling."

10. Fred Alan Wolf, author of *The Dreaming Universe,* has a good discussion of this placebo effect in *The Eagle's Quest: A Physicist's Search for Truth in the Heart of the Shamanic World* (New York: Simon & Schuster, 1992).

11. Some of the following material is from my essay, "Images from a Stolen Camera: An Autoethnographic Recursion," presented at "Transnational Korea: Division and Diaspora II," the Korean Studies Institute SSRC Conference, University of Southern California, Fall 1995. The essay is forthcoming in the conference volume edited by Michael Robinson, Nancy Abelman, and John Lie.

12. The next three paragraphs are adapted from my autobiographical novel, *Memories of My Ghost Brother* (New York: Dutton, 1996), pp. 239–241.

13. George Williamson told brilliant parable-like stories during his sermons, and they had a deep effect on me. Many years later I realized I could apply the same sort of layered narrative rhetoric by featuring my storyteller uncle in my novel.

14. This was a seminar on cognitive psychology at the University of California, Davis, with Charles Tartt, author of *Altered States of Consciousness.*

15. See Stephen LaBerge's now-classic work, *Lucid Dreaming* (New York: Ballantine, 1986).

16. From "10 Bulls," transcribed by Nyogen Senzaki and Paul Reps (comp.), *Zen Flesh, Zen Bones: A Collection of Zen and Pre-Zen Writings* (New York: Anchor/Doubleday, 1957), p. 152.

Chapter 7

The Labor of Compassion:
Voices of Churched Korean American Women

JUNG HA KIM

> When Chinese come to America, they start laundromats and
> Chinese restaurants; when Japanese come to America, they start
> business corporations; when Koreans come to America, they
> start their churches.

This overgeneralized and ethnocentric remark about Asian
Americans actually reveals at least one significant sociocultural fact about Korean Americans: their church growth.[1]
The traditional formula for estimating the Korean American
population in a given area—the number of Korean American
churches in the area multiplied by 500—reflects an astonishing and distinct characteristic of the highly churched Korean
American population in the United States.[2] Sociologists and
theologians agree that over 70 percent of Korean Americans
are self-claimed Christians compared to only 13 percent of the
total population in South Korea in 1982 and 18 to 21 percent
since 1986.[3] Such a dramatic increase of the churched population among Korean Americans living in the United States may
be attributed to the peculiar mission of Korean American

churches: on the one hand, they offer a vehicle for Americanization; on the other, they provide sites for the preservation and elaboration of Korean culture.

Conspicuously absent in the thesis of Christianization in either the Americanization or Koreanization process is a focus on Korean women's participation in the church, even though women constitute a majority of churchgoers across states. In fact, the so-called Christianization of Korean Americans is predominantly a feminization of churchgoers. Ironically, the study of churched Korean American women has been hindered by their shared membership with more conspicuous minority groups—namely Korean American men, with whom they share ethnicity, and other women of color, with whom they share gender. As a result, scholars tend to overlook Korean American women's experiences by assuming that their realities are identical to those of Korean American men or other women of color.[4] And although an increasing number of writers have addressed themselves to the Korean American church—its numerical growth, its schisms, its multifarious functions—none has focused specifically on women's experiences in a systematic way.[5] No published studies of the Korean American church have even considered the church experience within a gendered context. This chapter, therefore, addresses the following questions: Given that the Christian church is both patriarchal and potentially liberatory, and given that the Korean American church is supposed to minister to its members in multiple ways as a racial-ethnic institution within the dominant cultures, how do Korean American women experience their church? In particular, how does patriarchy operate within a Korean American church? How do Korean American women's hyphenated identities become socially and religiously organized? Is it possible to find a sense of "home" in an institution through inquiry into one's experiences of being a woman within the Korean American church context?

To address these questions I used participant observation,

in-depth interviews, oral histories, and written historical documents. Moreover, my research methods were instrumental for placing churched Korean American women's experiences and their own articulations at the center of this study. In my effort to examine the lives of churched Korean American women from the perspective of an "outsider within,"[6] I encouraged them to speak about their own lives and in their own terms—for many of these women suffer from "the cult of perfect language," which is a form of censorship based on racism, sexism, classism, and neocolonialism in the United States.[7] My work is significantly influenced by feminist methodologies.[8] Feminist research adds an important vantage point to qualitative research by considering gender as a central organizing feature of peoples' lives and thus an important theoretical construct. My participant observation and interviews were enhanced by "woman-to-woman talk."[9] Such talk is often qualitatively different from talk in gender-mixed groups for at least two reasons: the woman listener is more likely to listen attentively and seriously, and the woman speaker is more likely to use "language in nonstandard ways" for naming experiences.[10] Woman-to-woman talk among racially and ethnically similar persons gives speakers an opportunity to describe their worlds with language perhaps not utilized by the dominant groups of the society.

The church site chosen for the case study is the Kyo-whe,[11] where I was a member and have served as director of church education (DCE) for the past four years.[12] It is situated in an upper-middle-class neighborhood of a large city in the Southeast. The history of Kyo-whe's formation and its people are interrelated in that the first migration of Korean Americans into the area (and to other Southern states) occurred after the Immigration Act of 1965. Beginning with a few pioneers who came together to form the Kyo-whe in February 1971 as one of the growing cadre of "new immigrants,"[13] the historical documents of church directories demonstrate its steadily

Jung Ha Kim

increasing membership: 49 households as of 1985; 68 as of October 1988; 85 as of November 1989; and 101 as of June 1990. The steady growth of the church has not occurred without turmoil, however, given the schismatic tendency among the highly heterogeneous people who are its members. Within the past twenty-four years, for instance, the church has gone through eleven different pastoral leaders; I recall three different pastors' leadership in my four years of serving the church.[14]

Another difficulty in conducting a study of living subjects has to do with the differential alignment of power along lines of age, marital status, class, and occupational prestige among adherents of the church and between the researcher and participants. My socioreligious status in the Kyo-whe is as follows: unmarried (which can be translated as "not-yet-an-adult" according to Korean tradition), nonordained (often seen as "not as holy" as the ordained male ministers), relatively young (ageism is one of the powerful features of social relations in Korean culture), church-related professional woman (DCE). Thus I do not fit easily into the traditional category of church leader. Because of my nontraditional mixture of power and status, women of different status, prestige, and interests relate to me differently. And because of my official position in the church as DCE, I am keenly aware that when women are asked to participate in informal interviews, they may be reluctant to deny my request. Questions arise, then, about whether the issue of standard informed consent is sufficiently voluntary. Hence I was forced to come to terms with the realization that informed consent based on primary relationships is not a single contractual event but an ongoing process.

In the larger research project I devoted considerable attention to substantiate the claim that the Korean American church is a deeply gendered and racially and ethnically identified institution whose material and ideological arrangements reinforce and sometimes challenge churched Korean American women's construction of realities. To say that the church (or any other organization) is gendered means that "advantages and disadvantages, exploitation and control, action and emotion, meaning and identity, are patterned through and in terms of a distinction between male and female, masculine and feminine."[15] Insofar as these patterns systematically give males an advantage over females, it can be demonstrated that the church is a patriarchal institution.

With regard to material conditions, power structures within the church have typically excluded women from church leadership and religious authority. Controversies over women's ordination,[16] as well as differentiated dress codes and noninclusive language to define and ritualize various transitional events in human life,[17] can be cited as examples of women's exclusion from authority within the church. With regard to symbols and images, the Christian belief system represents a "culture" that defines and justifies its members' gender-biased worldviews.[18] Both the Old and the New Testaments are replete with calls for women's subordination (Ephesians 5:24), obedience (1 Corinthians 14:33–35), and submission (Leviticus 8, 9, 12:1–5, 15, 18, 21; Ephesians 5:22) to men as the God-ordained (hence natural and unquestionable) order. Thus the Korean American church places men behind the pulpit and women in the pews and kitchen, even though women constitute the majority of churchgoers in this patriarchal institution. At the same time, the very ethos and functions of the Korean American church are determined by the peculiar characteristics and needs of the hyphenated people, both women and men, who attend.

A closer look at church history from a cross-cultural perspective, however, reveals that Christianity has the potential to be both oppressive and liberatory at the same time. That is to say, Christianity has been used as a powerful tool for legitimating the multifaceted oppression of non-Western countries around the world (especially the Third World), for enslaving millions of African Americans, for colonizing (and

Jung Ha Kim

neocolonizing) the minds of minority groups, and for subordinating women globally. But Christianity has also been a powerful instrument for social change. With its preferential language for the poor and the oppressed (such as the Sermon on the Mount), the church liberated the lower and outcaste classes from illiteracy in Korea, mobilized the civil rights movement of the late 1960s in the United States, provided the biblical roots and language for Latin Americans to articulate their liberation theologies, and empowered women's struggles to transform the patriarchal basis of Christianity. Hence both the oppressive and the liberating potential of the Christian church and its theologies are the context within which churched Korean American women find themselves. At the same time, the Korean American church, as an ethnic religious institution within a dominant culture, is the focal point of sociocultural integration as well as the center of community life for both its female and its male members. While providing ethnic homogeneity in a highly pluralistic society, the Korean American church not only serves as a "megachurch,"[19] with a variety of programs and specific interest groups, such as educating recent arrivals for simple, everyday survival skills like shopping, driving, job hunting, and finding an apartment, but also offers psychological and spiritual solace for its members.

In the context of this deeply gendered and highly ethnicity-conscious institution, churched Korean American women recognize that their own church relegates them to secondary status and systematically excludes them from gaining public recognition. They are also aware that much of the church work is done by women, yet male church leaders tend to get the credit. As one woman in her mid-fifties commented:

> Is there anything that doesn't require women's work in the church? [We both laughed at this remark.] I really think, all the work that is related to the church is, in fact, women's work . . . that most of the church work is done by women, but men tend

to get all the credit. And I also think that that's just fine, because we women don't work for public recognition. If there are things that need to be done, then we just do them. That's all.

In short, the Korean American church is a highly contradictory location where a presumably universal gospel is preached in a particular tongue, understood by people of hyphenated identities, and experienced through distinct sociocultural lenses from various life circumstances. By juxtaposing patriarchal readings of the Christian gospel while beautifying and abstracting women's (especially Korean mothers') suffering as the highest form of human love and Christian calling, the Korean American church preaches quasi-Christian messages in the name of religion. To put it differently, the Korean American church as an ethnic institution provides religious explanations for its sexism and justifications for the pain experienced and pain endured in the lives of churched women. Furthermore, so long as churched Korean American women resist thinking of themselves as "100 percent American" and refuse to engage in collective amnesia of the culture they left behind, they are bound to feel an affinity toward the Koreanized Christian messages of women's suffering. These women, in turn, are called to sacrifice their interests as a gender group within their church in order to reaffirm their sense of loyalty to racial and ethnic identities as a minority group within the United States.

But by delving into what churched Korean American women say and listening to how they live everyday life, I became convinced that they are highly gender-conscious and self-selected survivors. A peculiar set of folk wisdom and the "hidden transcripts" among women in the context of the Korean American church demonstrates how they understand and articulate the seemingly oppressive experiences within their church:

Jung Ha Kim

- Men make the rules in the house and the church and we women follow them. But making rules is not as difficult as trying to follow them.

- Korean men are bossy. They insist that they come first; they speak the last word; and they always know better.

- Men think they are the ones who take care of women; but in reality we take care of men. Men don't know anything about women.

- God created Korean women very strong. They can survive anything.

Such handed-down wisdom shows that these women use what is traditionally known as "feminine," "deceptive," and "behind the scenes" language to their own advantage. Why do these women adhere to such seemingly oppressive gender roles and gender language within their church? Are there any advantages for women who insist on traditional understanding of gender? What are the costs? It is by asking these questions as another churched Korean American woman that I have encountered the unexpected reality: the Korean American church is an important location for both resistance and liberation.

Jean Lipman-Blumen has invented a term for the utilization of "intelligence, canniness, intuition, interpersonal skills, charm, sexuality, deception, and avoidance" in order to offset the control of those more powerful: he calls it "micromanipulation."[20] That is to say, since women have had little access to publicly acknowledged power and control, they have learned to use what resources they do have to survive by utilizing informal means of influence. Churched Korean American women also use extensive forms of nonverbal communication in the context of their church: frequent giggles, knowing glances, holding of hands, bitter smiles, light hitting on arms, and constant eye contact. All these nonverbal forms of communication and articulated wisdom for survival can be seen as instrumental for fostering their resistance and self-empowerment. James C. Scott has a term for verbal and non-verbal forms of "critique of power spoken behind the back of the dominant": he calls it a "hidden transcript."[21] "For any subordinate groups," Scott argues, "there is tremendous desire and will to express publicly what is the hidden transcript, even if that form of expression must use metaphors and allusions in the interest of safety."

Contrary to stereotypes, then, churched Korean American women are not all passive and victimized; indeed, they are social agents actively engaged in their own history making. Racism, sexism, Americanization, Koreanization, Christianization, and the process of immigration have not defeated these women in their struggle to maintain human dignity and give meaning to their everyday experiences in the United States. They took special pride in telling me how women have developed various strategies of micromanipulation and hidden transcripts in their church. They also described their struggles to be women, Koreans, Americans, and Christians, all at the same time, as the "labor of compassion." Paradoxically, however, in articulating the labor of compassion in their church, women's understanding and experiences of silence are placed at the center for achieving a sense of freedom, resistance, and liberation. During the Sunday worship service, for instance, the predominantly female laity has no formal channel through which to raise their concerns—except through learned silence as a powerful symbol for both submission and resistance. Of course I recognize that depending on how one conducts the study and constructs the reality, this learned silence may signify internalized submission or self-conscious expression of resistance. Listening to how these women speak about their own silence, however, has led me to conclude that it signifies neither passivity nor submission but a form of resistance. As a woman in her late thirties said: "Sometimes it's better not to verbalize what I really feel and think. In that way [through silence], I can do whatever I choose to do without unnecessary arguments and headaches." Another woman in her late fifties offered a theological grounding for her learned silence: "Even in the doctrine of Trinity, the quiet power of the Holy Spirit plays an essential role of a mediator between God the Father and Christ the Son." Within the context of the Korean American church, then, silence is not to be interpreted solely as manifested subordination. For "silence as a will not to say or a will to unsay and as a language of its own" has been understood and used by churched Korean American women as a powerful strategy for resistance.[22]

Furthermore, despite their seemingly docile silence, these women can learn to speak resistance in their own ways. They can express their deeply felt concerns by controlling the amounts they pledge to the church. Their very attendance at the church can be utilized politically as a last resort to resist the minister's covert dominance over them. One woman in her mid-forties told me: "We don't have much power in the church. But no one, not even the minister, can take away the power to withdraw from attending the church from us." In short, cultivating silence through knowing what not to say and when to keep quiet is often understood as a necessary growing experience for most churched Korean American women. One woman described what she means by "maturity" and "growing up as a woman" in the church:

> WOMAN: I hate some women in the church when they say "I can't do this and that because I am a woman." I think you just waste time asking men to do things for you. As you grow up, as a woman, you just have to know what to do.
>
> INTERVIEWER: What do you mean? What are the things that women are supposed to know?
>
> WOMAN: As women, we are supposed to know when to keep quiet and when not to say anything.

The Labor of Compassion

INTERVIEWER: How do we know when to keep silent?

WOMAN: (Looking at the interviewer with a puzzling smile.) You know. I'm sure you do. It comes to us as naturally as menstruation.

Through their explicit display of subjugation by silence and submission, churched Korean American women have also learned to hold onto the good that lies in playing the traditionally expected gender roles. Ironically then, through their engineering of learned silence and embracing of traditional gender language and roles, these women can experience both expected and unexpected rewards in their everyday lives. Furthermore, when they have gained a certain social status and power through relationship to a successful and respected man over a good part of their lives, there is little reason for them to give up these traditional roles, especially without alternative avenues for achieving status and power in the United States. When all is said and done, the women in my study pay little heed to the "women's freedom and liberation" talk of American feminism. In "this reversed world of human relationship in America," to borrow a churched woman's expression, the traditional gender roles and role expectations offer these women alternative ways to be women.

If churched Korean American women do in fact cultivate learned silence not merely as an act of submission, but also as a form of resistance and survival strategy, then the claim that "breaking the silence" by the oppressed is the unquestionable key to liberation must be reexamined. The most viable empowerment strategies of these women must be understood in their own terms rather than through some criterion for liberation. Perhaps not all attempts at liberation through micromanipulation are equally empowering, but they first must be understood in their own setting and evaluated in that context. Alice Walker writes in her much celebrated book, *The Color Purple*, that "it pisses God off if you walk by the color purple in a field somewhere and don't notice it."[23] And I dare say, I have seen the field of purple even in the context of the Korean American church.

Within this highly contradictory context of the Korean American church, my search was to elucidate various ways in which churched Korean American women find a sense of "home" (if they find it at all) in an institution where their ethnicity is valued but their gender is devalued. What I learned from this study points to a clearly shared reality that they do not readily find a sense of home in their church; instead, through constant struggle, they make a home for themselves. Together they strive to make a home mainly by using micro-manipulative survival skills and transmitting hidden transcripts from woman to woman and from one generation to the next. By refusing to be paralyzed by various forms of domination in their lives, they give meaning to their self-identity and dream of a better home for their American-born and raised descendants.

My study also points to the much neglected liberatory aspects of the Korean American church when women's experiences are placed at the center of the inquiry. Hence the study reminds us about the importance of avoiding an either/or construction of reality. Both material and ideological dimensions intersect to produce gender and ethnic identification. Nor do the coercive and voluntaristic aspects of gender/ethnic systems function as polar opposites. Rather, they operate fluidly and complexly along the various intersections of everyday life so that churched Korean American women produce their gender, ethnic, and religious identities in variable ways from one life circumstance or social situation to another. Furthermore, these women, as active social agents, have reaffirmed my speculations about hyphenated identities that reject neither the culture left behind nor the new culture. Nor do the oppressive and liberatory aspects of participating in church life function as polar opposites for churched Korean

American women. Rather, they operate intricately and often simultaneously along various dimensions of everyday life. These women's lives are not played out as victims of patriarchy or as liberators from various oppressive systems, but as both. The "both–and" focus enables us to comprehend the richness and complexity of such lives and thereby do them justice.

Notes

1. This work was first presented at the "Women and Religion" session of the American Academy of Religion in 1992. For the results of the larger research project see *The Bridge-Makers and Cross-Bearers: Korean American Women and the Church* (Atlanta: Scholar's Press, 1996).

2. In the mid-1980s the formula was revised to account for schisms producing a growing number of Korean American churches: today it should be the number of Korean American churches multiplied by 380 or 400 (New York: Christian Academy of New York, 1988); Y. Kim, "Church Growth: The Development of the Korean Church in America" (Ph.D. diss., California Graduate School of Theology, 1990).

3. Jong Young Lee, "On Marginality: Toward an Asian American Theology" (paper presented at the 1991 annual meetings of the American Academy of Religion in Kansas City, Kansas); Pyong Gap Min, "The Korean American family," in Charles H. Mindel et al., eds., *Ethnic Families in America: Patterns and Variations,* 3rd ed. (New York: Elsevier, 1983); Eui Hang Shin and Hyun Park, "An Analysis of Causes of Schism in Ethnic Churches: The Case of Korean American Churches," *Sociological Analysis: A Journal of the Sociology of Religion* 49(3) (Fall 1988):234–253.

4. Patricia Bell Scott and Gloria T. Hull, *Black Women in America: Social Science Perspectives* (Chicago: University of Chicago Press, 1989), discuss comparable problems for African American women: when race is discussed, audiences assume male gender; when women are discussed, audiences assume white women.

5. Kyong-Suk Cho, "Korean Immigrants in Greham, Oregon: Community Life and Social Adjustment" (master's thesis, University of Oregon, 1963); Bong-youn Cho, "Korean Religions and Cultural Activities in the U.S.," in Warren Y. Kim, ed., *Koreans in America* (Chicago: Nelson Hall, 1971); Dae Gee Kim, "Major Factors Conditioning the Acculturation of Korean Americans with Respect to the Presbyterian

Jung Ha Kim

Church in America and Its Ministry" (Ph.D. diss., Fuller Theological Seminary, 1985); Ilsoo Kim, *New Urban Immigrants: The Korean Community in New York* (Princeton: Princeton University Press, 1981); Won Moo Hurh, *Korean Immigrants in America: A Structural Analysis of Ethnic Confinement and Adhesive Adaptation* (Teaneck, N.J.: Fairleigh Dickenson University Press, 1981); Shin and Park, "An Analysis of Causes of Schism in Ethnic Churches"; David Kwan-sum Suh, *Korea Kaleidoscope: Oral Histories* (Sierra Mission Area, Calif.: Korean Oral History Project, United Presbyterian Church, 1983); Y. Kim, "Church Growth"; Warren Y. Kim, ed., *Koreans in America* (Chicago: Nelson Hall, 1971); Eui-young Yu, "Korean Communities in America: Past, Present and Future," *Amerasia Journal* 10 (1983):23–52.

6. Patricia Hill Collins, "Learning from the Outsider Within: The Sociological Significance of Black Feminist Thought," *Social Problems* 33(6) (December 1986):114–132, and *Black Feminist Thought: Knowledge, Consciousness, the Politics of Empowerment* (Boston: Unwin Hyman, 1990).

7. Mitsuya Yamada, "The Cult of 'Perfect' Language: Censorship by Class, Gender and Race" (paper discussed at the Asian American Women's meeting in Englewood, N.J., September 1992).

8. Judith Cook and Mary M. Fonow, "Knowledge and Women's Interests: Issues of Epistemology and Methodology in Feminist Sociological Research," *Sociological Inquiry* 56(1) (Winter 1986): 2–29; Judith Cook and Mary M. Fonow, eds., *Beyond Methodology: Feminist Scholarship as Lived Research* (Bloomington: Indiana University Press, 1991); Helen Roberts, ed., *Doing Feminist Research* (London: Routledge & Kegan Paul, 1981); Sarah Matthews, "Rethinking Sociology Through a Feminist Perspective," *American Sociologist* 17 (1982):29–35.

9. Dale Spencer, *Man Made Language* (London: Routledge & Kegan Paul, 1985); Marjorie DeVault, "Talking and Listening from Women's Standpoint: Feminist Strategies for Interviewing and Analysis," *Social Problems* 37(1) (February 1990); Clifford Geertz, *The Interpretation of Culture* (New York: Basic Books, 1973).

10. DeVault, "Talking and Listening," p. 97.

11. The pseudonym, "Kyo-whe" is a Korean word for the church.

12. Before deciding on the research site, I was confronted by several ethical and methodological concerns. Although I did not accept the position of DCE as an intentional "entree into the field," I felt that my commitment to the church and a sense of personal integrity in dealing with various relationships within the church were at stake. I struggled with lingering questions: Would the people perceive me as an opportunist who uses human relationships in order to collect data? Would my

relationships with people change because of my desire to do a case study of them? To what extent should I tell people about the intentions, goals, and analyses of the study? To what degree am I accountable to the people I study? Am I not living off less privileged people in order to gain access to the system of the more powerful? Would this study make any contribution to the people, to the Korean American church, and to the community as a whole? What about the question of objectivity? I decided to pursue the study for two major reasons: first, my stance as "outsider within" can provide a point of reference for understanding (*Verstehen* in the Weberian sense) the reality that is uncertain and unfamiliar from an outsider's perspective; second, most of my relationships with members of the Kyo-whe are built on solidarity from our commonly shared struggles as hyphenated people living in the United States, and this basic trust between fieldworker and hosts can enrich qualities of the data.

13. From an insider's perspective, perceiving Korean Americans as a "new immigrant" group is problematic. Although the "noticeable" number of Korean immigrants to the United States occurred after the 1965 Immigration Act and the racial-ethnic category "Korean" appeared for the first time in the U.S. Census in 1970, Korean Americans' history goes back to the year 1903. Hence Korean Americans who define the United States as their homeland need to reclaim their roots from a distorted American history.

14. According to "Methodists Keep Ministers Moving," *Atlanta Constitution* (30 June 1990), the average stay of a Methodist minister at a church is three to four years.

15. Joan Acker, "Hierarchies, Jobs, Bodies: A Theory of Gendered Organizations," *Gender and Society* 4(2) (June 1990).

16. Katie G. Cannon, *Black Women Ethics* (Atlanta: Scholars Press, 1988); Mary Daly, *The Church and the Second Sex* (Boston: Beacon Press, 1968), and *Beyond God the Father: Toward a Philosophy of Women's Liberation* (Boston: Beacon Press, 1973); Carter Heyward, "The Power of God-with-Us," *Christian Century* (14 March 1990); Meredith B. McGuire, *Religion: The Social Context* (Belmont, Calif.: Wadsworth, 1981).

17. Rosemary Radford Reuther, *Sexism and God-Talk: Toward a Feminist Theology* (Boston: Beacon Press, 1983); Pamela Dickey Young, *Feminist Theology/Christian Theology* (Minneapolis: Fortress Press, 1990).

18. Geertz, *The Interpretation of Culture*, p. 89.

19. Robert Wuthnow, *The Reconstruction of American Religion: Society and Faith Since World War II* (Princeton: Princeton University Press, 1988).

Jung Ha Kim

20. Jean Lipman-Blumen, *Gender Roles and Power* (Englewood Cliffs: Prentice-Hall, 1984). Socially legitimate and overt control by the dominant group is called "macromanipulation."

21. James C. Scott, *Domination and the Arts of Resistance: Hidden Transcripts* (New Haven: Yale University Press, 1990), p. 164.

22. T. Minh-ha Trinh, "Commitment from the Mirror-Writing Box," in Gloria Anzaldua, ed., *Making Face, Making Soul: Creative and Critical Perspectives by Women of Color* (San Francisco: Aunt Lute Foundation, 1990), p. 373.

23. Alice Walker, *The Color Purple* (New York: Washington Square Press, 1982), p. 178.

Chapter 8

Pilgrimage and Home in the Wilderness of Marginality:
Symbols and Context in Asian American Theology

SANG HYUN LEE

There was no particular problem with my life in this country when I thought of myself as a foreign student from Korea. All I had to do was study hard and get good grades. But when I began teaching in a small town in the midwest with the prospect of living my entire life here, something disturbing began to emerge in my consciousness. However long I stayed in this country, I seemed to remain an alien. This condition of being a stranger appeared to have two dimensions: one was the experience of being between two worlds, the Korean and the American, belonging to both in some ways, but not wholly belonging to either. The other element in my feeling as a stranger was the sense that I, as a nonwhite person, might never be fully accepted by the dominant group in this country.

Asian Americans' experience of marginality, therefore, is an experience of in-betweenness or being at the edge—an edge that has been made permanent, it seems, by the barriers set up by white racism. It is the predicament of a permanent liminality not given a fair chance to flourish.[1] Asian Americans are a diverse people who left home. We have been going through a wilderness of liminal in-betweenness and need reincorporation into a structure. We need to come home. But the dominant group in America resists our arrival and keeps us at the edge of this society. And in recent years the myth of Asian Americans as a model minority tries to keep hidden our predicament as perpetual strangers. It is indeed a testimony to the enduring human spirit that, in spite of relentless marginalization, there have been Asian Americans who exercise their liminal creativity to struggle for justice and a space we can call home.[2] And it is in this context of marginality and human struggle that the Asian American church is called upon to live out its faith and Asian American theology to do its reflective work.

In this brief essay I wish to ask a question: what are the important faith responses, both in word and deed, of the Asian American churches to their marginality? I will deal with this question by addressing two symbols—pilgrimage and home—that are important in the Asian American church. My discussion assumes two principles: first, that living Christian symbols exist not in abstraction but in concrete contexts; second, that historic Christian symbols are not just reappropriated and reinterpreted but continue to challenge and deepen the Christian church's faith responses. The historic Christian symbols live on by yielding to ever new contexts. But in a more fundamental way such symbols also reshape the life and work of Christians.

Pilgrimage in the Wilderness of Marginality

The image of the Christian believer as a pilgrim who does not absolutize one place or idea but is always ready to leave the present situation toward a God-promised goal has been important for the Asian American church.[3] Certain images from Letter to the Hebrews have been deeply meaningful to many Asian American Christians: the way Abraham obeyed and left home when he was called, "not knowing where he was to go," and the way he and his family sojourned in the wilderness as "strangers and exiles," seeking the true "homeland," "a better country," "the city whose builder and maker is God."

Most Asian immigrants, of course, do not come to America consciously thinking of themselves as pilgrims. They usually come here for very mundane reasons—for a better education, for a better financial future, and the like. And for some of them these dreams are fulfilled—sometimes beyond their expectations. Nevertheless, the Christian pilgrimage emerges as a compelling image as Asian immigrants invariably face uprootedness. Not only do they come to America unprepared for the consequences of leaving home but, as a nonwhite people, they encounter cold glances of disdain from the American public. So after a number of years in this country a crisis of sorts develops. In the secret places of their minds Asian immigrants ask themselves: Did we make a mistake? Is there any meaning in living as strangers? Most of them dare not voice these questions aloud because surrounding them in the living room are their own deeply Americanized children for whom home is nowhere but in America. And studies have shown that most Asian immigrants tend to shrink away from the cold winds of marginality and cling instead to the cozy comforts of their ethnic enclaves at the risk of bringing about a dangerous isolation from American society at large.[4]

It is in this context of "leaving home" and "arriving" in America that the image of Abraham's obedience to God's call has been invoked in the Asian American church. The challenge is to see the Asian immigrants' de facto uprootedness as an opportunity to embark on a sacred pilgrimage to some God-promised goal and, therefore, to believe that the exile's life can be meaningful. One of the hymns written by a Korean immigrant pastor has the following first stanza:

Sang Hyun Lee

Obeying when he was called, leaving home by faith,
Abraham made altar wherever he wandered.
We are all Abraham; let us learn of his faith;
Through our faithfulness to God, may God's own
   purpose fulfill.[5]

We must pause here, however, and ask whether the appropriation of the pilgrimage symbol has a sufficient regard for the context of Asian Americans. Although I myself have written and preached about the Asian immigrants' Christian calling to be pilgrims, I suspect that such talk may not go far enough in accounting for the full import of Asian Americans' marginality.[6] For Asian immigrants, to enter America is asking for trouble—namely, to become aware of their marginality. Therefore, it is not enough to call upon the Asian immigrant Christians to become pilgrims as white European immigrants and to enter American society. Their journeys differ.

What, then, is the particular meaning of the Asian Americans' pilgrimage into America? Why should they be asked to do something that is bound to bring them trouble? Beyond the secular goal of "making it in America," why should Asian Americans leave the comforts of their ethnic enclaves and mix with the majority people in America—at the risk of becoming marginalized? In thinking about this question, a passage from Richard Niebuhr's *The Meaning of Revelation* continues to have for me an irresistible quality. Niebuhr writes:

> He [Christ] is the man through whom the whole human history becomes our history. Now there is nothing that is alien to us. All of the wanderings of all peoples and all the sins of men in all places become parts of our past through him. . . . Through Christ we become immigrants into the empire of God which extends over all the world and learn to remember the history of that empire, that is of men in all times and places, as our history.[7]

Speaking from his radical monotheism perspective, Niebuhr regards all parts of the world and all aspects of human history as the realm of God's activity and thus sacred though finite. It is the responsibility of a faithful Christian, then, to make a pilgrimage to every part of history and to every place of the world and to include them in his and her remembering.

But what does it mean to make every part of human history our own? I suggest that to get at the specific implication for Asian Americans we must pay more attention to the Asian American Christians' own experience of making a pilgrimage into America.[8] The tragic events of 1992 in Los Angeles are particularly instructive. The initial reaction of the Korean immigrants in Koreatown was one of surprise. How could this happen in America? Many of these Korean immigrants were living in ethnic self-confinement and had not really entered American society. What happened to them on 29 April was a coerced entrance into American realities: a painful lesson in their own marginality in American society. What resulted, in other words, was awareness.[9]

Awareness then led to sympathy and solidarity. First- and second-generation Korean Americans suddenly forgot all their generational conflicts and joined together in relief work and marched in a peace demonstration. A young Korean American woman told me that the pain she felt at the sight of other Koreans suffering told her that she was Korean after all. Korean American and African American churches came together in various ways to worship, to share each others' experiences, and to discuss ways of helping each other in their common struggle for justice and human dignity. Being consciously at the margin of society gave them the capacity to recognize others at the margin; this capacity was also a capacity for solidarity. To put it in Victor Turner's language, having become aware of their alienation from American society and thus in a sense freed from the dominant social structure, Korean immigrants became consciously liminal and thus open to the experience of *communitas*.[10] Whatever else it may mean to become pilgrims for Asian Americans, it does mean to become self-conscious strangers and thereby to become capable of solidarity with other strangers.

All this suggests that creative and redemptive events occur at the in-between and often despised margins of this world. Margins, in other words, can be creative centers. Is it any accident, then, that we find the following words in Letter to the Hebrews?

> So Jesus also suffered outside the gate in order to sanctify the people through his own blood. Therefore let us go forth to him outside the camp, bearing abuse for him. For here we have no lasting city, but we seek the city which is to come. [13:12–14]

In this passage pilgrimage theme and redemption theme come together. "Outside the camp" is where Jesus began his redemptive project.[11] And it is the pilgrims who know that "here we have no lasting city" and are willing to follow Christ to the margins that participate in Jesus' project. And these pilgrims are not alone but have Jesus as "the pioneer and perfecter" of their faith. In other words, something more than sheer human courage is going on here. There is behind all this an intentionality of God's own self, God's own journey, and God's own project.

God's Household for Strangers on the Margin

To be pilgrims and self-conscious strangers on the margins, therefore, can lead to an experience of *communitas* and solidarity. But we cannot stay in such ecstatic moments indefinitely. Asian American pilgrims, like all mortal humans, need a hospitable structure for belonging. We need a home. And as many people know, in the Korean American community it is the ethnic church, more than any other institution, that has played the greatest role in meeting this need for belonging. The church is the home, or at least a home away from home, for many Asian immigrants and their succeeding generations.[12]

According to the biblical scholar John H. Elliott, the "home for the homeless" is precisely the way 1 Peter in the New Testament conceives of the essential nature of the church as the eschatological community itself. According to Elliott, "the Good News offered by 1 Peter to the socially marginalized Christians in Asia Minor was not an ephemeral 'heaven is our home' form of consolation but the new home and social family to which Christians can belong here and now . . . a supportive circle of brothers and sisters." And "status here is not gained through blood ties nor by meeting social prerequisites; it is available to all classes and races of mankind as a divine gift."[13] They remain despised strangers in society; but in the *oikos,* the household of God, everything has changed. They are the elect of God: "But you are a chosen race, a royal priesthood, a holy nation, God's own people. . . . Once you were no people but now you are God's people; once you had not received mercy but now you have received mercy" (2:9–10).

As Asian Americans come together in their ethnic churches, sit next to each other, worship together, eat together, and work and play together, we experience an inversion of status, turning upside down the way we are viewed in the society outside. In this way, the church as the household of God takes an ethnically particular form in the Asian American context. But the Asianness of the Asian American church is nothing to apologize about; ethnicity in this case can be an instrument of the church's redemptive function. When Asian Americans are marginalized and made homeless because of our ethnicity, how can a church be a home to us if it does not affirm the dignity of our ethnicity? As the Japanese American theologian Roy Sano puts it, "liberation *through* ethnicity"

Sang Hyun Lee

and not "*from* ethnicity" has to be an essential function of the Asian American church.[14] The symbol "household of God," then, has to be contextualized in this way in the Asian American context of marginality.

For the second and later generations, their particularity as Asian Americans takes the form of an in-between ethnicity— a hyphenated synthesis that is neither just Asian nor just American. First-generation immigrants experience an in-betweenness, too, but their rootedness in their homeland and the strong first-generation church comfort them. But later generations often feel alienated both from their parents' first-generation church and community as well as from American society. In other words, neither the Asian community nor the American quite accepts them for what they are. The Asian American church as a household of God must become a place where the second and later generations are accepted as we are —neither just as Asian nor just as American but as a new synthesis of the two with an integrity all our own.[15] In the Asian world, we are often criticized for not being Asian enough; in American society, we are looked down upon for not being American enough. In the household of God, we shouldn't have to be enough anything—except to be what we are and have faith in Christ.

Another way to look at the particularity of Asian American ethnicity is to point to its fundamentally dynamic and open character. Asian American identity is not an eternally fixed reality; it is in the making. And the making of this something new requires the creative energies inherent in the liminal condition of Asian Americans. One of the essential tasks of the Asian American church, then, is to liberate the creativity of the in-between people by affirming them for what they are. The household of God, in other words, has to be a place where Asian Americans can dream dreams. Gaston Bachelard observes that home is a place "that protects the dreamer, allows one to dream in peace."[16]

The Asian American church, then, must affirm all the particularities of Asian Americans in their new emerging ethnicity. But to be a true embodiment of the household of God, the Asian American church also has the challenge to become ever more inclusive—both internally and externally. There is one area where most Asian American churches have a long way to go in becoming a true embodiment of the household of God: the place of women. Asian American women are marginalized not only in American society but within the Asian American community itself. Much of the economic success of many Asian immigrants is due to the inordinate amount of labor provided by women at business places. But women do not enjoy the same status and privileges as men either at home or at church.[17]

What Asian American women, especially the first generation, are up against is the whole Confucian metaphysics with a conception of household in which women exist primarily to serve men.[18] The household metaphor, therefore, is ambiguous for Asian American women. The Asian cultural ideology about women needs to be purged and corrected by the reality of the biblical household of God. And the church as household needs to be presented as a liberating household in which the usual ideas of women are turned upside down. Liberated from their double marginalization, the creative energies of Asian American women's two-sided in-betweenness can be set free—their liminality as women and their liminality as Asian American.[19]

The symbol of the household of God also challenges the Asian American church to become inclusive in its relations with other peoples and other churches. To affirm the Asian American ethnicity, in all its particularities, is an essential dimension of the Asian American church as a church. But the ethnic particularity must not be absolutized. Whenever this absolutizing happens, the demonic consequences of ethnocentrism are perpetuated—this time in its Asian American

Sang Hyun Lee

form. The Asian American church, in short, has a most delicate and difficult calling: to affirm its ethnic particularity against racism while at the same time resisting the temptation toward self-enclosure and constantly to move beyond itself toward others. To be at home in the household of God, in other words, is to be at home in such a way that one does not fear the margins—that is to say, one never ceases to be a pilgrim.

In sum, the two historic symbols of the Christian faith—pilgrimage and home—manifest their original power in new ways when they are appropriated in the Asian American context of marginality. Pilgrimage for marginalized people means the willingness to face up to one's marginality and to join with other strangers at the margins. But it is precisely our pilgrimage, our freedom from the idolatrous centers of the world, that prepares us for an experience of the reality of the household that God is building for all humankind. Pilgrimage and home, then, go together. This can only be so because, in the final analysis, pilgrimage and home are connected by a story that is God's own story.

God's Own Story

In conclusion, then, we ask: What is God's own story in which pilgrimage and home have their foundation and unity? What I have been saying here suggests an answer I can only offer without elaboration. God, too, is a pilgrim who left home. Not that God was not perfect from eternity but rather that God wanted to repeat God's inner life of loving community now in time and space.[20] But God's own world did not welcome God. God was not accepted by the idolatrous and absolutized centers of this world and thus became stranded in the wilderness of marginality. So the marginalized pilgrim God began God's project of building the loving community in the margins of the world. This project will be a struggle because

Pilgrimage and Home

it is carried out in the margins. But because it is God's own project it cannot fail.

And because this project is God's own, it is a project and a story that all of God's creation, regardless of race, is invited to join. To do so, however, means they must first become pilgrims and embrace their own wilderness in their own ways. The Asian American theology in the context of marginality, in short, is an invitation for all to meet in the margins as fellow strangers and to stand by each other in solidarity as we join in God's own joyous struggles to build the household of God where all of God's creation can come and be at home.

Notes

1. One of my earliest attempts to use the concept of marginality as a hermeneutical principle for Asian American theology was: "Called to Be Pilgrims: Toward a Theology Within the Korean Immigrant Context," in Byong-suh Kim and Sang Hyun Lee, eds., *The Korean Immigrant in America* (Montclair, N.J.: Association of Korean Christian Scholars in North America, 1980), pp. 37–74.

2. The literature on marginality and liminality is considerable. Three works that have been important in my own thinking: Everett V. Stonequist, *The Marginal Man: A Study in Personality and Culture Conflict* (New York: Russell & Russell, 1937); H. F. Dickie-Clark, *The Marginal Situation: A Sociological Study of a Coloured Group* (London: Routledge & Kegan Paul, 1966); Victor Turner, *The Ritual Process: Structure and Anti-Structure* (Ithaca: Cornell University Press, 1969). For an account of the Asian American struggles see Glenn Omatsu, "The 'Four Prisons' and the Movement of Liberation: Asian American Activism from the 1960s to the 1990s," in Karin Aguilar-San Juan, ed., *The State of Asian America: Activism and Resistance in the 1990s* (Boston: South End Press, 1994), pp. 19–69.

3. The meaning of the pilgrimage symbol I am adopting follows closely that of J. B. Soucek, "Pilgrims and Sojourners: An Essay in Biblical Theology," *Communio Viatorum* 1 (1958):3–17. I have also found helpful Richard Niebuhr's observation: "Pilgrims are persons in motion—passing through territories not their own—seeking something we might call completion, or perhaps clarity will do as well, a goal to which only the spirit's compass points the way." See "Pilgrims and

Sang Hyun Lee

Pioneers," *Parabola* 9(3) (1984): 7. Definitions of the term "pilgrimage" range from strict to comprehensive. H. B. Partin, for example, finds four essential elements in pilgrimages: separation, journey to a sacred place, a fixed purpose, and a hardship. See H. B. Partin, "The Muslim Pilgrimage: Journey to the Center" (Ph.D. diss., University of Chicago, 1967), quoted in William G. Johnson, "The Pilgrimage Motif in the Book of Hebrews," *Journal of Biblical Literature* 97(2) (1978):244. Another anthropologist, Alan Morinis, offers a much broader definition. The term "pilgrimage," according to Morinis, "can be put to use wherever journeying and some embodiment of an ideal intersect." See "Introduction: The Territory of the Anthropology of Pilgrimage," in Alan Morinis, ed., *Sacred Journeys: The Anthropology of Pilgrimage* (Westport, Conn.: Greenwood Press, 1992), p. 3. For a discussion of the metaphor of pilgrimage with a different application from mine see Margaret Miles, "Pilgrimage as Metaphor in a Nuclear Age," *Theology Today* 45(2) (July 1988):166–179.

4. Won Moo Hurh and Kwang Chung Kim, *Korean Immigrants in America: A Structural Analysis of Ethnic Confinement and Adhesive Adaptation* (Rutherford, N.J.: Fairleigh Dickinson University Press, 1984), pp. 84–86 and 146–149.

5. Byung-sup Bahn, *Jil-Geu-Reut-Gat-Un-Na-Eh-Ge-Do* (Even for me an earthen vessel) (Seoul: Yang-Suh-Kuk, 1988), p. 97.

6. I have benefited from numerous other theological reflections by Asian American scholars. In addition to those mentioned elsewhere, see also Roy I. Sano, *From Every Nation Without Number: Racial and Ethnic Diversity in United Methodism* (Nashville: Abingdon Press, 1982); Wesley S. Woo, "Theological Themes," *Asian Pacific American Youth Ministry* (Valley Forge: Judson Press, 1988), pp. 11–22; Ha Tai Kim, *Tai-Pyong-Yang-Geun-Neu-Kanaan-Tang* (The land of Canaan across the Pacific) (South Pasadena, Calif.: Korean Church of the Pacific, 1979); Fumitaka Matsuoka, *Out of Silence: Emerging Themes in Asian American Churches* (Cleveland: United Church Press, 1995). For a theological interpretation of marginality different from my own see Jung Young Lee, "Marginality: Multi-Ethnic Approach to Theology from an Asian American Perspective," *Asian Journal of Theology* 7(2) (1993):244–253.

7. Richard Niebuhr, *The Meaning of Revelation* (New York: Macmillan, 1962), p. 116.

8. Darryl M. Trimiew, in an African American context, critiques and learns from Richard Niebuhr's thought. See his *Voices of the Silenced: The Responsible Self in a Marginalized Community* (Cleveland: Pilgrim Press, 1993).

9. Elaine H. Kim has written: "What [Korean immigrants] experi-

enced on 29 and 30 April was a baptism into what it really means for a Korean to become American in the 1990s." See her "Home Is Where the *Han* Is: A Korean American Perspective on the Los Angeles Upheavals," in Robert Gooding-Williams, ed., *Reading Rodney King/Reading Urban Uprising* (New York: Routledge, 1993), p. 219, quoted in Nancy Abelmann and John Lee, *Blue Dreams: Korean Americans and the Los*

Angeles Riots (Cambridge, Mass.: Harvard University Press, 1995), p. 24. For other insightful analyses of the Los Angeles uprising see Edward T. Chang and Russell C. Leong, eds., *Los Angeles—Struggles Toward Multi-ethnic Community* (Seattle: University of Washington Press, 1994); Sung Do Kang, ed., *Riot or Revolution?: A Theological Reflection on the L.A. Uprising* (Los Angeles: Korean Caucus, Cal-Pac Annual Conference of the UMC, 1994).

10. See Turner, *The Ritual Process,* pp. 94–203.

11. See Helmut Koester, "'Outside the Camp': Hebrews 13:9–14," *Harvard Theological Review* 55 (1962):299–315; William G. Johnson, "The Pilgrimage Motif in the Book of Hebrews," *Journal of Biblical Literature* 97(2) (1978):239–251. For an important study of Letter to the Hebrews by an Asian American theologian see Roy I. Sano, *Outside the Gate: A Study of the Letter to the Hebrews* (Cincinnati: United Methodist Church, 1982). For an instructive essay on the themes of home and Christ "outside the camp" see Charles C. West, "Where Is Our Home and Who Is Welcome in It?" *Presbyterian Outlook* (10 June 1985):14–15.

12. In the case of Korean immigrants, for example, almost 70 percent are affiliated with Korean immigrant churches, and about 85 percent of them attend church regularly. See Hurh and Kim, *Korean Immigrants in America,* pp. 129–169.

13. John H. Elliott, *A Home for the Homeless: A Sociological Exegesis of I Peter—Its Situation and Strategy* (Philadelphia: Fortress Press, 1981), pp. 127, 130–131, 199. Elliott draws a sharp distinction between, on the one hand, the "heavenly home" beyond time and history of Letter to the Hebrews and, on the other, the "house of God," a place of belonging here and now, of 1 Peter; see pp. 129–132 and 224–227. Even if we accept this distinction, surely we would need both the transcendent dimension of the ultimate realization for God's kingdom in Letter to the Hebrews as well as the kingdom's this-worldly embodiment in 1 Peter.

14. Roy I. Sano, "Ministry for a Liberating Ethnicity: The Biblical and Theological Foundations for Ethnic Ministries," in Roy I. Sano, comp., *The Theologies of Asian American and Pacific Peoples: A Reader* (Berkeley: Asian Center for Theology and Strategies, Pacific School of Religion, 1976), p. 291.

15. See Won Moo Hurh, "Toward a New Community and Identity:

Sang Hyun Lee

The Korean-American Ethnicity," in Kim and Lee, *The Korean Immigrant in America*, pp. 1–25.

16. Gaston Bachelard, *The Poetics of Space* (Boston: Beacon Press, 1969), p. 6, quoted in Sharon Daloz Parks, "Home and Pilgrimage: Companion Metaphors for Personal and Social Transformation," *Soundings* 72(2–3) (Summer–Fall 1989): 304.

17. Kwang Chung Kim and Won Moo Hurh, "The Wives of Korean Small Businessmen in the U.S.: Business Involvement and Family Roles," in Inn Sook Lee, ed., *Korean American Women: Toward Self-Realization* (Mansfield, Ohio: Association of Korean Christian Scholars in North America, 1985), pp. 1–41. For a good anthology of articles on Asian American women's experiences see Asian Women United of California, eds., *Making Waves: An Anthology of Writings by and about Asian American Women* (Boston: Beacon Press, 1989).

18. See Inn Sook Lee, "Korean American Women and Ethnic Identity," in Sang Hyun Lee and John V. Moore, eds., *Korean American Ministry* (expanded English ed.) (Louisville: Presbyterian Church (USA), 1993), pp. 192–214; Soon Man Rhim, "The Status of Women in Traditional Korean Society," in Harold H. Sunoo and Dong Soo Kim, eds., *Korean Women in a Struggle for Humanization* (Memphis: Association of Korean Christian Scholars in North America, 1978), pp. 11–37; Minza Kim Boo, "The Social Reality of the Korean American Women: Toward Crashing with the Confucian Ideology," in Lee, *Korean American Women*, pp. 65–93.

19. For a discussion of women's "experience of nothingness" and its creativity see, for example, Carol Christ, *Diving Deep and Surfacing: Women Writers on Spiritual Quest* (Boston: Beacon Press, 1980), pp. 9–14.

20. The idea of the creation as God's "repetition" of God's inner being comes from Jonathan Edwards. See his "Concerning the End for Which God Created the World," in Paul Ramsey, ed., *Works of Jonathan Edwards*, vol. 8: *Ethical Writings* (New Haven: Yale University Press, 1989), p. 433.

PART III

Creations of Spirit

This part of the book turns to memoir, poetry and short stories in recognition of the fact that the study of religion must incorporate people's lived experiences. Asian American religions are more than an academic affair, and the following contributions ground religion in the personal spaces that give it power and meaning. Albert Saijo is one of the original beat poets associated with Jack Kerouac and Lew Welch; in Chapter 9 his poetry reflects his encounters with Zen Buddhism. As a Muslim child growing up in India, Saleem Peeradina notes in Chapter 10 that by his adult years, "my growing skepticism had gradually erased from the sky the face of God." And yet, in the move from Bombay to a small, midwestern U.S. town, he rediscovered his faith and the Koran in the face of racism directed against Islam and Muslims. His defense of what was once left behind is also done for the sake of his Asian American children. In Chapter 11 a poem by Meena Alexander explores the meanings of race, religion, and nation from Sarajevo to India.

Allan DeSouza in Chapter 12 tells two stories within one narrative, moving back and forth between a boy's sexual com-

ing of age and historical texts on the first Jesuit missionary to Asia, St. Francis Xavier. A South Asian artist born in Kenya, DeSouza writes about the convergence of colonialism, religious experience, and migration. The choices that are made, like the narratives themselves, matter because they are integral to the **234** *definition of the self and one's place in the larger scheme of things. In Chapter 13 the scents of post-riot Los Angeles mix with religious imagery in a richly textured poem by Russell Leong.*

Chapter 9

Bodhisattva Vows

ALBERT SAIJO

BODHISATTVA VOWS TO BE THE LAST ONE OFF
THE SINKING SHIP—YOU SIGN UP & FIND OUT IT'S
FOREVER—PASSENGER LIST ENDLESS—SHIP
NEVER EMPTIES—SHIP KEEPS SINKING BUT
DOESN'T GO QUITE UNDER—ON BOARD ANGST
PANIC & DESPERATION HOLD SWAY—TURNS
OUT BODHISATTVAHOOD IS A FUCKING JOB LIKE
ANY OTHER BUT DIFFERENT IN THAT THERE'S NO
WEEKENDS HOLIDAYS VACATIONS NO GOLDEN
YEARS OF RETIREMENT—YOU'RE SPENDING ALL
YOUR TIME & ENERGY GETTING OTHER PEOPLE
OFF THE SINKING SHIP INTO LIFEBOATS BOUND
GAILY FOR NIRVANA WHILE THERE YOU ARE
SINKING—& OF COURSE YOU HAD TO GO & GIVE
YOUR LIFEJACKET AWAY—SO NOW LET US BE
CHEERFUL AS WE SINK—OUR SPIRIT EVER
BUOYANT AS WE SINK

Chapter 10

Erasing God

SALEEM PEERADINA

Either because I was the first child or because I displayed a combination of talents—for singing, for art, for ranking first in school—I became the family's showpiece for guests.

More so than in most families where kids are thrust forward with pride—much to the children's own bashfulness and glee—I got more than my share of public pats and praises. This put into my head the notion that I was somehow special, creating in me the desire to please, making me dependent—I realized too late—on the need for approval. As a spur to action, this is neither unnatural nor exceptional; it has largely been a force for the positive although it has led me into behavior and situations I didn't necessarily enjoy or want to be in. But this back-patting was far better than the active discouragement and constant putdowns I began to receive from my father when I was old enough to assert my wishes and pursue my own peculiar logic. So successful was he in undermining my self-confidence that I had to fight the temptation to fail in order to prove him right, and therefore push the blame for my failure on him. This had two outcomes: all I needed to challenge my ability to succeed in a task was an obstacle—and I would go for it. On the flip side, a model that struck too close to home, as a reminder of my father's obstructive will, created in me untold anxieties of failure.

All that was still in the future. Right then, at age six, I was basking in the warmth of approval generated by my grandparents' monopoly of my talents. They believed I should be learning to read the Koran—since what use was the God-given gift of learning if not pressed into the service of his word? Bapaji initiated me into the holy book, and after his death Ma continued to teach me. After her passing, a *mullasaahib* was retained. He came every day from Bandra (where my father had a clinic) waddling on a twisted knee—as much a trademark as the aroma of attar that surrounded him, as *paan* and long hair were the insignias of my music teacher who taught me the harmonium. *Janaab,* as the *mullasaahib* was referred to, was a good teacher who occasionally rewarded my diligence by removing the wad of cotton from his ear and rubbing the attar onto my shirt!

I was making rapid progress through the thirty chapters— the earlier a Muslim child accomplished the feat, the prouder the family—and the day I finished the Koran, a celebration was held in which I presented a recital, *mithai* were distributed, and a garland of flowers was strung around my neck. I remember the day clearly—sitting crosslegged in a newly stitched *kurta* and pajama, an embroidered cap on my head, the Koran on a reading stand on the floor. The room floated in a haze of incense; beaming onlookers circled me.

This was one kind of initiation—a far more pleasant one than the earlier mandatory one that put the stamp on my Muslim identity by literally scalping my genitals. The job that is conducted routinely now in hospitals, the week a male child is born, was at that time done privately anytime between the ages of three and six. I was five when the circumcision was done.

I was seated in the *diwankhana* on a small wooden platform—an object of ritual also used in weddings—and a man who smelled of a strange mixture of attar and iodine was talking to me. His beard, dyed with henna, was orange and on his shoulder was a checked white and yellow napkin. The family waited in the wings as the man's hypnotic voice directed my gaze up to the tiled roof sloping high above wooden beams.

"Look, a golden sparrow," he exclaimed, with the timing of a magician.

Everything happened at once in that moment of betrayal: my eyes, seeking the elusive golden sparrow in the rafters above, misted with tears as a stab of pain hit my pelvic region. As swiftly as the operation had taken place, I was quickly bandaged and bundled off crying to sleep. Over the next couple of days, the bandage was removed, the wound dabbed, cleaned, and swaddled in a new bandage. I could see raw pink flesh peeping out of a folded ring of skin with smudges of dried blood. I also remember a momentary, sharp twitch of pain accompanied by a pleasant relieving sensation while I attempted to urinate. I was wearing only a shirt and in bed. A little stool covered with white cloth was placed over my pelvic area to keep away the flies and mosquitoes! All the while, I was terribly aware of the deep public interest in my private parts and the open discussion of this major event. Even at five, it was a humiliating experience.

After my official induction into the faith, my religious education proceeded via theory as well as through ritual. The Koran was to be read every day. My father set the example in this regard—a habit he maintained for the rest of his life without a single lapse. It was the only religious ritual he observed, though later on in his fifties he took up fasting as well. Every morning after his bath, he unfolded the holy book from its leather cover, carried it to his favorite corner, and the house was filled with the loud, not very melodious in his case, guttural sounds of Arabic—something we recognized as sacred though we didn't comprehend its meaning. In Fufijan's (father's sister) house in Dongri, there was the tradition of tuning into the daily Koranic recital over the radio—the mellifluous sound awash in the house was a kind of consecration in itself, a morning hour inaugural of the day's oncoming rhythms, just as the beating of the *nagaara* in the mausoleum next door and the call of the muezzin from the mosque's minaret worked as a sort of spiritual disinfectant for the entire neighborhood. Reading the Koran was mostly a mechanical ritual—most lay Muslims have only a reading knowledge of Arabic, though many read Urdu translations as well. My mother always perused a Gujarati translation along with the Arabic. Wanting at some point to learn the text myself, I delved into the English version in my teens. Perhaps it was a premature effort; perhaps it was the Victorian translation; or perhaps I expected to be charmed by prophetic exploits remembered from my mother's telling. All in all, the encounter was a severe disappointment to my fanatical structure of faith not yet besieged by doubts.

My mother, who also prayed *namaaz* and kept track of festivals, holy days, and death anniversaries, like most women was the de facto keeper of the family faith. While ours was not a remotely fundamentalist ideology, either in belief or in practice, the men of the house went through long vacations from faith punctuated by bouts of faithfulness. I towed along with two uncles to the mosque and to the Mohorrum discourses. What has always seemed to be universal among Muslims is the selective participation in ritual, a kind of synecdochic adherence to spiritual accountability. For some it is the Friday noon public prayers; for others it is making pilgrimages to assorted *durgahs;* for still others it is distributing largesse to the poor and needy—a single mode of religious devotion repeatedly enacted to the benign neglect of all others. For my father, the daily recital of the Koran was the extent of his summation of the faith. For my oldest uncle, it was the *magrib namaaz* offered at dusk and the periodic attendance of public discourses similar to revival meetings.

I enjoyed the fact that the location of the mosque—unlike Hindu, Christian, or Parsi trips to the temple, church, and *agiari* respectively—was inseparable from the neighborhood *paan* and *bidi* kiosks and the Irani and Chiliya restaurants. All over Bombay where *durgahs* and mosques are situated, a colorful street life is intimately tied to these places including, sometimes, dens of iniquity. The fairs associated with *durgahs*—especially the Mahim fair, which we visited annually—were keenly awaited. A special brand of *barfi* (evaporated, moist cream of milk) that we bought from the fair used to be the highlight for my father and the kids. Later, when we were all grown up and hated the crowds and noise, I would make a quick dash to the fair only to bring home the *barfi*. More than Juhu Beach, the popular sea resort, it was the Mahim seafront, where the ferries unloaded black sand from Ghodbunder, that was our favorite snacking place for *bhelpuri* and *kulfi*. Either the whole family went in the evening or the women and children made a day of it, spending the afternoon visiting an old surviving *nanima* of my mother's in Mahim, and then coming to the beach in the evening.

So it was the setting for the feasts and the surrounding exhibits, rather than the main religious menu, that defined my understanding of Muslim ways. I'm not sure it was different for the adults. The Irani café was the place for cold Duke's lemonade and the Chiliya establishment the place for *panikum chai*, an addictive brew if ever there was one. This was always a male affair. Like the butcher shops, the Chiliya restaurants were not considered wholesome places for the women, a segregation common in the Muslim world to protect women from the gaze and undesirable comments of the male. The typical café had mirrors all around, yelling waiters who slapped ice cold tumblers of water and steaming tea (layered with cream for me) on marbletop tables, and the radio going full blast. Two cups of tea were usually split into two portions; one person drank out of the saucer. The most impressive part for me was the verbal bill, always accurate, shouted out by the waiter (who never wrote down any of the orders he was taking from numerous tables) to the man in charge at the counter where we paid. Some Sunday evenings at home we supped on fried potato and onion fritters, or French toast, and washed down the meal with Chiliya tea. I was usually the errand boy with the tin kettle, delivering the tea.

Within the house, too, my religious sense was nurtured by the frills and celebrations rather than the serious core of prescribed religious tenets. *Lobaan,* an aromatic coal, was regularly burnt in the evening, and I was in charge of dispersing the scented fumes by carrying the earthenware bowl of glowing embers through all the rooms. In the Muslim household, this is the fragrance associated with sundown and the winding down of day to the hum of mosquitoes. At other times, when grace had to be said over a specially cooked meal of *sevaiyya* or *seera,* and rice and mutton curry, incense sticks were lighted and the vapors of food blended enticingly with the flavor of incense, leaving an indelible impression of the event that was being commemorated—usually the death anniversary of one of my grandparents or the birthday of a saint or some form of thanksgiving.

A figure imprinted on my memory screen is the *fakir* who showed up late evenings. On our upper-floor veranda we waited for the sound of his scuffling gait. Dressed in a long *jabba* with beads around his neck and a scarf around his head, he came with a kerosene lamp and recited a short prayer in slow, high-pitched, guttural accents. Then he would look up for the coin wrapped in a calendar date leaf to be flung down to him. We felt sorry for his failing eyesight which had trouble locating the drop of the coin. He was a childhood icon, an exponent of the saintly and the dispossessed, the angel in disguise who dropped in uninvited and left blessings in the wake of those who heeded his call.

Idd was *the* big feast following the month of Ramadan. The family fasted during the holy month, but most of us observed only the "big" fasts—the nineteenth, twenty-first, twenty-third, and twenty-seventh. To fulfill the obligations of fasting was a test of our infantile courage. But the fun part was always the camaraderie—setting the alarm for four in the morning; gulping the last desperate sips of water before sunrise; finding things to do during the day to keep our minds off food; keeping busy without exhausting ourselves. Evenings it was the dragging minutes, the cooking of special foods at home, or items bought on the street that made us dizzy with impatience. The whole neighborhood wore a festive look with restaurants churning out piles of *samosas* and *kabaabs;* vendors retailing fruit sherbets, ice cream, and, yes, dates—and finally the breaking of the fast. It was a dawn to dusk affair every day for thirty days.

A neighborhood like Minara Masjid in the Muslim *mohulla* between J. J. Hospital and Crawford Market, about which I had heard glowing accounts, I got to experience only years later when I began visiting my wife's family in the area. It is truly the most exotic place during Ramadan—virtually the whole street for several blocks springs to life in the evening, burgeoning with mouthwatering varieties of gourmet delights, vanishing into the blazing sunlight during the day to reappear again toward evening.

Since the Islamic calendar is based on the twenty-eight-day lunar cycle, the year is shorter by four weeks. Consequently, Ramadan traverses the length of the Roman calendar and appears in different seasons in the yearly cycle. The summer months, often in 110-degree temperature, are the hardest to endure. Never motivated enough to maintain the strict regimen, I skipped many of the fasts and finally gave up fasting altogether. But I was always in awe of the orthodox followers who not only stuck to this thirty-day undertaking but went about their business as usual, heat or no heat. The servants, the manual laborers, the millworkers, the taxi drivers, sweated it out without the least bit of fuss—an indication of the discipline and sacrifice fasting entails: giving the appetite a rest; understanding the deprivation of those for whom hunger is a daily reality; sharing with them the morsels you eat. Aside from practicing temperance, evoking empathy and social consciousness, and heightening spiritual awareness, the month is to be spent in prayer and meditation in addition to the abstinence from food and water. The physical benefits of cleansing and dieting so evident in this ritual would alone make it a valuable creed for anyone to follow. It is this practical dimension of Islam that made the most sense, not the historically dated, culture-specific statement of prohibitions and commands dogmatically preached by the *maulvis.*

A song sung by Mohommed Rafi containing a parable is played all over, ad nauseum, during Ramadan. It concerns a boy who insists on fasting though, young as he is, it is not incumbent upon him to do so. By evening he is very feeble, and his anxious family tries hard to make him give up the fast. Adamant, the boy breathes his last before the sun sets. In answer to his devotion and steadfastness, God sends an angel to restore him to life. The implications of this sacrifice and this miraculous resurrection are spelt out lyrically as the song ends. It is a song that touches every believer deeply, imparting the message to those who waver in their resolve. It moved me too, but not enough to convert me.

There is another song, "Parwardigar-e-aalum," also sung by Rafi in the film *Hatim Tai,* that recounts episodes from the lives of the prophets—a song that brought tears to my mother's eyes whenever I sang it. She wept too, I suspect, from the knowledge that the song's sanctity did not rub off on me.

Erasing God

On the eve of Idd, the sighting of the moon is both a joyous occasion and, of late, a matter of controversy among egotistical mullahs who employ different criteria for a valid sighting, a pointless and tasteless affair as far as the general populace is concerned. In tribal Saudi Arabia where the religion was founded, the observance of Idd must have been based on local sightings of the moon. The communication systems that make possible the transmittal of the news have changed the rules by which an event like the sighting of the new moon can be declared to have occurred. If the sky is overcast in Bombay, for example, and the moon is reported to have been sighted in Hyderabad or Ahmadabad, a war of nerves could be let loose by the skeptical Bombay mullah who cannot stand to have his authority flouted by mullahs from other regions. So, in practice, Idd is celebrated on different days in the country, much to the annoyance of everybody concerned. The designated holidays have to be moved, and the bickering often causes bitterness among various Muslim constituencies (and amusement among their non-Muslim onlookers).

To the general Muslim populace in the street, the problem is much more practical: cooking, shopping, and sending invitations to family and friends are seriously disrupted and a last-minute frenzy is evident everywhere. The problem is compounded especially when the sky is overcast and the announcement of the sighting is made late in the night. Shopping for perishable ingredients like milk for the feast next day has to be held in abeyance until the last moment. While most families have been sewing new clothes for Idd, hordes of people go on a last-minute shopping spree after the moon is sighted. Extra milk is ordered for preparing *seerkhurma*—that deliciously rich concoction made of vermicelli, nuts, raisins, and dry dates. All our non-Muslim well-wishers who visited were served *seerkhurma,* and those who were invited for dinner usually got mutton or chicken roast with *naan* and *biryani*—the perennial Muslim standbys for all celebrations.

To the non-*namaazi* males in the family, the public Idd prayer was the one to which they faithfully subscribed. The *idgah* was about a mile's distance from the house and after being freshly bathed and clothed and perfumed (Muslims in general, particularly on festive days, follow prophetic precedent and douse themselves with attar!), we would join the stream of Muslims winding its way to the open-air prayer ground. The veranda, as always, provided a ringside view of street theater. In the early morning half-light, the dust-coated street and the dilapidated shops always took on the coloring of stage props as someone prompted cues from the wings and the action got going: first, a few early souls in sparkling white *kurta* pajamas, then a steady trickle of bodies, then bunches of people on foot, punctuated by truckloads of devotees as they went roaring by screaming *"Allahoakbar!"* By the time we joined the flow—we were invariably late, waiting for father to finish his toilet—the street was surging with freshly groomed, brightly clothed men moving in a procession toward the designated site. There were hundreds of people already gathered on the grounds so we always found a place in the rear and lined up on newspapers (father's idea of disposable prayer mats!) at the tail end of the congregation.

At the conclusion of the formal prayer, which lasted about thirty minutes, people embraced and hugged, said "Idd Mubarak," and dispersed. For us, the next stop by public transport was the cemetery at Versova where we paid our respects to Ma and Bapaji—as sacred a tradition in the family as the Idd celebration. Then began the round of visits, chiefly to an uncle's house; then his family would visit ours. After lunch—over which the women had been slogging all morning—and siesta we would await further visits in the evening from relatives living in town. Since ours was the "big" house, the one the founding fathers built, it was always the place for reunions. Along with the food and the piety this was an unchanging feature of Idd celebrations. The other constant was *mawa* cakes from Merwan bakery on Grant Road, potato chips from Golden Wafers, and other *mithai* from Eros Sweets. This most special combination of treats was exclusively reserved for Idd Day. The cakes were avoided at other times as an unnecessary expense that involved a special trip to town; the potato chips were frowned upon as an unhealthy indulgence, permitted only on Idd and sometimes on birthdays. After each of us got jobs and had money in the pocket, we changed the rules by treating the family to frequent "festival day" feasts.

Bedtime prayers were a must and existed in a predictable personal cosmology. God was kind, benevolent, and merciful and he ruled in heaven. And if you were good and obeyed your parents and performed your duties and didn't hurt anybody, God would reward you. Then there was the devil and hellfire, and if you cheated or lied or did other unacceptable things, you would be punished—forever. Which child in the Judeo-Christian-Islamic religious traditions has not been subjected to the terrors of this damnation? The vivid mental imagery through which this irredeemable worldview is presented ruled my imagination until my late teens. Later, for a dozen years or so, I became an agnostic; still later, I emerged from these extreme positions with a view tempered by life's realities and the influence of other spiritual topographies.

The blow to a simpleminded concept of religious morality cultivated through mechanical observance of ritual came from the marked discrepancy between precept and practice—a phenomenon so blatant it eventually knocked the faith out of me. It didn't require a great deal of thinking—just a little—to figure out that noble intentions and holy postures did not add up to a morally upright existence; that mechanical acts of charity provided a license to commit rationalized acts of robbery in business; that public display of piety was often a cover-up for a private reign of terror.

Saleem Peeradina

The family, ironically, provided the worst models of hypocrisy. The stamp of approval among Muslims universally for a gold standard of faith is the dark mark on the forehead—the sign of a true *namaazi* who prays five times a day, a ritual that involves touching your forehead to the ground. "Only the lucky few," my mother used to insist, "acquire this mark. They have bowed their heads to God so many thousands of times that the telltale mark works as a signature of their devotion." What she was implying was clear: this should be a lesson to the defaulters, the disbelievers, and the plainly skeptical, like me.

One of her brothers-in-law, my father's sister's husband, was the exemplar in this respect. And I had no objection to him since, by all accounts, he was a straight and virtuous man at all times, in public and in private. And I had no reason to doubt this in the future either—Yusufalibhai was indeed the ideal son, husband, father, professional man, and law-abiding citizen. He was generous, tolerant, and scrupulous in his dealings at all levels; he was also the most widely informed of anyone in the family, whose counsel in matters financial, business, ethical, and religious was keenly sought. My trouble was my other uncle, father's eldest brother—Pappa to everyone after Bapaji's death—who also displayed his mark of religious orientation prominently. He was known to have been an abusive husband and parent, had put his two daughters in an orphanage in Poona after his wife's death, and was generally a loser in whatever he undertook in terms of a job, which was usually an on-off proposition. He lived on the income from the inheritance his father had set up as a trust for his sons. His favorite posture was sitting cross-legged on a wooden bench near the door of his room, smoking *bidis,* watching the world go by.

He was fun for the kids because he was uncouth, entertaining, and the butt of jokes from Mahmood, which he guffawed away mostly (and at other times got howling mad).

Erasing God

The hollering during quarrels—all my father's family is *loud*
—was great fun, and he would often stomp out in indigna-
tion, or sulk in a corner, and I would be the diplomat dispatched to tempt him back to the gathering. We shared some
amount of empathy—perhaps because our birthdays coincided.

Since he was a widower whose kids were away, he was also
the effective babysitter for the family. Kite-flying expeditions
to the beach with a *firkee* of *manja* and dry snacks—*sev-kur-*
mura-boondi was typical—were the most popular under
Pappa's tutelage. Later, daylong swimming picnics with him
and Mahmood at Marve and Aksa Beach were the most
delightful times of our childhood. A collective memory shared
among my brother, cousin, and me is of the time when a high
wave at Aksa took Pappa by surprise. He usually minded the
towels and clothes on the beach, but the wave swept him off
balance and soaked his pajama and *kurta!* Good sport that he
was, he laughed with the rest of us.

I still couldn't reconcile Pappa's professed religiosity with
his nasty temper, his vile language when he was provoked, his
treatment of his daughters, and his total surrender to a direc-
tionless existence. I now understand his need for spiritual bal-
last. What I saw at the time was the deliberate and manipulative use of a religious facade to hoodwink the unwary. His
piety was a mirage to deflect attention from questionable
behavior and what were simply unpleasant personality traits.

Actually it was my naive idealism that was under assault.
My father was next. As the bully in him gradually began to
emerge and his total domination of my mother was recklessly
revealed before my unbelieving eyes, the clay feet of my idols
stood exposed. Although my father never constructed the
elaborate machinations of religious guile devised by seasoned
practitioners of deceit, the daily morning recital of the Koran
—his only badge of religious affiliation—appeared more and
more a hollow exercise, more a habit, like going to the bath-

room every day. The performance of that ritual had no connection with anything that went before or after. In fact, right before he took up the holy book, he might be harassing my mother about something; and soon after he finished reading, he would go after the sweeper in a most offensive manner.

My father's (as well as my mother's) attitude to servants was perhaps typical of their generation's—they were to be treated as irresponsible and undeserving (my parents' favorite term of condemnation), coerced into performing their chores, given leftovers to eat, paid poor wages, and yelled at consistently. I hated my father's triumphant expression when the servants groveled. I could never forgive my father for his failure to rise above his middle-class prejudices, for his inability to apply the axioms of Islamic brotherhood and equality to the daily contexts of living, and for his high-minded, self-righteous stance. The more moralistic his tone and the more offensive his attitude, the hollower his advocacy of the Koran.

The *tasbeer* or rosary is another icon of Muslim religious exhibitionism I came to abhor. My reasoning was simple. If you wanted to chant God's name by repeating a word or phrase continually in your mind (which is what the beads help you do), why not dispense with the cosmetic trimmings of sanctified jewelry and meditate upon the words in your mind? Of course, the rosary is just an object to train your concentration. But displayed in a social setting or a business situation, it can earn you a tactical advantage by pulling a kind of spiritual wool over people's eyes. Stories I heard during my high school years about priests involved in financial scams and sexual misdemeanors served to taint other religions as well. The Hindus, I learned, discriminating against women and perpetuating the caste system, were equally guilty. Figures of religious authority in all religions, it seems, propagated their virtues to the gullible, brainwashed the young, but practiced the most expedient and cynical version of the faith themselves.

Eventually I pared institutionalized religion down to the

essentials: the simple personal aspects of faith embodied in the individual's relation to God as well as the value system that one may attempt to follow in one's private and social affairs. Ethical value systems are common to most religions, although cultural norms of behavior produce variations in style and intensity. In radically polarized situations, these differences become emotionally charged and ethically volatile, leading to bitter feuds and long-lasting historic sieges. The Hindu-Muslim warfare, the Sunni-Shia standoffs, the Protestant-Catholic fighting never seem to end.

Back then, the steady stripping away of my venerated beliefs left me with nothing. My elders had left me in the lurch. I saw the world of adults embroiled in conspiracy and treachery. Everything on the surface was just an act; the reality below was grim, shameful. As I looked up into the blue, I saw a vast emptiness: my growing skepticism had gradually erased from the sky the face of God.

For the better part of fifteen years—all through college, my abbreviated teaching career, and my return to student life in the United States in the early seventies—that face stayed invisible and ensured that my faith would remain marginal.

Since God had ceased to preside in the theater of my religious imagination, I abandoned all Islamic ritual except the annual Idd *namaaz,* which I joined only to save the family's face. Bowing and touching forehead to the ground, I felt no devotion stirring in me. The absence of God from my personal cosmology produced no qualms of conscience; instead, I felt strangely liberated. This sense of optimism was of course linked to the intellectual climate of the time. Sartre, Camus & Co., whose writings I devoured, were the rage on college campuses; lesser luminaries like Ayn Rand were even more potent in molding impressionable undergraduate minds like mine.

A *Time* magazine cover that posed the question, IS GOD DEAD?, put a stamp of approval on the virtues of skepticism. Benign indifference toward divine absence produced a new sense of individual responsibility. It was this combination of the ideological and the personal that fired my spirit during those years.

It wasn't until I was in my mid-thirties that the faith which had so far lain in deep freeze began to thaw, and the face that had been smudged blue began to emerge. I recorded the precise moment of this emergence in a poem I wrote after the birth of my daughter:

STRANGE MEETING I

With the visible signs
        of his first child
God loomed into view. Before her time
                her message
Came through. Unborn, her heart

Pounded, clear as hoofbeats.
        Long before she broke
The waters, she pronounced—
        I exist, I exist.
Her heart, the size of a seed

Embedded in a lump of clay
        had been pulsing
For millions of years. Yearning
                to ride the air
To attach itself to the flesh of its father.

God alone could have sowed this urge
                in the womb's
Ancient slush. To initiate him
                into the mystery

Erasing God

Of His life-giving breath. And to give

Immensity to his joy, He blew the dust
                    that lay ahead.
Time collapsed. The child's galloping years
                    diminished
His own, until a full-grown woman

Sat by his bedside, stroking his hand,
                    chilling him
To the bone. From that day, he opened
                    to a new life
Drinking deep from the dark pool

Of the child's eyes which held his own
                    in a spell—
As if this child had summoned him
                    to a great height
And what he saw was his own soul

Revealing to him the face
                    of a timeless love
That took his breath away.
                    The earth

Glided on.
And God stood, watching.

This assertion of spirituality was for me a pantheistic feast—a celebration that had at its core a poetic mystery. I was still, obstinately, a nonsubscriber to the official doctrine and far removed from the easy commerce that hardcore followers established with the Deity.

In the late eighties, a major period of adjustment opened up with the migration of my four-member family from Bombay to a small town in the upper midwest. Located forty miles south of Ann Arbor, thirty miles west of Toledo, Ohio, and

Saleem Peeradina

seventy-five miles southwest of Detroit, this town of 22,000 is popularly described as strategically isolated. Despite its two colleges, it is a provincial and conservative town; its 12 percent Hispanic population owes its ancestry to migrant farm labor that came from Texan border towns in the 1940s; its prime position on the Underground Railroad to the north, duly recorded in the Museum of African American History in Detroit, has thrust on it minor fame. In comparison to larger and more celebrated neighbor cities that boast sizable Asian populations, including Dearborn, which has the largest single concentration of Middle Eastern Muslims and *halal* meat shops in Michigan, Adrian's international flavor is modest—a smattering of South Asians and Southeast Asians, mostly professional. Among the fifteen families from the Indian subcontinent, half a dozen are Muslim with persuasions ranging from strictly traditional to extremely liberal.

Tradition intensifies in families whose religious beliefs seem besieged by a secular culture. This is a commonplace observation in the pan-Islamic world not under Muslim political rule. In practice, this means following the more orthodox customs of sending children to "Sunday" school, building mosques and setting up public prayer congregations, imposing dress codes on adolescent females, prohibiting dating, eating *halal* meat only, and observing all the other rituals required of a God-fearing Muslim. We saw each of these manifestations practiced in varying degrees among the families we came to know in the area. We experienced friendly and, on one occasion, coercive pressure to join in these practices. We stuck to our resolve. My wife practiced the personal and private version of the faith she had always followed—praying the *namaaz*, reading the Koran, and fasting whenever it did not conflict with work and school. After two decades of an incorrigible nonpartisan reputation, I was not about to lapse back into the niceties of formal religion or pay lip service to its most superficial claims.

But in the seven years we have been here, a curious development has entered our lives. This has opened for us, as representative Muslims, a new role as spokespersons and, sometimes, defenders of the faith in the American classroom. With America's mass media so devoted to giving a bad press to Muslim fundamentalists, it is hard for students to get information that is free from bias. Among those who study world religions, history, literature, anthropology, and politics, the need to gather historical facts, anecdotal evidence, and first-person accounts is never fulfilled by texts alone or their American interpreters. My wife, who has the greater claim to speak on the subject, having studied Islamic culture in college, is regularly invited to address students and even ministers in the local diocese. Having walked the same Bombay streets and scanned the same newspaper headlines and gossip columns as Salman Rushdie, and sharing some of the same religious concerns that he poses in *The Satanic Verses,* I was in a better position to explain Rushdie's phenomenal achievement as a novelist and to contextualize the Muslim world's outrage against his so-called heretical stance.

Far from renegade status, even farther from fundamentalist positions, my wife and I are neither unique nor different from thousands of other immigrant Muslims whose credibility is easier to behold and whose perspective is taken seriously. The lesson, in student minds, of the particular character and features of Islam and its place alongside the world's other theologies, is well learned.

Personally, for us, having mingled with Palestinian Muslims, Iraqi, Pakistani, and Bangladeshi Muslims, in addition to Indian Muslims, we have discovered enough common features of domestic and social practice to establish a comfortable degree of interaction. The degree to which our customs and expressions coincide is often astounding and amusing—another affirmation of the ties that bind us across geographical boundaries and national frontiers.

Saleem Peeradina

As they were already facing multiple adjustments—including changes of schools in the first two years and the acquiring of language fluency (adapting their British-Indian accent to the local accents heard in the classroom)—we decided to spare the children the rigors of Sunday school in Arabic. Besides, the nearest mosque—a beautiful, imposing structure built by local Muslims—was in Perrysburg, Ohio, some forty miles from our town. Seven years later, we cannot say for sure that we made the best choices on behalf of the children. They do not have a religious identity other than what they have absorbed in the domestic setting. They do have a spiritual sense and a belief in God. We've taught them to offer bedtime prayers. Among the things they have lost the most precious is the knowledge of Hindi: they are one more statistic in the brutal logic of assimilation. But erasures, whether metaphysical or historical or those dictated merely by expediency, are hardly permanent; they have a way of resurfacing when the time is right. A whole generation of Hispanic children, forcibly disconnected from their language, is now relearning Spanish in school and in college.

When the need asserts itself, our children will move in the direction of their own individual searches. Relearning the language and rediscovering religion—not necessarily Islam—may well be two of the central components of those searches.

Glossary

Indian words whose meanings are not implied in the text are explained here in the order they appear in the essay.

mullasaahib teacher
paan digestive made from betel leaf, lime paste, areca nut, and other condiments
janaab sir
mithai sweets
nagaara big drum
namaaz Muslim prayer

Mohorrum days of mourning for the prophet Ali's martyrdom

durgah mausoleum

magrib sundown

agiari Parsi fire temple

bidi indigenous cigarette rolled in tobacco leaf

bhelpuri a type of Indian fast food made from puffed rice and other ingredients

kulfi Indian ice cream

panikum chai tea with generous helping of cream

sevaiyya, seera cooked desserts made of vermicelli and rice flour respectively

fakir ascetic

jabba flowing robe

Idd Muslim feast following Ramadan

samosas, kabaabs appetizers

mohulla neighborhood

maulvi religious instructor

naan thick flat bread

biryani fancy dish of rice and meat

idgah prayer ground

Allahoakbar God is great

firkee of *manja* a roll of string treated with crushed glass

Saleem Peeradina

Chapter 11

San Andreas Fault

MEENA ALEXANDER

And if I cried, who'd listen to me in those angelic orders?

—Rilke

I: THE APPARITION

Too hard to recall each grass blade, burn of cloud
in the monsoon sky, each catamaran's black sail.
Nor very easily could we make ourselves
whole through supplication
before and after—the jagged rasp of time
cooled by winds brushing the Pacific.
The brown heart rocking, rocking
ribs dashed to the edge of San Andreas Fault.

Suddenly I saw her, swathed in silk
seemingly weightless, nails pried into rock
rubber boots dangling over the gorge:

"This morning light over water
drives everything out of mind, don't you agree?

I know the Ganga is like nothing else on earth
but now I fish here
San Andreas suits me: salmon, seaperch, striped bass."

Montara, Moss Beach, Pescadero, Half Moon Bay,
North American names quiver and flee, pink shrubs
stalks of the madrone, speckled heather rooting in clumps
and under it all, earth's fault where her voice worked free:

"Saw him walking with you, holding hands in sunlight
two of you against a wall, hands, face, eyes all shining
he had a brown paper bag, you nothing, how come?"

Feet hot against madrone roots, veins beating indigo
to the rift where her thighs hung musically
unbuckling gravity, I set my face to her squarely:

"Come to America so recently
what would you have me carry in my hands?
In any case why bring in a man I hardly see any more?"

II: FLAT CANVAS

Once waiting for him in the parking lot
right by the muddied pool where wild dogs congregate
—he was often late—I let the sunlight bathe my face.
Stared into water, saw myself doubled, split
a stick figure, two arms bloodied with a bundle
racing past parked cars of third world immigrants.

Then I saw him sprinting by my side:
"Teeth, Teeth, Teeth"
he cried, his body bolted down, a dream
by Basquiat, flat canvas, three pronged heart, broken skull
laced with spit, skin stretched over a skeleton pierced with nails
Gray's Anatomy in one hand, in the other, the Bible.

Meena Alexander

In Malayalam, Hindi, Arabic, French he cried out
turning to English last, as the continental coast broke free
riveting Before and After, jumpstarting reflection.
The Angel of Dread wings blown back
neck twisted over mounds of rubble
doorposts with blood of the lamb smeared on.

And faintly visible under jarring red
words like Progress, Peace, Brotherly Love,
One Nation under God, *all that stuff.*

III: FUNERAL SONG

I sensed his breath on my neck,
he needed to suck me into eternity
press thumbs against my throat, set a paper bag
against my thighs warm with the hot dog he got on the cheap
from the corner store by the supermarket wall.
"Real American hot dog, sauerkraut and all" he boasted
till the tears took hold.

He pressed me tight against a tree
in full sight of an Indian family
struggling with their groceries, thrusting
harder as breath came in spurts—
a funeral song he learnt from his mother
the words from Aswan filling me:

"You have crossed a border, never to return.
Stranger in this soil, who will grant you burial?
Neck of my beloved, who will grant you burial?
Eyes, lips, nose, who will shield you from sight?"

Tighter and tighter he squashed me
till figs of the fruit tree burst loose
and fit to faint I thrust my fist
into his blue cotton shirt, cast myself free.

San Andreas Fault

IV: PACKAGE OF DREAMS

Late at night in Half Moon Bay
hair loosed to the glow of traffic lights
I slit the moist package of my dreams.

Female still, quite metamorphic
I flowed into Kali ivory tongued, skulls nippling my breasts
Durga lips etched with wires, astride an electric tiger

Draupadi born of flame, betrayed by five brothers
in the banquet house of shame.

In the ghostly light of those women's eyes
I saw the death camps at our century's end

A woman in Sarajevo shot to death
as she stood pleading for a pot of milk
a scrap of bread, her red scarf swollen
with lead hung in the linden tree.

Turks burnt alive in the new Germany
a grandmother and two girls
cheeks puffed with smoke
as they slept in the striped blankets
bought new to keep out the cold.

A man and his wife in Omdurman
locked to a starving child, the bone's right
to have and hold never to be denied
as hunger stamps the light.

In Ayodhya, in Ram's golden name
hundreds hacked to death, the domes
of Babri Masjid quivering as massacres begin—
the rivers of India rise mountainous,
white veils of the dead, dhotis, kurtas, saris,
slippery with spray, eased from their bloodiness.

Meena Alexander

Shaking when I stopped I caught myself short
firmly faced her: "What forgiveness here?"
"None" she replied. "Every angel knows this.
The damage will not cease and this sweet gorge
by which you stand bears witness.

"Become like me a creature of this fault."

She said this gently swinging to my side
body blown to the fig tree's root.

"Stop" I cried. "What of this burden?
The messy shroud I stepped into?
Ghostly light, senseless mutilations?"

Her voice worked in my inner ear
sorrow of threshed rice,
cadences of my mother tongue loosed in me:

"Consider the glory of the salmon
as it leaps spray into its own death
spawn sheltered in stone under running water.
That's how we make love—Can you understand?
Each driven thing stripping itself
to the resinous song of egg and sap
in chill water.

"Sometimes I think this is my mother's country
she conceived me here, legs splayed, smoke in her eyes
in the hot season when gold
melts from chains, beads, teeth
and even the ceremonials of the dead
dwelt on in Upper Egypt dissolve away."

"We are new creatures here.
Hooking fish in San Andreas we return them to the fault
perch, black salmon, the lot.

"When the walls of your rented room
in Half Moon Bay fall away
consider yourself blessed.

"Snows of the Himalayas
that murmur in your mother's songs
once came from the rainclouds high above this coast
cradling the rafters of the seven heavens."

Meena Alexander

Chapter 12

Once Bitten

ALLAN DESOUZA

*hey mary full o grace hall obe thy name
thy kindom come thy wil be done as tis in
heaven hol mary mother o god pray for
ours in san lead us not into temptation
but dliver us from evil amen*

Somehow it comes out all wrong. Even after five years of reciting it—is it thirty? maybe even forty or fifty?—times a day, every day, Luke still can't remember it or distinguish it from a jumble of other prayers. The words collapse into each other, forming one long, uninflected monotone.

It is just after the evening meal. Luke and his parents sit in the dining room with the main light and the TV switched off. Flickering shadows are cast against the rose-patterned walls from a host of candles. White-bodied, golden-haloed, they dispel the darkness like a legion of God's angels, guardians of the innocent and just.

The son, his father, and mother nestle their rosaries in their laps, counting off the prayers with each bead. They used to kneel to pray; Luke can't remember when they began to merely sit. Did God mind? Was he displeased that they put their own comfort before obeisance? He never gave them a sign, which they took for tolerance, even negligence, on his part. When it is Luke's turn to recite, he begins "Heymary, fullograce murmur, murmur . . . holymary, motherogod . . . murmur, murmur, murmur—." "Start again! Do it properly!" his mother shouts. And he begins over, only marginally less inarticulate. The words which tumble out of his mouth are a litany whose meaning he never once stops to consider; but in some dark corner of his psyche they have taken root, smearing their tincture over everything he does, everything he is. Luke is not a heathen, one to whom the Word has not yet reached. He is worse. He has fallen from grace. He is one for whom the angels weep.

In order to stabilize the Portuguese hold in Goa and promote allegiance to the land, intermarriage between Portuguese men and native women of light complexion was encouraged, particularly with the Muslim women whose husbands and relatives had been killed during the Portuguese invasion. The spoils of war. Female slaves also included other local women, Africans, Arabs, Asians from Pegu, Siam, and China, and it was not uncommon to encounter harems of up to six slaves. The benefits of commerce. The women were baptized and received Christian names. Should a prospective wife or other female slave die without receiving Confession and Holy Communion, a fine was imposed upon her master. The penance of religion.

Dominus vobiscum, et cum spiritu tuo.

Was that right? He can't remember anymore, but sometimes these phrases suddenly pop up in his memory, like snatches of pop songs whose tunes have infiltrated the brain to never again be dislodged. Jostling for primacy against the unending lists of Latin nouns, verbs, tenses, and declensions —*declina, -as, -at, -amus, -atis, -ant*—and the interminable catechisms—who made me? God made me; why did he make me? silence—are the more succulent, illicit memories of being an altar boy.

Allan DeSouza

He removed his short trousers and underpants after slipping into the black, ankle-length cassock. With his shoes and socks still on, he looked cherubic as he filed into the church behind the priest. Behind the mask of his penitential face, he reveled in being shamelessly naked under his cassock before a churchful of decent, righteous people. And now, when he closes his eyes and allows his senses to take him back, he can still recall the heady aroma of incense, the rainbow hues of sunlight as it filtered through the stained glass windows, and most of all, the swish and sway of the cotton fabric caressing his thighs.

"*. . . We came here simply to get money by any means and to rob through usury and other evil devices. . . . And despite all this, they make an annual confession and receive their Lord without restitution, and I see this daily. . . . I believe that even if an apostle of Christ our Lord came here, he would be of little profit to their souls. This is why St. Thomas said to our Lord when he sent him here: "Lord, send me wherever you will, but not to the Indians!" . . . [The Portuguese] are led solely by their sensuality and say: "Why did I come to the Indies if it was not to make a fortune?" Bishop of Dume to King of Cochin, 1522.*

The two altar boys lapped at the priest's sonorous words as he raised the chalice of wine to the heavens, bowing their heads in earnest deference as if they actually believed in its transubstantiation into blood. After mass, when Father Gomes had changed and gone out to the front of the church to socialize with parishioners, they lingered behind, playing in the sacristy. Still dressed in their black cassocks and lace-trimmed surplices, they chased each other round the pews.

It was something about their vestments, their *dresses,* which lent their game a sacrilegious tinge, which increased the thrill of chasing and being chased—of being so *unchaste.* When caught, they tickled each other, squirming and giggling, trying desperately to stifle their shrieks of pleasure.

On a sunny spring morning in 1541, the Spanish-born Francis Xavier left the court of King John III in Lisbon to become the first Jesuit missionary to Asia. He landed in Goa, a little over a year later, on an evening in May 1542, just as the sun was setting.

Known by all as the "holy priest," Francis visited people's houses, collecting alms for the poor and the sick. Sometimes, if the man had female slaves, Francis would enter and sit with the household: "When there were already children of the union, he had them called and caressed them. He also had their mother come. He praised her good features, when this was possible, and frequently at this first visit urged his friend for the sake of his good name and for the honor of his children and their mother to be married in the church with his slave. When the concubine was dark in color and ugly featured, he employed all his eloquence to separate his host from her. He was even ready, if necessary, to find for him a more suitable mate." Francis Xavier, procurer, patron saint of Goa.

By the time Luke was ten, his blasphemies had been exposed and he was forbidden from serving mass. At eleven, he stopped attending church. By twelve, his parents had given up enforcing the rosary as a nightly ritual. Religion slowly retreated from their house as prayer books and rosaries were relegated to tissue-lined boxes in the attic.

Yet once a Catholic always a Catholic, the Jesuits say, eulogizing their own powers of indoctrination. Once the heart is infiltrated, religion is not so easily dispelled. The expulsion of God serves only to extend an invitation for his nemesis, the Devil.

Ringing a little silver bell, Francis Xavier stood at street corners and called out, "Faithful Christians, friends of Jesus Christ, send your sons and daughters and your slaves, both men and women, to learn about the faith, for the love of God." When a sufficient crowd had gathered, he led the Credo: "I believe in God, the Father Almighty, the Creator of heaven and earth. I believe in Jesus Christ, his only Son, our Lord. I believe that he was conceived of the Holy Spirit and born of the Virgin Mary. I believe that he suffered under Pontius Pilate, was crucified, died, and was buried. I believe that he descended into hell, and

*that on the third day he arose from the dead. I believe that he
ascended into heaven and sits at the right hand of God, the
Father Almighty. I believe that he will come from heaven to
judge the living and the dead. . . . I believe in the resurrection of
the body. I believe in life everlasting. Amen."*

Despite his apostasy and excommunication, it could be
said (and it once had been) that Luke was a religious, even
pious, child. He continued to believe in the man Jesus who is
called Christ. He believed in his angels. He believed in his
tempter, the fallen Lucifer. He believed. As he grew older, he
didn't relinquish his faith but diverted it, staunchly practicing
a religion of the body, a paradise incarnate replete with temptation. Longing for an all-but-naked man on a cross, a man
who offered his flesh and blood to be consumed. Ahh, that
was not abstract faith but a matter of aching desire.

*Finally, he would ask his assembled congregation, "Do you
believe that there is a hell, that is, an everlasting fire, where
everyone who dies outside the grace of God will be tortured forever? That there is a paradise and an everlasting happiness,
which the good will enjoy who have ended their lives in God's
grace? That there is a purgatory, where souls make satisfaction
to the divine justice for a period of time as they atone for the
punishment due to their sins, which although they were forgiven
them during life still were not entirely expiated before they
died?"*

As a child, Luke believed that salvation waited in the guise
of a Christ rendered as a blond-tressed, blue-eyed, Californian
surfer in flowing white robes. The discrepancy between
Christ's visage and his own had never struck him as anom-
alous: after all, it was Christ's very difference, and the distance
between his perfection and the flaws of the abject, the dark—
with their black hair, brown eyes, brown skin—that caused
them to deny their heathen lives, to give up their old ways and
become followers. It was submission—the calluses on bent
knees—that saved lost souls and created disciples.

Christ waited, Luke had been taught, at the end of a

Once Bitten

beaten track of renunciation, abstinence, and a little self-mortification to strengthen the resolve. But sinner that he was, he should not sully the divine ears with his tarnished voice. He should beg the saints for their intercession.

And after each question his listeners—slaves who could vividly imagine the lash of everlasting punishment—would cross their arms over their breasts and reply, "Yes, Father, with the grace of God, we believe this."

Luke closes his bedroom door firmly and wedges a chair under the handle. From his bookshelves he takes down a hefty volume, *The History of European Painting,* and opens it to a dog-eared, full-page reproduction of St. Sebastian. He undresses, watching his body in the wardrobe mirror. Naked, he ties one of his mother's scarves around his waist in imitation of the saint's loincloth. A trace of her smell on the scarf now rubbing against his skin adds further weight to his anticipation.

Using the painting for guidance, he clamps clothespins onto his body in the exact places where Sebastian was pierced, working upwards from the shin, to the thighs, the stomach, sides, chest, neck, to the forehead. Forehead, neck, chest, sides, stomach, thighs, shin. As each pin bites, Luke feels the surge and retreat of blood.

He stands on a chair to remove a Barbie and a GI Joe doll, each dangling from a ribbon fashioned into a noose and tied to a nail on the wall. He slips his left hand through a noose and pulls it taut with his right. He repeats the movement with his right hand and pulls the noose closed with his teeth. With his hands held in place he steps down off the chair so that his arms are pulled up over his head in imitation of Sebastian. The tableau is complete. The operation has been carried out with a calm and efficiency born of practice.

Speaking in pidgin Portuguese for the benefit of his illiterate audience, Francis added, "You, O Lord, have created me, and not my father or my mother, and you have given me a body and

Allan DeSouza

soul and all that I have. And you my God, have made me to your likeness, and not the pagodas which are the gods of the heathens in the form of irrational cattle and beasts of the devil. O you heathens, how great is the blindness of your sins that you make God out of beasts and the devil, since you pray to him under their forms! O Christians, let us give praise and thanks to the triune God for having revealed to us the faith and true law of his son Jesus Christ!"

The muscles in his arms soon begin to twitch and flex. He tries to keep them locked in position but they shake with the exertion, the shudders starting from his raised ribcage and passing through his shoulders to his biceps and forearms. He can't hold his arms up any longer and lets them sag. As they recuperate, his respite is punctured by a fresh agony at his wrists as the thin ribbon cuts into the meager flesh. He welcomes the familiarity of the pain and lets his attention scan it before letting it return to the clothespins. By rotating his focus from one source of torment to another he can maintain and extend the pain threshold.

From Goa, Francis traveled south and east, proselytizing and baptizing, arriving seven years later at Kagoshima, Japan, on 15 August 1549. Declared the "Apostle of Japan," on his arrival he observed that "the Japanese are the best of the peoples discovered up to now and it seems to me that there will not be another to better them," adding, "among the infidels." Japanese monks welcomed the Jesuit missionaries, believing them to be monks from Tenjiku, their name for India.

He leans back against the wall, dizzy with pain and euphoria, the blinding light of heavenly agony flooding his temples. Tears showering his cheeks, he moans and sobs, thrashing about like a speared puppy. The pain escalates, permeating his entire body. He surrenders, accepts, and bathes in Sebastian's denied desire. Beyond pain, beyond sensation, the blood stops flowing and his limbs turn cold and purple: all pleasure gone. Sliding his hands free from the crimson ribbon constraints, he begins the task of removing the pegs and massaging his seared nerves. Despondently, he watches the carmine flush of blood spread back into the blue, livid flesh. How weak was his body, deserting him before the ultimate pleasure, leaving him instead the lonely, desolate spiral down from glory into the mire of mortal mundanity.

Beneath the outward appearance of subjugation, Luke feels strengthened by his submission to pain. It creates an entrance, a pathway for his mind, into an almost sexual penetration of his body.

Despite his praise for the Japanese, Francis condemned what he called their "three Great Vices: abortion and infanticide; idolatry; and the abominable sin. "So awful was the last for the goodly priests that even its name could not be uttered. The Japanese not only continued to indulge their sin but laughed in the streets at the strangers who tried to forbid it.

During the day, Luke dutifully served his Lord, and at nights he received his reward. In febrile dreams he enveloped Luke and applied the salve of his tongue to Luke's undeserving flesh.

Waking from such dreams had opened Luke's mind to the first stirrings of doubt. Perhaps there was another way, another equally tortuous path to his arms. Perhaps he should put the ascetic on hold and concentrate on earthly indulgence until, becoming so sated, there would remain no weakness, no temptation in his body, and he would be free to fully embrace the heavenly.

Legend held that homosexuality was brought to Japan from China by the monk Kukai in the first year of the Daido era, or AD 806. Kukai's other achievement was the invention of Kana, the phonetic writing system. That erudition and sensuality were both attributed to him was a natural expectation from any who followed the Rishu-kyo sutra or, to use its Sanskrit name, Adhyardhar satika Prajnaparamita.

He told himself that in his budding youthfulness, he had

been given a body designed for the pleasures of the earth. When he stood in front of the mirror stroking the lines and developing curves of his body, he was easily convinced of the argument and decided there and then that it was his spiritual obligation to follow his body's lead and fulfill its purpose.

When temptation befell him, he barely hesitated, and leapt headlong into abomination.

To say that voluptuousness is pure is a truth of the state of boddhisattva.

To say that desire is pure is a truth of the state of boddhisattva.

To say that physical pleasure is pure is a truth of the state of boddhisattva.

To say that sounds are pure is a truth of the state of boddhisattva.

To say that tastes are pure is a truth of the state of boddhisattva.

To say that tangible things are pure is a truth of the state of boddhisattva.

To say that visual forms are pure is a truth of the state of boddhisattva.

And why? It is because all dharmas, all creatures, are in essence pure.

They pass each other in the street. He is the kind of person Luke's parents warn him about. But by now, so is Luke. They meet on Sunday mornings in the park when Luke would once have been at church. It isn't a case of one leading the other, nor is it a cautionary tale of youthful corruption; more a search for glimpses of heaven.

And God? God is a surge of heat to dripping loins.

ohgod.ohgodohgodohgod

For those with senses to feel and imaginations to interpret, Luke's transition from child to adulthood was marked, not by his fall nor by an abandonment of the quest for salvation, but by its substitution with a pursuit of sanctity.

Once Bitten

Like grace, sanctity is an absorption and elevation of the physical into a divine transformation, so that the earthly would glow with a transcendent light. From the depths shines the beauty of sanctity, for only the most debased, the most vilified—the outcast—can raise itself through each layer of sediment and encompass the totality of the physical.

Seekers of salvation are ultimately passive in their quest as salvation has to be bestowed by a higher authority; whereas sanctity, aggressive in its total acceptance, is self-activated.

Luke seeks a place where laughter might greet the street corner sermons of Francis Xavier.

All desire is pure.

He feels vindicated.

Unknowingly retracing the mythical path taken by the "heinous sin," Francis sets out for China, which he had always dreamed of converting. Never reaching his goal, he died on 3 December 1552, on the island of Shangchwan [Sanchon], in sight of the elusive mainland, and accompanied only by Christovao, an Indian servant, and Antony China, "a Chinese boy who had been in Goa so long that he had forgotten his mother tongue."

Francis's body, sealed in a lime-filled coffin to hasten its decomposition, was later disinterred and discovered to be in perfect condition, as if it was freshly dead. It was returned to Goa, arriving in March 1554. News of its uncorrupted condition spread rapidly and soon the streets of Velha Goa were jammed with throngs of the faithful and the simply curious. The number of people at the funeral was so great that the viewing of the body took three days.

Caught in the frenetic euphoria of the moment, a woman bit off one of Francis's toes. A few years later, another toe was bitten off. In 1614, the Pope in Rome was filled with the same passionate fervor and at his command, the right arm was ripped out and sent to him. One-armed, de-toed, the body was transferred to the Church of Bom Jesus in Old Goa, where it still remains and where it was regularly displayed to crowds of pilgrims.

Allan DeSouza

In 1974, however, after its final display, the Church authorities decided that what the Lord had preserved was being gradually corroded by human zeal. And so ended the four hundred years of Francis Xavier's expositions.

When Luke went in search not of faith but of memory's stories, he visited Bom Jesus. As he stepped out of the searing, noonday sun into the church interior, he expected to enter cool, somber darkness. Instead, he was momentarily blinded by cascades of dazzling light, reflected and deflected off every surface. Walls, ceiling, altars, chalices, statues, candlesticks were all gilt-covered and reeked of gold. Swirling pillars rose in serpentine coils to angels' eyries. Elaborate carvings filigreed every curve and angle, overwhelming Luke's vision with soaring flights of baroque opulence.

And amidst this display whose fatuous brilliance eclipsed the heathen sun, his eyes alighted upon two silver caskets, no bigger than jewel boxes. When he asked a worshiper what lay within, he was told that they contained the digested and regurgitated but resiliently fresh toes of the Holy Priest.

Note

The account of St. Francis Xavier is based on Georg Schurhammer, *Francis Xavier, His Life, His Times,* vol. 2: *India 1541–45* (Rome: Jesuit Historical Institute, 1977), and Harold S. Williams, *Foreigners in Mikadoland* (Tokyo: Tuttle, 1963).

Chapter 13

Unfolding Flowers, Matchless Flames

RUSSELL C. LEONG

I

"Tell me my name,"
I ask Sifu, as ashes
turn the City of Angels blue.
"Wait until
Buddha's birthday."

Tip by singed fingertip,
the ends of orange punk sticks
tinge the burning days of L.A.
Firefighters in bulletproof vests
catapult through flames
prod mini-malls to fall faster
without falling upon
the arms of mothers,
fathers, daughters, sons, who,
picking through the rubble of barrios
outfit their desire, abandon
their plantation names.

II

Santa Ana winds
carry the haze away.
Not even Buddha's hand
can bring back
those who have lost
their breath and beauty here.

If he were walking with straw sandals
across these bruised
boulevards, among people buying
yesterday's bread and milk, queuing
for a bus downtown, skateboarding
on Venice Beach this afternoon,
would he recognize the Pure Land
in the West,
the country whereby
we sought rebirth?

III

From above,
the sun heats Gautama's head.
From below,
snails glide up his thighs,
arms, neck, forming
a moist helmet
around his brow.

On the concrete ramp
which divides the Harbor freeway
a Mayan hawks baskets
of strawberries, purplish in the heat.
Two days after the fires,
the same man beckons me to buy

Unfolding Flowers, Matchless Flames

just as he did before.
Leaving the plundered pyramid
of L.A. in the rearview mirror,
I drive south toward the temple
in Little Saigon.

IV

White clouds,
breathe in.
Green waves,
breathe out.

"Crossing the gulf to Siam,"
said Sifu, "I left my country
on a wooden boat. Topside,
I turned my legs inward
into a lotus form
right foot over left thigh
left foot over right thigh.
My thumbs traced
a triangle just below my belly;
my half-closed eyes met
the hunger of pirates
on ships about to rob us.
They stopped twice, then left, but
it was not my sight that saved us."

Now a knit cap shields his head,
a yellow mantle warms his shoulders.
He lifts his teacup.
"Americans bombed Baghdad,
now burn their own cities.
Always, what we do returns to us—
unfolding flowers, matchless flames."

Russell C. Leong

V

Palm trees cool
the smoldering skies.
I cannot read the sutras
written upon the leaves.

Wanting her child back
a mother with a dead boy
sought Gautama, who told her:
"Bring me a punk stick
from a house
in which no one has died."
Far and wide she searched the town
until friend and folk thought her mad.
No house lay untouched.
Each held the spirit
of one who had perished.

VI

Saigon, 1963
Thich Quang Duc,
a buddhist monk,
protests the regime.
Petrol transforms
his flesh into petals
of flame. His heart
beats intact in the ashes.

All night we clean the temple.
Tomorrow marks the 2536th year
of Buddha's birth.
Men whitewash the walls,
scrape paint off windowpanes,

Unfolding Flowers, Matchless Flames

shake out rugs. In the kitchen
women wash baskets of mungbeans,
sort red papayas, green pears.
I place chrysanthemums
into four urns. A gray
mouse runs among the flowers.

The temple becomes alive at dawn,
a boat of passengers moving to the mallet
of the wooden fish drum.
Set low on a table,
the bronze Gautama surveys
his shallow pond, a glass bowl
filled with water and rose petals.
Some bathe the buddha figure,
others mist themselves with water.

"Each day, dust gathers
upon us; each day,
we forget his face," says Sifu.
With others, I listen.
I don gray robes,
and vow to uphold the Three Jewels
gleaming in the dust.

VII

In Buddha, I seek refuge.
In his teachings, I seek refuge.
In his community, I seek refuge.

"Tinh Thanh—
Reaching Calmness is your temple name."

So these words are spoken.
So these words are written.
So these words are understood.

Russell C. Leong

Yes, three times I repeat
and bow again.

On my hands and feet
I carry the smoke
of incense,
exit the temple door,
put on my shoes.

Entering the freeway on-ramp,
I return through disputed
red and blue territories.
I recall what Sifu said:
"Everyone in Saigon
was fighting over the land.
I built a treehouse, three times
the span of my outstretched arms.
I lived in the tree, suspended
between earth and sky.
Through leaves and branches,
I could hear cursing and singing.
I could smell cooking.
How far I have come
to tell you your name."

Asian American Religion:
A Selected Bibliography

MARJORIE LEE AND JUDY SOO HOO

This is a revised version of "Asian American Religion: A Special Topics Bibliography," originally published in *Amerasia Journal* 22(1) (Spring 1996). Since its last compilation, new sources have been published, and in this update forty-one citations have been selected from the 1996 and 1997 annual bibliographies of the journal. A number of citations are annotated for clarity.

Some 370 citations, arranged by general religious categories for convenience, are listed here. The final category, "Other Religious Issues," contains citations on various religious subjects that were not particular to any one category but contributed to the evolving nature of religious studies in the field of Asian American studies. Citations were indexed using the following category headings:

Buddhism
Christianity: Catholicism
Christianity: Protestantism
Hinduism
Islam
Mormonism
General Religion

Shamanism

Sikhism

Other Religious Issues

As this bibliography is primarily academic in orientation, it is not wholly reflective of the actual religious life and experiences of Asian American communities. Indeed, the study of religious life in Asian America is still in its formative stages. This bibliography reflects what has surfaced and, we hope, provides resources for further study and research.

Buddhism

Akiyama, Linda Cummings. "Reverend Yoshio Iwanaga and the Early History of Doyo Buyo and Bon Odori in California." M.A. thesis, University of California, Los Angeles, 1989.

Batchelor, Stephen. *The Awakening of the West: The Encounter of Buddhism and Western Culture.* Berkeley: Parallax Press, 1994.

Biographical History of Hawaii Hongwanji Ministers. Honolulu: Hawaii Hongwanji Ministers' Association, 1991.

Browning, James Clyde. "Tarthang Tulku and the Quest for an American Buddhism." Ph.D. dissertation, Baylor University, 1985. Study of a Tibetan Buddhist expatriate's efforts to adapt his religion to the United States.

Burford, Grace. "Lao Retrospectives: Religion in a Cultural Context." *Journal of Refugee Resettlement* 1(3) (May 1981):50–58.

Campbell, Milo K. "The Influence of Buddhism on the Transitional Southeast Asian Refugee Student." *Religion and Public Education* 16(2) (Spring–Summer 1989):279–282.

Canda, E. R., and T. Phaobtong. "Buddhism as a Support System for Southeast Asian Refugees." *Social Work* 37(1) (January 1992): 61–67.

Cordes, Helen. "Buddhism American Style: Too White, Too Elite? Is It Even Buddhism?" *Utne Reader* (January–February 1995):16.

Dart, John. "U.S. Buddhist Group Approves Marriage-Like Rites for Gays." *Los Angeles Times* (1 July 1995):B5. Shift in policy by Soka Gakkai International, which claims 300,000 followers and is based in Santa Monica, California.

Davis, Susan. "Mountains of Compassion: Dharma in American Concentration Camps." *Tricycle: The Buddhist Review* (Summer 1993):46–51. Buddhism among Japanese Americans during the wartime internment.

"Dharma, Diversity and Race." *Tricycle: The Buddhist Review* (Fall 1994). Special issue on Buddhism and race.

Farber, Don. *Taking Refuge in L.A.: Life in a Vietnamese Buddhist Temple*. New York: Aperture Foundation, 1987. Photographs by Farber with text by Rick Fields and an introduction by Thich Nhat Hanh.

Fields, Rick. "Confessions of a White Buddhist." *Tricycle: The Buddhist Review* (Fall 1994):54–56.

"Fifty-Three Temples In and Around Seattle." *Tricycle: The Buddhist Review* (Fall 1994):46–47. Map of Buddhist temples (Cambodian, Chinese, Japanese, Korean, Laotian, Thai, Tibetan, Vietnamese, and "other") in Seattle area.

Foye, Addie. "Buddhists in America: A Short, Biased View." *Tricycle: The Buddhist Review* (Fall 1994):57.

Gussner, R. E., and S. D. Berkowitz. "Scholars, Sects and Sanghas, I: Recruitment to Asian-Based Meditation Groups in North America." *Sociological Analysis* 49(2) (Summer 1988):136–170.

Hasegawa, Atsuko, and Nancy S. Shiraki, eds. *Hosha: A Pictorial History of Jodo Shinshu Women in Hawaii*. Honolulu: Hawaii Federation of Honpa Hongwanji Buddhist Women's Associations, 1989.

Heifetz, Julie Ann. "The Role of the Clergy at the Vietnamese Buddhist Temple in Los Angeles as Culture Brokers in Vietnamese Refugee Resettlement." M.A. thesis, University of Houston, 1980.

Hong, Peter Y. "Tibetan Monks Bring Tranquility to the Mean Streets of Los Angeles." *Los Angeles Times* (17 August 1995):B4.

Honpa Hongwanji Mission of Hawaii. Centennial Publication Committee. *A Grateful Past, A Promising Future: Namu Amida Butsu, 100 Centennial Commemoration, 1889–1989*. Honolulu: Honpa Hongwanji Mission of Hawaii, 1989.

Hori, Victor Sogen. "Sweet-and-Sour Buddhism." *Tricycle: The Buddhist Review* (Fall 1994):48–52. North American Buddhism.

Ichikawa, Akira. "A Test of Religious Tolerance: Canadian Government and Jodo Shinshu Buddhism During the Pacific War, 1941–1945." *Canadian Ethnic Studies* 26(2) (1994):46–69.

Kalab, Milada. "Buddhism and Emotional Support for Elderly People." *Journal of Cross-Cultural Gerontology* 5 (1990):7–19. Role of Theravada Buddhism in the lives of Cambodian elders.

Kashima, Tetsuden. *Buddhism in America: The Social Organization of an Ethnic Religious Institution.* Westport, Conn.: Greenwood Press, 1977.

———. "The Buddhist Churches of America: Challenges for Change in the 21st Century." *Pacific World: Journal of the Institute of Buddhist Studies* 6 (Fall 1990):28–40.

Khmer-Buddhist Educational Assistance Project. *Buddhism and Khmer Society: Three Talks to Khmer Monks and Novices.* Amherst, Mass.: Khmer-Buddhist Educational Assistance Project, 1990. Three sermons by the Venerable Hok Savann of the Pagode Khmer du Canada on reaching Khmer refugees.

Lee, Elisa. "Tricycle Magazine Explores Buddhism's Evolution." *Asian Week* (30 July 1993):1. Buddhism in the United States.

Levin, Claudia, and Lawrence R. Hott. *Rebuilding the Temple: Cambodians in America.* Santa Monica: Florentine Films, 1991. Video documentary.

McLellan, J. "Religion and Ethnicity: The Role of Buddhism in Maintaining Ethnic Identity Among Tibetans in Lindsay, Ontario." *Canadian Ethnic Studies* 19(1) (1987):63–76.

Minatoya, Lydia. *Talking to High Monks in the Snow: An Asian American Odyssey.* New York: HarperCollins, 1992.

Moiliili Hongwanji Mission. *85th Anniversary, 1906–1991: Nurture Today, Hongwanji's Tomorrow.* Honolulu: Moiliili Hongwanji Mission, 1991.

"Monks Put Healing Art on Display." *Los Angeles Times* (6 August 1995):J2. Tibetan Buddhist art.

Morreale, Don, ed. *Buddhist America: Centers, Retreats, Practices.* Santa Fe: John Muir Publications, 1988.

Mortland, Carol A. "Khmer Buddhists in the United States: Ultimate Questions." In *Cambodian Culture Since 1975: Homeland and Exile,* edited by May M. Ebihara, Carol A. Mortland, and Judy Ledgerwood. Ithaca: Cornell University Press, 1994.

Mullens, James G. "Buddhism and the West." *Journal of the Buddhist Council of Canada* 2 (1988).

Mullins, M. R. "The Organizational Dilemmas of Ethnic Churches:

A Case Study of Japanese Buddhism in Canada." *Sociological Analysis* 49 (Fall 1988):217–233.

Nakayama, Takeshi. "Woman Minister Sues Buddhist Churches of America for Sexual Harassment, Discrimination." *Rafu Shimpo* (4 May 1995):1. Ordeal of Rev. Carol Himaka.

Nguyen, Son Xuan. "Evangelization of Vietnamese Buddhist Refugees." D.Min. dissertation, Claremont School of Theology, 1985.

Pais, A. J., and E. Sanders. "Transplanting God: Asian Immigrants Are Building Buddhist and Hindu Temples Across the U.S." *Far Eastern Economic Review* (23 June 1994):34–35.

Pan, Philip P. "Temple Finding Acceptance in Neighborhood." *Los Angeles Times* (29 July 1993):B7. Hsi Lai Temple in Hacienda Heights, Los Angeles County, is the largest Buddhist temple in the western hemisphere.

Phan, Chanh Cong. "The Vietnamese Concept of the Human Soul and the Rituals of Birth and Death." *Southeast Asian Journal of Social Sciences* 21(2) (1993):159–198.

Pitzer, Kurt. "March of the Monks." *Los Angeles Times* (14 September 1994):B1. Members of Wat Thai Temple make weekly procession in North Hollywood.

Santoki, Mark. "Young Buddhist Association Struggles to Make Centennial." *Rafu Shimpo* (18 March 1995):1.

Snow, David Alan. "The Nichiren Shoshu Buddhist Movement in America: A Sociological Examination of the Value Orientation, Recruitment Efforts, and Spread." Ph.D. dissertation, University of California, Los Angeles, 1976.

Sugunasiri, Suwanda H. J. "Buddhist Organizational Unity in Canada." *Karuna: A Journal of Buddhist Meditation* 5 (1988).

———. "Buddhism in Metropolitan Toronto: A Preliminary Overview." *Canadian Ethnic Studies* 21(2) (1989):83–103.

Tuck, Donald. *Buddhist Churches of America: Jodo Shinshu.* Lewiston, N.Y.: Edwin Mellen Press, 1987.

Tworkov, Helen. "The Mushroom Monk: Nyogen Sensaki." *Tricycle: The Buddhist Review* 2(3) (Spring 1993):8–9. Profile of Buddhist monk Nyogen Sensaki who was interned with Japanese Americans during World War II.

———. *Zen in America: Five Teachers and the Search for American Buddhism.* New York: Kodansha, 1994.

Van Esterik, Penny. *Taking Refuge: Lao Buddhists in North America.* Tempe: Program for Southeast Asian Studies, Arizona State University, 1992.

Watada, Terry. *Bukkyo Tozen: A History of Jodo Shinshu Buddhism in Canada, 1905–1995.* Toronto: HpF Press and Toronto Buddhist Church, 1996.

Wilkinson, Stephen L. "Nichiren Shoshu Sokagakkai in America: An Analysis of Ultimate Concerns Between 1960 and 1965." Ph.D. dissertation, University of Iowa, 1975.

Yoo, David. "Enlightened Identities—Buddhism and Japanese Americans of California, 1924–1941." *Western Historical Quarterly* 27(3) (Fall 1996):281–301.

Christianity: Catholicism

Avella, Steven M. "Transformation of Catholic Life in the Twentieth-Century West: The Case of the Diocese of Sacramento, 1929–1957." *California History* 72(2) (Summer 1993):150–169. Includes some information about the Holy Family Japanese Mission in Sacramento during World War II.

Boniog, Emil T. "A Value-Driven Strategy to Plant, Grow, and Multiply Filipino-American Churches in Los Angeles." Ph.D. dissertation, Biola University, 1996.

Crews, Noemi, and Timothy Chan. "A Pictorial History of the Catholic Chinese Center in Los Angeles Chinatown." *Gum Saan Journal* (Chinese Historical Society of Southern California) 13(1) (June 1990):1–23. Photographs with an introduction by Ruby Ling Louie.

Dart, John. "Filipino Services Offer Touch of Home." *Los Angeles Times* (25 December 1993):B4. Filipinos in Los Angeles Catholic archdiocese (425,000) are second-largest ethnic group.

"Is Religion Worth It?" *Tanawin* (January 1993):13. Filipinos and the Catholic church.

LaFleur, Mary Hope. "Catholic Education in Japan as Seen Through the Eyes of Twenty Alumni." M.A. thesis, University of California, Los Angeles, 1994. Interviews with Japanese Americans at Maryknoll Church in Los Angeles.

Lee, E. Mei-Hwa. "Vietnamese Catholics: Making Places in Baton Rouge." M.A. thesis, Louisiana State University, 1990.

Nash, Jesse W. *Vietnamese Catholicism.* Harvey, La.: Art Review Press, 1992. Study of Vietnamese Catholics in New Orleans.

Nordheimer, Jon. "A Different Holiday for Vietnamese Catholics." *New York Times* (23 November 1995):B7(L). Feast of 100 Martyrs.

Olen, Helaine. "Manhattan Catholic School's Vitality Fueled by New Generation of Immigrants." *Los Angeles Times* (7 October 1995):A15. Asian American immigrant enrollment into school.

Pereyra, Lillian A. "The Catholic Church and Portland's Japanese: The Untimely St. Paul Miki School Project." *Oregon Historical Quarterly* 94(4) (Winter 1993–1994):399–434.

Rondineau, Rogatien. "My Ten Years in the Cambodian Catholic Apostolate in the United States: A Missionary's Reflections." *Migration World* 20(4) (1992):26–28.

Saint Ann's Church and School, 1841–1991, 150th Anniversary, a Bright Future, a Proud History. Honolulu: Presentation Press, 1991.

Shen, Louis. "Growing Up in the Church: China and the U.S.A." *America* (23 January 1993):10–12. A Chinese Catholic priest in China and the United States.

St. Raphael's Parish, 1841–1991. Koloa, Hawai'i: Saint Raphael's Church, 1991.

Vaughan, Laurence S. *A Chronicle of the Maryknoll Fathers and Brothers in Hawaii, February 4, 1927–September 1, 1990.* Maryknoll, N.Y.: Maryknoll Fathers and Brothers, 1990.

Walker, Maria J. "A Song in South Philadelphia: St. Thomas Aquinas Church." *Migration World* 20(3) (1992):25–27. Vietnamese refugees and the Catholic Church.

Weber, Rev. Francis. "Christ on Wilshire." *TM Weekly Herald* (10 November 1989):23. History of St. Basil's Church in Los Angeles, a church with Pilipino members.

Christianity: Protestantism

Ahn, Yoo Kwang. "The Usefulness of Selected Programs in the Contemporary Christian Family Life Movement for Korean Family Life in New York City." Ph.D. dissertation, New York University, 1986.

Appleby, Jerry L. *The Church in a Stew: Developing Multicongregational Churches*. Kansas City, Mo.: Beacon Hill Press, 1990.

Au, May, and Cynthia Ping. "A New Testament: Towards a Culturally Inclusive Christianity." *Slant: UC Berkeley's Asian Pacific Newsmagazine* (April 1992):17.

Baglo, Ferdy. "Chinese Ministry in Canada." *Canadian Lutheran* 2(2) (February 1987):12–15.

Baluarte, Librado L. "A Ministry to Filipino-Americans." Ph.D. dissertation, United Theological Seminary, 1989.

Brock, Rita Nakashima. "On Mirrors, Mists, Murmurs, and the Way Toward an Asian American 'Theology.'" *Drew Gateway* 58 (Spring 1989):65–81.

Busch, Briton C. "Whalemen, Missionaries, and the Practice of Christianity in the Nineteenth-Century Pacific." *Hawaiian Journal of History* 27 (1993):91–118.

Cang, Ruth. "Cultural Adaptive Styles and Mental Health Attitudes of Chinese-American Christians." Psych.D. dissertation, Rosemead Graduate School of Professional Psychology, 1980.

Capps, Lisa Louise. "Concepts of Health and Illness of the Protestant Hmong." Ph.D. dissertation, University of Kansas, 1991.

Carvajal, Doreen. "Trying to Halt 'Silent Exodus.'" *Los Angeles Times* (9 May 1994):A1. Korean American ministers reach out to keep younger immigrants as church members.

Chan, Kim Man. "Mandarins in America: The Early Chinese Ministers to the United States, 1878–1907." Ph.D. dissertation, University of Hawai'i, 1981.

Chan, Samuel Sum-yee. "Growing Chinese Boomer Churches in Toronto." D.Min. dissertation, Fuller Theological Seminary, 1991.

Chandler, Russell. "Churches Reach Out to Asian-Americans." *Los Angeles Times* (11 August 1991):B1. Profile of True Light Chinese Presbyterian Church in Los Angeles and Evergreen Baptist Church in Rosemead, California.

Chang, Ryun. "Korean Churches in Los Angeles Metropolis in Relation to Present Status and Future Prospects." M.A. thesis, University of California, Los Angeles, 1989.

Chao, Samuel H. "The Ethnic and Cultural Role of the Chinese Church in North America." *Chinese Around the World* (Hong Kong) (January 1988):5–8.

Bibliography

Chen, Noah. "Evaluation and Projection of the Ministry of the Chinese Christian Church in Metuchen, New Jersey." D.Min. dissertation, Drew University, 1978.

Cho, Brandon Inkyun. "Towards an Authentic Korean-American Worship." D.Min. dissertation, Claremont School of Theology, 1987.

Cho, Kun-Kap. "The Possible Faith Formation in the Experience of the Asian American Community." Ph.D. dissertation, Claremont School of Theology, 1985.

Cho, Sung-Whan. "Personal and Spiritual Growth of a Korean-American Congregation." D.Min. dissertation, Drew University, 1984.

Choe, Asbury Jongsu. "The Development of Guidelines for the Transgenerational Summer Internship Program of the Korean-American United Methodist Churches." D.Min. dissertation, Eastern Baptist Theological Seminary, 1987.

Choi, Jong E. "Comparison of Childrearing Attitudes Between Church-Related Korean American Immigrant Parents and Korean Parents." Ph.D. dissertation, University of North Texas, 1992.

Choi, Tom. "Christian Love: Homosexuality and the Church." *KoreAm Journal* (August 1993):14.

Chung, Do-ryang. "A Study of the Korean Immigrant Church Growth Through the Bible Study Movement." Ph.D. dissertation, Fuller Theological Seminary, 1988.

Church of the Holy Cross. *Church of the Holy Cross: One Hundred and Beyond, 1891–1991.* Hilo, Hawai'i: Church of the Holy Cross, 1991.

Churches Aflame: Asian Americans and United Methodism. Nashville: Abingdon Press, 1991.

Codman-Wilson, Mary L. "Thai Cultural and Religious Identity and Understanding of Well-Being in the U.S.: An Ethnographic Study of an Immigrant Church." Ph.D. dissertation, Garrett Evangelical Theological Seminary, 1992.

"Comprehensive View of the Korean American Churches." *KoreAm Journal* (5 March 1991):13–30. Series of articles on the role of the church in the Korean community.

Connor, John Harold. "A Relationship Study Between the Wesleyan

Church and the Los Angeles Based Korean Wesleyan Churches."
M.Th. thesis, Fuller Theological Seminary, 1986.

Cornell, George W. "Most Americans Identify with Christian Faiths."
Los Angeles Times (5 March 1991):F15. Reports results from ICR
Survey Research Group of Media, Pennsylvania, that 86.5 percent
of Americans identify with Christian denominations and that
most Asian Americans are also Christians.

Dabagh, Jean L., and Suzanne Espenett Case. *Central Union Church,
1887–1988, Honolulu, Hawaii: One Hundred One Years.* Honolulu: Central Union Church, 1988.

Dart, John. "Korean Congregations May Break with Church." *Los
Angeles Times* (21 August 1993):B4. Ministers are angered by
Christian Reformed Church's move to ordain women; 1,400-
member Los Angeles Korean Christian Reformed Church—second largest congregation in the 311,000-member denomination—
may secede.

*The Diversity of Discipleship: Presbyterians and Twentieth-Century
Christian Witnesses.* Louisville, Ky.: Westminster/John Knox
Press, 1991. Includes essays by Michael J. Kimura Angevine and
Ryo Yoshida, "Contexts for a History of Asian-American Presby-
terian Churches: A Case Study of Japanese-American Presbyte-
rians' Early History"; and Sang Hyun Lee, "Korean-American
Presbyterians: A Need for Ethnic Particularity and the Challenge
of Christian Pilgrimage."

Engh, Michael E. "A Most Excellent Field for Work: Christian Missionary Efforts in the Los Angeles Chinese Community,
1870–1900." *Gum Saan Journal* (Chinese Historical Society of
Southern California) (June 1992):1–15.

Evangelical Lutheran Church in America. *Report on Multicultural
Mission Strategy.* Chicago: Commission for Multicultural Ministry, Evangelical Lutheran Church in America, 1991.

Fein, Helen. *Congregational Sponsors of Indochinese Refugees in the
United States, 1979–1981.* Cranbury, N.J.: Fairleigh Dickinson
University Press, 1987.

Fong, Jessica Yi Ping. "Faith: A Multifarious Blend." *Momentum*
(University of California, San Diego) (February–March 1994):10.
Asian Pacific American churches in San Diego.

Fong, Kenneth James Uyeda. "Insights for Growing Asian-American Ministries." D.Min. dissertation, Fuller Theological Seminary, 1990.

———. "On the Need to Dispel 'Model Minority' Myth." *Los Angeles Times* (20 December 1993):B5. Asian American Christians and the "model minority" myth.

Frank, Kurt Weldemar. "The Resettlement of a Vietnamese Refugee Family by the Drexel Hill Baptist Church (a Case Study)." D.Min. dissertation, Eastern Baptist Theological Seminary, 1978.

Gallagher, Mark Edward. "No More a Christian Nation: The Protestant Church in Territorial Hawaii, 1898–1919." Ph.D. dissertation, University of Hawai'i, 1983.

Hagiya, Grant John. "Japanese-Americans and the Christian Church: The Struggle for Identity and Existence." D.Min. dissertation, Claremont School of Theology, 1978.

Harris, Scott Collins. "Korean Church Growth in America, 1903–1990: History and Analysis." Ph.D. dissertation, Southwestern Baptist Theological Seminary, 1990.

Hayashi, Brian Masaru. "The Untold Story of Nikkei Baptists in Southern California, 1913–1924." *Foundations* 22 (October–December 1979):313–323.

———. *"For the Sake of Our Japanese Brethren": Assimilation, Nationalism, and Protestantism Among the Japanese of Los Angeles, 1895–1942.* Stanford: Stanford University Press, 1995.

Hertig, Young Lee. "The Role of Power in the Korean Immigrant Family and Church." Ph.D. dissertation, Fuller Theological Seminary, 1991.

Ho, Phu Xuan. "The Christian Ministries to the Vietnamese Refugees in Orange County, California." D.Min. dissertation, Claremont School of Theology, 1986.

Hole, J. Wesley. "History of the Los Angeles Chinese United Methodist Church." *Gum Saan Journal* (Chinese Historical Society of Southern California) (December 1990):11–19. Excerpts from the church's one hundredth anniversary book.

Hsu, Chung-Chang David. "The Mission Strategic Analysis of Taiwanese Church in North America: A Case Study of Evangelical Formosan Church." Th.M. dissertation, Fuller Theological Seminary, 1990.

Hurh, Won Moo, and Kwang Chun Kim. "Religious Participation

of Korean Immigrants in the United States." *Journal for the Scientific Study of Religion* 29(1) (March 1990):19–34.

Inglis, David Jackson. "Change and Continuity in Samoan Religion: The Role of the Congregational Christian Church." Ph.D. dissertation, University of New South Wales, Australia, 1993.

"Jitsuo Morikawa: Prophetic and Proactive." *American Baptist Quarterly* 12(2) (June 1993). Special theme issue on the impact of the late Japanese Canadian minister; includes commentaries by Paul M. Nagano and Lloyd K. Wake.

Jordan, Philip D. "Immigrants, Methodists and a 'Conservative' Social Gospel, 1865–1908." *Methodist History* 17(1) (1978):16–43. Includes discussion of the attitudes of Methodist missionaries toward China and the church's subsequent position on Chinese emigration to the United States.

Jun, Sung Pyo. "Power Relations in Churches: Bases of Power and Motivations for Striving for Power in American and Korean Churches." Ph.D. dissertation, University of Minnesota, 1991. Study of immigrant churches.

Jun, Yong Jai. "A Holistic Evangelization of Korean Churches in the Los Angeles Area." D.Min. dissertation, Claremont School of Theology, 1984.

Kanda, Michael T. "Faith and Fellowship." *Pacific Ties: UCLA's Asian Pacific Islander Newsmagazine* (February 1994):3. Asian American Christian fellowships at UCLA.

Kang, K. Connie. "Church Provides One-Stop Center for Koreans' Needs." *Los Angeles Times* (23 October 1992):A1. Profile of Young Nak Presbyterian Church of Los Angeles and its seven thousand members, the largest Korean American church in the United States.

Kasmin, Barry A., and Seymour P. Lachman. *One Nation Under God: Religion in Contemporary American Society.* New York: Harmony Books, 1993. Includes data on Asian American religious affiliations; states that Protestants account for the largest number of churchgoers (33.6 percent).

Kastens, Dennis A. "Nineteenth Century Chinese Christian Missions in Hawaii." *Hawaiian Journal of History* 12 (1978):61–67.

Katz, Nathan. *Tampa Bay's Asian-Origin Religious Communities.* Tampa: National Conference of Christians and Jews, 1991.

Kennedy, John W. "Mission Force Looking More Asian in Future." *Christianity Today* 38(2) (7 February 1994):48–49. Asian American attendance increasing at InterVarsity Christian Fellowship mission conference.

Kim, Ai Ra. "The Religious Factor in the Adaptation of Korean Immigrant 'Ilse' Women to Life in America." Ph.D. dissertation, Drew University, 1991.

Kim, Dae Gee. "Major Factors Conditioning the Acculturation of Korean-Americans with Respect to the Presbyterian Church in America and Its Missionary Obedience." Ph.D. dissertation, Fuller Theological Seminary, School of World Mission, 1985.

Kim, Hae-Jong. "Use of Class Meeting for Unifying Pastoral Ministry and for Church Growth in the Korean-American Immigrant Churches." D.Min. dissertation, Drew University, 1984.

Kim, Han G. "Changing Values of Korean Immigrant Churches in Southern California." M.A. thesis, California State University, Chico, 1982.

Kim, Illsoo. "Problems of Immigrant Society and the Role of the Church with Reference to the Korean Immigrant Community in America." *Korea Observer* 7(4) (1976):398–431.

———. "Organizational Patterns of Korean-American Methodist Churches: Denominationalism and Personal Community." In *Rethinking Methodist History,* edited by Russell Richey and Kenneth E. Rowe. Nashville: United Methodist Publishing House, 1985.

Kim, Jung Ha. *Bridge-Makers and Cross-Bearers: Korean-American Women and the Church.* Atlanta: Scholars Press, 1997.

Kim, Kerry Y. "The Role of Korean Protestant Immigrant Churches in the Acculturation of Korean Immigrants in Southern California." Ph.D. dissertation, University of Southern California, 1992.

Kim, Kwang Suh. "The Effectiveness of Sessions in Korean Immigrant Churches in Southern California." D.Min. dissertation, Claremont School of Theology, 1983.

Kim, Mikyoung. "Korean-American Clergymen's Views on Mental Health and Treatment." Ph.D. dissertation, University of California, Berkeley, 1990.

Kim, Nak-In. "A Model Ministry to Transitional and Second Generation Korean-Americans." D.Min. dissertation, Claremont

School of Theology, 1992. Focuses on Korean United Methodist Church in Los Angeles, California.

Kim, Paul Soung-Wook. "Developing and Conducting a Membership Training Course for Members of the North United Methodist Church's Korean Congregation in Indianapolis." D.Min. dissertation, Drew University, 1981.

Kim, Sang-Mo. "A Process of Growth in Christian Experience Through Small Group Sharing and Searching: For Constituent Members in a Korean-American Congregation." D.Min dissertation, Drew University, 1979.

Kim, Stephen K. "Pastoral Care to Asian American Families." *Military Chaplains' Review* (Summer 1992):19–28.

Kim, Woong-Min. "History and Ministerial Roles of Korean Churches in the Los Angeles Area." D.Min. dissertation, Claremont School of Theology, 1981.

Kim, Yong Choon. "The Nature and Destiny of Korean Churches in the United States." *Journal of Social Science and Humanities* (Republic of Korea) 67 (1989):33–47.

Klootwijk, Eeuwout. "Christian Approaches to Religious Pluralism: Diverging Models and Patterns." *Missiology: An International Review* 21(4) (October 1993):455–468. Special theme issue.

Kung, Peter. "The Story of Asian Southern Baptists." *Baptist History and Heritage* 18(1) (1983):49–58.

Kuramoto, Mary Ishii. *Dendo: One Hundred Years of Japanese Christians in Hawaii and the Nuuanu Congregational Church.* Honolulu: Nuuanu Congregational Church, 1986.

Kusel, Ronald Julius. "Church Growth Plans in a Multicultural Setting: First Lutheran Church of Long Beach." Ph.D. dissertation, Fuller Theological Seminary, 1990. Includes a chapter on "cross-cultural" ministries to Cambodia refugees in California.

Kwak, Rev. Dong Chang. "Mending Broken Immigrant Lives." *Los Angeles Times* (24 June 1995):B7. Korean immigrant minister takes up issues relating to elderly Korean homeless.

Kwon, Oh-Dal. "The Growth of the Korean Church in America." M.Th. thesis, Fuller Theological Seminary, 1986.

Kwon-Ahn, Young Hee. "The Korean Protestant Church: The Role in Service Delivery for Korean Immigrants." D.S.W. dissertation, Columbia University, 1987.

Kyung, Chung Hyun. *Struggle to Be the Sun Again: Introducing Asian Women's Theology*. Maryknoll, N.Y.: Orbis Books, 1990.

Lee, Chang Soon. "Growth Ministry in Korean Immigrant Churches." D.Min. dissertation, Claremont School of Theology, 1978.

Lee, Chull. "Social Sources of the Rapid Growth of the Christian Church in Northwest Korea: 1895–1910." Ph.D. dissertation, Boston University, 1997.

Lee, D. John, and Mark Kane. "Multicultural Counseling: A Christian Appraisal." *Journal of Psychology and Christianity* 11(4) (Winter 1992):317–325.

Lee, Elizabeth, and Kenneth A. Abbot. "Chinese Pilgrims and Presbyterians in the U.S. 1851–1977." *Journal of Presbyterian History* 55 (Summer 1977): 125–144.

Lee, John Keunyung. "Developing a Lay Ministry to Increase Pastoral Care Services to an Immigrant Korean Church Community." D.Min. dissertation, Drew University, 1984.

Lee, Joon-Young. "New Church Development Strategy: A Case of Collegial Ministry of a Clergy Couple." D.Min. dissertation, Claremont School of Theology, 1987. Study of Korean-American clergy.

Lee, Jung Young. "Search for a Theological Paradigm: An Asian-American Journey." *Quarterly Review: A Scholarly Journal for Reflection on Ministry* 9 (Spring 1989):36–47.

Lee, Samuel K. "Pros and Cons of English-Only Korean American Churches." *KoreAm Journal* (7 December 1990):36.

Lee, Soon Jung. "The Role of the Korean Immigrant Church in the United States for Contemporary World Mission." M.Th. thesis, Fuller Theological Seminary, 1983.

Lee, Warren W. *A Dream for South Central: The Autobiography of an Afro-Americanized Korean Christian Minister*. San Anselmo, Calif.: Advanced Pastoral Studies, San Francisco Theological Seminary, 1993.

Liestman, Daniel. "'To Win Redeemed Souls from Heathen Darkness': Protestant Response to the Chinese of the Pacific Northwest in the Late Nineteenth Century." *Western Historical Quarterly* 24 (May 1993):179–202.

Lim, Hakchoon. "A Proposed Liturgical Model of 'Chumorye' for

Korean United Methodist Churches in America." D.Min. dissertation, Claremont School of Theology, 1996.

Liu, Chao-Ying. "The Structure of Chinese Church in Los Angeles Area." M.A. thesis, Fuller Theological Seminary, School of World Mission, 1991.

Liu, Felix Fu-Li. "A Comparative Study of Selected Growing Chinese Churches in Los Angeles County." D.Miss. dissertation, Fuller Theological Seminary, School of World Mission, 1981.

Lundell, In-Gyeong Kim. *Bridging the Gaps: Contextualization Among Korean Nazarene Churches in America*. New York: P. Lang, 1995.

MacPhail, Elizabeth C. "San Diego's Chinese Mission." *Journal of San Diego History* 23 (Spring 1977):9–21.

Maefau, Mila. "The Samoan Churches in Southern California: Their Needs, Development, and Search for Identity." D.Min. dissertation, Claremont School of Theology, 1977.

Maffly-Kipp, Laurie F. *Religion and Society in Frontier California*. New Haven: Yale University Press, 1994. Information about early Chinese immigrants.

Mark, Diane Mei Lin. *Seasons of Light: The History of Chinese Christian Churches in Hawaii*. Honolulu: Chinese Christian Association of Hawai'i, 1989.

Marocco, James Dwight. "Dealing with Demonic as a Dimension of Growth of First Assembly of God, Maui (Hawaii)." D.Min. dissertation, Fuller Theological Seminary, 1988.

Maxwell, Carol J. C. "White Like Them: Asian Refugees in a White Christian Congregation." *City and Society* 3(2) (December 1989): 153–164. Study of Laotian refugees in an evangelical church in St. Louis, Missouri.

Menton, Linda K. "A Christian and 'Civilized' Education: The Hawaiian Chief's Children's School, 1839–50." *History of Education Quarterly* 32 (Summer 1992):213–242.

Miller, Char, ed. *Missions and Missionaries in the Pacific*. New York: Edwin Mellen Press, 1985.

Min, Pyong Gap. "The Structure and Social Functions of Korean Immigrant Churches in the United States." *International Migration Review* 26(4) (Winter 1992):1370–1394.

Misumi, Diane M. "Asian-American Christian Attitudes Towards

Counseling." *Journal of Psychology and Christianity* 12(3) (Fall 1993):214–224.

Mizuki, Rie Honda. "Differential Components of Assertiveness in Asian-American Christians." Ph.D. dissertation, Fuller Theological Seminary, 1991.

Mochizuki, Ken. "Reasons for Attending Nikkei Churches Change Over the Years." *Northwest Nikkei* (June 1993):1.

Mondello, Salvatore. "The Integration of Japanese Baptists in American Society." *Foundations* 20 (July–September 1977):254–263.

Morikawa, Jitsuo. "Toward an Asian American Theology." *American Baptist Quarterly* 12(2) (June 1993):179–189.

Moyer, Linda Lancione. "From Laos to Oakland: Personal Perspective." *Christianity and Crisis* 46 (1986):334–345.

Murakami, May. "Ethnic Hymnody in Asian American Churches." *Reformed Liturgy and Music* 21 (Summer 1987):154–155.

Nagano, Paul M. "Out of the Shadows: A New Chapter in Pacific Rim and Asian American Stories for the Journey." *American Baptist Quarterly* 10 (June 1991):137–147.

Nagata, Judith. "Is Multiculturalism Sacred? The Power Behind the Pulpit in the Religious Congregation of Southeast Asian Christians in Canada." *Canadian Ethnic Studies* 19(2) (1987):26–43.

Nam, Moon Hee. "The Role of the Korean Immigrant Church for the Korean Bilingual/Bicultural Education in the Los Angeles Area." D.Min. dissertation, Claremont School of Theology, 1984.

National Council of Churches. *Indicators of Institutional Racism, Sexism and Classism.* New York: National Council of Churches, n.d.

National Council of the Churches of Christ. "Growth of Korean American Christian Churches." *NCCC Newsletter* (January 1987). Data on Korean American Christian churches during the past ten years.

Neves, Paul K. "Na Huihui a Makali'i (The Cluster of Little Eyes)." *Mission Studies* 10(1–2) (1992):15–22. Hawaiian sovereignty and the church.

Ng, David. *People on the Way: Asian North Americans Discovering Christ, Culture, and Community.* Valley Forge, Pa.: Judson Press, 1996.

Ng, G. A. "Family and Education from an Asian North American

Perspective: Implications for the Church's Educational Ministry."
Religious Education 87(4) (Winter 1992):52–61.

———. "Toward Wholesome Nurture: Challenges in the Religious
Education of Asian North-American Female Christians." *Religious
Education* 91(2) (Spring 1996):238–254.

Ng, Johnny. "1850–1989, Growth of Chinese Churches." *Asian Week*
(8 September 1989):14. Chinese churches in San Francisco.

Ng, John Lai. "Cultural Pluralism and Ministry Models in the Chinese Community." D.Min. dissertation, Fuller Theological Seminary, 1985.

Nisei Christian Oral History Project. *Nisei Christian Journey: Its
Promise and Fulfillment*. San Francisco: Japanese Presbyterian
Conference and Northern California Japanese Christian Church
Federation, 1988.

———. *Nisei Christian Journey: Its Promise and Fulfillment*. Vol. 2.
San Francisco: Japanese Presbyterian Conference and Northern
California Japanese Christian Church Federation, 1991.

Oden, T. C. "Manhattan's Cloud of Witnesses." *Christianity Today*
37 (19 July 1993):13. Chinese Methodist Church.

Paek, Woon Young. "Worldview Change and the Korean-American
Youth Ministry in the Korean Immigrant Church." D.Min dissertation, Fuller Theological Seminary, 1989.

Pai, Hyo Shick. "Korean Congregational Church of Los Angeles:
The Bilingual Ministry and Its Impact on Church Growth."
D.Min. dissertation, Fuller Theological Seminary, 1987.

Paiva, Carlos. "The Talk of the Community." *City Times* section of
Los Angeles Times (9 October 1994):23. Angelia Lutheran Church
in Los Angeles offers services to five language groups, including
Koreans.

Palinkas, L. A. *Rhetoric and Religious Experience: The Discourse of
Immigrant Chinese Churches*. Fairfax, Va.: George Mason University Press, 1989.

Park, Jang Kyun. "A Study on the Growth of the Korean Church in
Southern California." D.Min. dissertation, Claremont School of
Theology, 1979.

Park, Kwang Ja. "A Challenge for Cross-Cultural Mission Among
Korean-American Churches." D.Miss. dissertation, Fuller Theological Seminary, 1992.

Park, Sharon. "New Directions: Church Works for Better Relations Between Korean and African Communities." *Pacific Ties: UCLA's Asian and Pacific Islander Newsmagazine* (April 1993):47.

Pascoe, Peggy. "Gender Systems in Conflict: The Marriages of Mission-Educated Chinese American Women, 1874–1939." *Journal of Social History* 22(4) (Summer 1989):631–652.

Pouesi, Daniel I. "The Samoan Church: Is It Losing Touch?" *Malama* (Summer 1987):7–17.

Prieto, Jaime Guerrero. "The Development of a Filipino Ministry in Honolulu with the Hawaii Baptist Convention." D.Min. dissertation, Eastern Baptist Theological Seminary, 1986.

Rauchholz, Roland Albert. "Strategy to Produce Mission-Oriented Churches in Micronesia." Ph.D. dissertation, Biola University, 1989.

Rhee, Amos Seung-Woon. "Stabilizing and Vitalizing the Church Membership of Central Korean Church of Yonkers, New York." Ph.D. dissertation, Drew University, 1981.

Riccardi, Nicholas. "Congregants Mourn Church's Latest Fire." *Los Angeles Times* (29 June 1994):B1. Wilshire United Methodist Church in Los Angeles has eight services every Sunday in four languages—English, Korean, Spanish, and Tagalog.

Rim, Joseph Byong-Gin. "A Comparison of the 'Word and Life' Church School Curriculum of the Korean Presbyterian General Assembly with the United States of America 'Living the Word' Church School Curriculum of Joint Educational Development, 'Christian Education: Shared Approaches.'" Ph.D. dissertation, New York University, 1991.

Sanjek, Roger, ed. *Worship and Community: Christianity and Hinduism in Contemporary Queens.* Flushing: Asian/American Center, Queens College, City University of New York, 1991.

Sasaki, Shiro J. "Various Problems and Biblical Solutions Facing the Japanese Ministry in the Pacific Northwest." D.Min. dissertation, Western Conservative Baptist Seminary, 1984.

Shin, E. H., and H. Park. "An Analysis of Causes of Schisms in Ethnic Churches: The Case of Korean-American Churches." *Sociological Analysis* 49 (Fall 1988):234–248.

Shoaf, Norman L. "Christians Must Challenge Racism." *Plain Truth* (February 1993):14–20.

Silva, Glenn. "A Comparative Study of the Hymnody of Two Hawaiian Protestant Denominations: Ho'omana Ia Iesu and Ho'omana Na'auao." Ph.D. dissertation, University of Washington, 1989.

Smith-Hefner, N. J. "Ethnicity and the Force of Faith: Christian Conversion and Khmer Refugees." *Anthropology Quarterly* 67 (January 1994):24–34.

So, Anthony Ping-kam. "Church-Based Marriage Enrichment Program for Chinese New Immigrant Couples: Ministry and Evangelistic Dimension." D.Min. dissertation, Fuller Theological Seminary, 1992.

Stepp, Theodore J. "Serving Samoan Youth in Honolulu: Culture, Religious Education, and Social Adjustment." M.A. thesis, University of Hawai'i, 1989.

Stone, Holly. "'The Proper Way to Pray': Description of a Korean-American Youth Service Prayer." *Working Papers in Educational Linguistics* 8(2) (Fall 1992):89–105.

Taillez, Daniel. "A New Heart: Hmong Christians in America." *Migration World* 21(2–3) (1993):36–38.

Tapp, Nicholas. "The Impact of Missionary Christianity upon Marginalized Ethnic Minorities: The Case of the Hmong." *Journal of Southeast Asian Studies* 20(1) (1989):70–95.

Tsia, Andrew Ing-shih. "A Five-Year Church Growth Plan for the South Pasadena (California) Chinese Baptist Church." Ph.D. dissertation, Fuller Theological Seminary, 1989.

Ukosakul, Chaiyun. "A Study of the Patterns of Detachment in Interpersonal Relationships in a Local Thai Church (Christian)." Ph.D. dissertation, Trinity Evangelical Divinity School, 1994.

Vergara, Alex Ravelo. "Filipino Ministry in Hawaii: Past, Present and Future." D.Min. dissertation, Claremont School of Theology, 1986.

———, ed. *Waves, 1888–1988: The United Methodist Church of Hawaii: A Centennial Jubilee.* Koloa, Hawai'i: Taylor Publishing, 1988.

Vinluan, Vivencio L. "A Design for an Intentional Ministry for Filipinos in Southern California." D.Min. dissertation, Claremont School of Theology, 1979.

Williams, Raymond Brady. *Christian Pluralism in the United States:*

The Indian Immigrant Experience. New York: Cambridge University Press, 1996.

Winland, Daphne N. "Christianity and Community: Conversion and Adaptation Among Hmong Refugee Women." *Canadian Journal of Sociology* 19(1) (Winter 1994):21–45.

Wong, David. "A Church Planter's Manual for Chinese Churches in America." D.Min. dissertation, Trinity Evangelical Divinity School, 1984.

Woo, Wesley. "Presbyterian Mission: Christianizing and Civilizing the Chinese in Nineteenth Century California." *American Presbyterians* 68 (Fall 1990):167–178.

Yamada, Yutaka. "Purifying the Living and Purifying the Dead: Narratives of Religious Experience of Japanese-Americans and Caucasian Members of World Messianity, Los Angeles, California." Ph.D. dissertation, University of North Carolina, 1984.

Yeung, Alexander Kwok-wing. "Toward a Strategy for Developing a Ministry to the Canadian Born Chinese in the Context of the Chinese Immigrant Family." D.Min. dissertation, Fuller Theological Seminary, 1987.

Yiu, Nelson K. "Contextualizing Pastoral Care and Evangelism to Reach a North American Chinese Community: Using Laity in Premarital Preparation." D.Min. dissertation, North American Baptist Seminary, 1990.

Yoo, Hwa-Ja. "Differences in Selected Cultural Values and Religiosity Between Christian Korean Adults and College-Age Young People, and Christian Komerican Adults and College-Age Young People." Ph.D. dissertation, Biola University, Talbot School of Theology, 1993.

Yoo, Jae-Yoo. "A Study of Preaching in Four Growing Korean Immigrant Churches." Ph.D. dissertation, Claremont School of Theology, 1993.

Yoo, Tai Young. "Walking on a Narrow Way: Shaping a Model of Ministry for the Korean-American Church." Ph.D. dissertation, Drew University, 1992.

Yoshida, Ryo. "A Socio-Historical Study of Racial/Ethnic Identity in the Inculturated Religious Expression of Japanese Christianity in San Francisco, 1877–1924." D.Th. dissertation, Graduate Theological Union, 1989.

Zackrison, James Willard. "Multiethnic/Multicultural Ministry in the 1990s: With Special Emphasis on the Seventh-Day Adventist Church in North America." D.Min. dissertation, Fuller Theological Seminary, 1991.

Hinduism

Barot, Surendra P., and Tarulata S. Barot. "Changing Patterns of Hindu Marriages in Foreign Lands." M.A. thesis, California State University, Dominguez Hills, 1987. Focuses on Hindus in Southern California.

Dhruvarajan, Vanaja. "Conjugal Power Among First Generation Hindu Asian Indians in a Canadian City." *International Journal of Sociology of the Family* 22(1) (Spring 1992):1–33.

Faris, Gerald. "Hindus' Plan for Temple in Norwalk Encounters Unfriendly Neighbors." *Los Angeles Times* (21 July 1992):B3. Controversy surrounding proposed temple in Los Angeles County community.

Goa, David J., Harold G. Coward, and Ronald Neufeldt. "Hindus in Alberta: A Study in Religious Continuity and Change." *Canadian Ethnic Studies* 16 (1984):96–113.

Gottesman, Jill. "East Meets West: Hindu Congregation Wins OK for Temple by Adopting Mission Design." *Los Angeles Times* (22 July 1994):B1. Controversy regarding proposed temple in Norwalk in Los Angeles County.

Martin, Claudia E. "Oranges and Peanuts: Latino Immigrants Working to Survive." *Pacific Ties: UCLA's Asian and Pacific Islander Newsmagazine* (April 1993):10–11. Growth of anti-immigrant sentiment in Los Angeles.

Mehta, Mahesh J. "Hindus in the United States of America." *VHP Newsletter* 5 (Winter 1990):1–3.

Narayan, Kirin. "Refractions of the Field at Home: Hindu Holy Men in America in the Nineteenth and Twentieth Centuries." *Cultural Anthropology* 8 (1993):476–509.

Nye, Malory. "Temple Constructions and Communities: Hindu Constructions in Edinburgh." *New Community* 19(2) (January 1993):201–215.

Pais, A. J., and E. Sanders. "Transplanting God: Asian Immigrants Are Building Buddhist and Hindu Temples Across the U.S." *Far Eastern Economic Review* (23 June 1994):34–35.

Parekh, Bhikhu. "The Living Ramayana: 'Cultural Text of Overseas Hindus.'" *Little India* (April 1994):30–34.

———. "Some Reflections on the Hindu Diaspora." *New Community* 20(4) (July 1994):603–620.

Pattabhiram, B. "Hindu Temple Priests in America." *Hinduism Today* 8 (November–December 1986).

"Popularity of Hinduism, Related Teachings Rises in U.S." *Los Angeles Times* (12 August 1995):B4.

Sanjek, Roger, ed. *Worship and Community: Christianity and Hinduism in Contemporary Queens.* Flushing: Asian/American Center, Queens College, City University of New York, 1991.

Tallapragada, Sridhar. "Hindu Revival Stirs College Campuses." *Little India* (June 1994):10–24.

van der Veer, P., and S. Vertovec. "Brahmanism Abroad: On Caribbean Hinduism as an Ethnic Religion." *Ethnology* 30 (April 1991): 149–166.

Vertovic, Steven. "Religion and Ethnic Ideology: The Hindu Youth Movement in Trinidad." *Ethnic and Racial Studies* 13(2) (April 1990):225–249.

Williams, Raymond B. *Religions of Immigrants from India and Pakistan: New Threads in the American Tapestry.* New York: Cambridge University Press, 1988.

Islam

Barboza, Steven. *American Jihad: Islam After Malcolm X.* New York: Doubleday, 1994.

Buchsbaum, Herbert. "Islam in America." *Scholastic Update* (22 October 1993):15–16.

Dart, John. "A Closer Look at Islam in the West." *Los Angeles Times* (10 December 1994):B4. Nearly 80 percent of the 1,046 Muslim congregations in the United States and Canada were formed in the past twenty-five years, according to a survey directed by the Islamic Resource Institute of Fountain Valley, California.

————. "State's 1st Muslim Library Reopens in Canoga Park." *Los Angeles Times* (31 January 1995):B1. Muslim Public Library in San Fernando Valley has a collection of more than 2,000 books, magazines, and videotapes.

Dawoodjee, Aisha. "East to West: Chinese Muslims Claim Islam Was More Visible in China." *Al-Talib: The Muslim Newsmagazine at UCLA* (June 1992):11. Chinese Muslims in Southern California.

Deshpande, Shekhar. "Demonizing Islam." *Little India* (March 1995):63–64.

Dev, Nisha. "Cham Muslims Escape Religious Persecution: Cambodian and Vietnamese Make a New Start in Southern California." *Al-Talib: The Muslim Newsmagazine at UCLA* (June 1992):10.

Haddad, Yvonne Zazbeck, ed. *The Muslims of America.* New York: Oxford University Press, 1991.

Haddad, Yvonne Yazbeck, and Jane Idleman Smith. *Mission to America: Five Islamic Sectarian Communities in North America.* Gainesville: University Press of Florida, 1993. Includes information about Pakistani and Indian Muslims in the United States.

Huda, Qamarul. "Silent Majority of the Muslim World: The Largest Muslim Group in the World Preserves Its Cultural Identity in the U.S." *Al-Talib: The Muslim Newsmagazine at UCLA* (June 1992):14. Indonesian Muslims in Los Angeles.

Islam, Naheed. "Belly of the Multicultural Beast." *Little India* (August 1994):56–59. Need for Indian Americans to examine their own hegemonic role in the region and the United States.

Malla, Muhammad Akil. "Dietary Changes of Muslims in the United States." Ph.D. dissertation, Washington State University, 1990. Study of Muslims from Bangladesh, India, Indonesia, Malaysia, and Pakistan.

Mateen, Bushra Gohar. "I Take My Religion Seriously." *Pakistan Link* (19 April–2 May 1992):26. A Pakistani-American's perspective on Islam.

"Muslims in America: Can They Find a Place in American Society?" *CQ Quarterly* (30 April 1993). Special theme issue; 24.4 percent of Muslims in the United States are South Asians.

Njeri, Itabari. "Chinese Muslims Struggle to Forge Distinct Identity." *Los Angeles Times* (6 September 1990):E1. Chinese Muslims in the United States.

Quick, Abdullah Hakim. "Muslim Rituals, Practices and Social Problems in Ontario." *Polyphony: The Bulletin of the Multicultural History Society on Ontario* 12 (1990):120–124.

Quraishi, Ibrahim. "Will Islam Ever Merit 'PC' Protection?" *Los Angeles Times* (1 June 1995):B7.

Rizvi, Talha. "An Island of Islam: It Ain't No Club Med." *C/S, Con Safos* (Summer 1995):12–13. Muslim youth in Los Angeles.

Wormser, Richard. *American Islam: Growing Up Muslim in America*. New York: Walker, 1995.

305

Mormonism

Bishop, M. Guy. "Waging Holy War: Mormon-Congregationalist Conflict in Mid-Nineteenth-Century Hawaii." *Journal of Mormon History* 17 (1991):110–119.

Britsch, R. Lanier. *Moramona, the Mormons in Hawaii*. Laie, Hawai'i: Institute for Polynesian Studies, 1989.

Chazanov, Mathis. "Spreading the Word." *Los Angeles Times Westside* (20 February 1994):14–18. Work of Mormons in Los Angeles in ethnic communities, including Tongan, Korean, and Hawaiian.

Shaffer, Donald R. "Hiram Clark and the First LDS Hawaiian Mission: A Reappraisal." *Journal of Mormon History* 17 (1991):94–109.

Webb, Terry Douglas. "Mormonism and Tourist Art in Hawaii." Ph.D. dissertation, Arizona State University, 1990.

———. "Missionaries, Polynesians, and Tourists: Mormonism and Tourism in La'ie, Hawai'i." *Social Process in Hawaii* 35 (1994): 195–212.

Whitehurst, James. "Mormons and the Hulas: The Polynesian Cultural Center in Hawaii." *Journal of American Culture* 12 (Spring 1989):1–5.

General Religion

Alexander, H. A. "Ethnicity and Gender Issues in Multicultural Religious Education." *Religious Education* 88(3) (Summer 1993): 330–495.

Barkan, Elliott R. "Race, Religion, and Nationality in American Society: A Model of Ethnicity—From Contact to Assimilation." *Journal of American Ethnic History* 14(2) (Winter 1995):38–75.

Bibby, Reginald W. *Unknown Gods: The Ongoing Story of Religion in Canada*. Toronto: Stoddart, 1993.

Bobilin, Robert T., and Joan Chatfield. "Religion in Hawaii." *Mission Studies* 10(1–2) (1992):48–52.

Cadière, Léopold. *Religious Beliefs and Practices of the Vietnamese*. Translated by Ian W. Mabbett. Victoria, Australia: Centre of Southeast Asian Studies, Monash University, n.d.

Chang Chou, Shih-Deh. "Religion and Chinese Life in the United States." *Studi Emigrazione* 28(103) (1991):455–464.

Corpuz-Brock, Jane. "Gospel, Cultures, and Filipina Migrant Workers." *International Review of Mission* 85(336) (January 1996): 63–84.

Ehara, Jun D. "Ministry to the Japanese Ethnic Community in the United States of America." D.Min. dissertation, Claremont School of Theology, 1980.

Fenton, John Y. *Transplanting Religious Traditions: Asian Indians in America*. New York: Praeger, 1988.

Gans, Herbert J. "Symbolic Ethnicity and Symbolic Religiosity: Towards a Comparison of Ethnic and Religious Acculturation." *Ethnic and Racial Studies* 17(4) (October 1994):577–592.

Goh, Francis Swee-Huat. "A Ministry to New Asian Immigrants in Monticello, New York." D.Min. dissertation, Drew University, 1980.

Han, Young-Taek. "The Church as a Reconciling Community: Toward the Mission of Korean Immigrant Churches (California)." D.Min. dissertation, Claremont School of Theology, 1996.

Hunsberger, George R., et al. "Selected Annotated Bibliography: Multicultural Ministry in North America." *Missiology: An International Review* 21(4) (October 1993):501–505. Special theme issue.

Kim, Ai Ra. *Women Struggling for a New Life*. Albany: State University of New York Press, 1996. Korean American women's religious life in New Jersey.

Kleiber, Margrethe S. C. *Report on Asian Ministry: June 1993 (Evangelical Lutheran Church in America)*. Chicago: Asian Ministries

Program, Commission for Multicultural Ministries, 1993. Report on pastoral and counseling work with Asian Americans.

Kosmin, Barry A. *Research Report—The National Survey of Religious Identification 1989–90 (Selected Tabulations)*. New York: Graduate School and University Center of City University of New York, 1991.

Leong, Russell C. "Litany." *Tricycle: The Buddhist Review* (Fall 1994):58–63. Reflections on Christianity and Buddhism.

Lewis, Robert E., Mark E. Fraser, and Peter J. Pecora. "Religiosity Among Indochinese Refugees in Utah." *Journal for the Scientific Study of Religion* 27(2) (1988):272–283.

Lin, Keh-ming, Lina Demonteverde, and Inocencia Nuccio. "Religion, Healing, and Mental Health Among Filipino Americans." *International Journal of Mental Health* 19(3) (Fall 1990):40–44.

Lippy, Charles H., and Peter W. Williams, eds. *Encyclopedia of the American Religious Experience: Studies of Traditions and Movements*. New York: Scribner's, 1988.

Louie, Alvin. "Case Studies of the Mother-Daughter Model of Church Planting in North American Chinese Churches." D.Min. dissertation, Dallas Theological Seminary, 1995.

Ma, L. Eve Armentrout. "Chinese Traditional Religion in North America and Hawaii." In *Chinese America: History and Perspectives*. San Francisco: Chinese Historical Society of America, 1988.

Matsuoka, Fumitaka. *Out of Silence: Emerging Themes in Asian American Churches*. Cleveland: United Church Press, 1995.

Melton, John Gordon. *The Encyclopedia of American Religions*. 2nd ed. Detroit: Gale, 1987.

Moore, David. *Transitional World Religions*. Minneapolis: Minneapolis Public Schools, 1990. Study plan for high school students; includes a section on Hmong belief systems.

Moseley, Romney. *No Longer Strangers: Ministry in a Multicultural Society*. Toronto: Anglican Book Centre, 1993.

Muhler, William Mead. "Religion and Social Problems in Gold Rush California: 1849–1869." Ph.D. dissertation, Graduate Theological Union, 1989.

Nash, Jesse W., and Elizabeth Trinh, eds. *Romance, Gender, and Religion in a Vietnamese-American Community: Tales of God and*

Beautiful Women. Lewiston, N.Y.: E. Mellen Press, 1995.

Paige, Glenn D., and Sarah Gilliatt, eds. *Nonviolence in Hawaii's Spiritual Traditions.* Honolulu: Center for Global Nonviolence Planning Project, Spark M. Matsunaga Institute for Peace, University of Hawai'i, 1991.

Pozzetta, George, ed. *The Immigrant Religious Experience.* New York: Garland, 1991.

Rutledge, Paul James. "The Role of Religion in Ethnic Self-Identity: The Vietnamese in Oklahoma City, 1975–1982." Ph.D. dissertation, University of Oklahoma, 1982.

Southard, Naomi, and Ruth Nakashima Brock. "The Other Half of the Basket: Asian American Women and the Search for a Theological Home." *Journal of Feminist Studies in Religion* 3 (Fall 1987):133–150.

Shamanism

Bosley, Ann. "Of Shamans and Physicians: Hmong and the U.S. Health Care System." M.A. thesis, Hampshire College, 1985.

Cheon, Jun Ku. "Liberating Shamanism: A Spiritual Resource for Korean Christians." D.Min. dissertation, Claremont School of Theology, 1996.

Jang, Nam Hyuck. "Shamanism in Korean Christianity: Evaluating the Influence of Shamanism on Perceptions of Spiritual Power in Korean Christianity." Ph.D. dissertation, Fuller Theological Seminary, 1996.

Jin, Hee Keun. "Preaching in the Korean Presbyterian Church with Insights from a Shamanistic Worldview." D.Min. dissertation, Fuller Theological Seminary, 1996.

Sikhism

Bhachu, Amarjet S. "A Shield for Swords." *American Criminal Law Review* 34 (Fall 1996):197–224. Laws that restrict the ability of Sikhs to carry *kirpans* (swords with religious significance).

Kennedy, Des. "A Temple in Paldi: A Vibrant Sikh Centre in Logging Country." *Canadian Heritage* 14(3) (Fall 1988):27–29.

Ahn, Duk-Won. "A Strategy of Laity Training for Church Growth: The Case of Young Nak Presbyterian Church of Los Angeles." D.Min. dissertation, Fuller Theological Seminary, 1993.

Bankston, Carl L., III, and Min Zhou. "The Ethnic Church, Ethnic Identification, and the Social Adjustment of Vietnamese Adolescents." *Review of Religious Research* 38(1) (September 1996):18–37.

Breyer, Chloe Anne. "Religious Liberty in Law and Practice: Vietnamese Home Temples and the First Amendment." *Journal of Church and State* 35(2) (Spring 1993):367–404.

"Building Human and Spiritual Bonds Across the Pacific." *Ampo* 20(3) (1989):52–56. Interview with Lopeti Senituli, general coordinator for the Pacific Concerns Resource Center of the Nuclear-Free and Independent Pacific.

Burwell, Ronald J., Peter Hill, and John F. Van Wicklin. "Religion and Refugee Resettlement in the United States: A Research Note." *Review of Religious Research* 17(4) (1986):356–366.

Chace, Paul G. "The Oldest Chinese Temples in California: A Landmarks Tour." *Gum Saan Journal* (Chinese Historical Society of Southern California) (June 1991):1–19. Profile of Bok Kai Temple in Marysville, Liet Sheng Kung in Oroville, Won Lim Miao in Weaverville, Kuan Ti Temple in Mendocino, and Wu Ti Miao in Cambria.

Chang, Soo-Chul, Hyun-Sook Kim, and Sook-Ja Chung. "Korean Woman Jesus: Drama Worship." *Journal of Women and Religion* 13 (1995):45–51. Play excerpt.

Chao, Ching–Lung Raymond. "Pastoral Strategies for Dealing with Depression in Chinese Church Context." D.Min. dissertation, Fuller Theological Seminary, 1995.

Choe, Joon Soo. "Biblical Resources for Pastoral Care and Counseling for Marital Conflicts in Korean Immigrant Families." D.Min. dissertation, Drew University, 1994.

Chung, Angie. "Rev. Madison T. Schockley: Working for 'Positive Exchange.'" *Korea Times English Edition* (5 October 1994):6. Efforts of African American minister to build interracial coalitions for understanding.

Clark, Karen. "Hanford's Chinatown Revolved Around Taoist Temple: Armona's Chinatown Once Rivaled Hanford's." *Chinese Historical Society of America Bulletin* 19 (February 1984).

Clarke, Peter, and Jeffrey Somers, eds. *Japanese New Religions in the West*. Richmond, England: Curzon Press, 1994.

Coleman, Graham, ed. *A Handbook of Tibetan Culture: A Guide of Tibetan Centres and Resources Throughout the World*. Boston: Shambhala, 1994.

Conroy, Hilary, and Sharlie Conroy Ushioda. "A Review of Scholarly Literature on the Internment of Japanese Americans During World War II: Toward a Quaker Perspective." *Quaker History* 83 (Spring 1994):48–52.

Dahl, Winifred Lucille. "Religious Conversion and Mental Health in Two Japanese American Groups." Ph.D. dissertation, University of California, Berkeley, 1975.

Dart, John. "Southern Baptists Vote to Issue Apology for Past Racism." *Los Angeles Times* (21 June 1995):A28. Asian American Baptists.

Davidson, Jack. "Hmong Ethnohistory: An Historical Study of Hmong Culture and Its Implications for Ministry." Ph.D. dissertation, Fuller Theological Seminary, 1993.

Dolnick, Janis Lee. "Fear, Acceptance and Denial of Death: Their Relationship to Afterlife Beliefs, Exposure to Death, and Connectedness to Religious Orientation." Ph.D. dissertation, California Institute of Integral Studies, 1987. Based on research of Hindus, Buddhists, Catholics, Protestants, Jews, and atheists at San Francisco State University.

Dubin, Zan. "Keeping Faith." *Los Angeles Times* (5 June 1995):E1. Describes rise of activity in private religious practices in Los Angeles, including those of Buddhists such as Luu Kim-Chi at Lien Hoa Temple in Garden Grove, Orange County.

Fisher, Bob. "Mining the Spiritual Layers of *Heaven and Earth*." *American Cinematographer* (February 1994):36–41.

Gazzolo, Michele B. "Spirit Paths and Roads of Sickness: A Symbolic Analysis of Hmong Textile Design." M.A. thesis, University of Chicago, 1986.

Grandin, Elaine, and Merlin B. Brinkerhoff. "Does Religiosity

310

Encourage Racial and Ethnic Intolerance?" *Canadian Ethnic Studies* 23(3) (1991):32–47.

Han, Jung Mi Lim. "A Pastoral Strategy for Interracial Marriages of Korean Women to American Servicemen." D.Min. dissertation, Columbia Theological Seminary, 1986.

Ichinotsubo, Tammy H. "Shame-Proneness in Asian American and Caucasian American Christian families." Ph.D. dissertation, Fuller Theological Seminary, 1994.

Kassel, Marleen. "Two Japanese New Religions in Flushing: The Tenrikyo Mission and the Nichiren Shoshu Daihozan Myosetsu Temple." *Long Island Historical Journal* 5(1) (1992):81–90.

Kim, Jung Sup. "The Relationship Between Virtue and Acculturation Among Korean American Young Adults in Korean Churches in Southern California." Ed.D. dissertation, Biola University, 1993.

Kim, SeungHee Lisa. "The Influences of American Gospel Music on the Korean Church." M.Th. thesis, Louisville Presbyterian Theological Seminary, 1996.

Kolb, Michael J. "Monumentality and the Rise of Religious Authority in Precontact Hawai'i." *Current Anthropology* 35(5) (December 1994):521–547.

Kortz, Larry. "Multiculturalism: How Well Are We Doing?" *United Church Observer* 57(3) (September 1993):17–21.

Leduc, Louis S. "Migration and Religion: Ministering to Lao Refugees in the United States." *Migration World* 21(1) (1993):26–30.

Lee, Helen. "Silent Exodus: Can the East Asian Church in America Reverse the Flight of Its Next Generation?" *Christianity Today* 40(9) (12 August 1996):50–54. Includes related article on Asian American pastors.

Melton, John Gordon. *Encyclopedic Handbook of Cults in America*. New York: Garland, 1986.

Misumi, Diane Minekoh. "Effects of Psychoeducation on Asian-American Christian Attitudes Towards Counseling." Ph.D. dissertation, Fuller Theological Seminary, 1993.

Moss, David M. "Internment and Ministry: A Dialogue with Joseph Kitagawa." *Journal of Religion and Health* 32(3) (1993):163–178.

"Multicultural Ministry." *Missiology: An International Review* 21(4) (October 1993). Special theme issue.

Okihiro, G. Y. "Religion and Resistance in America's Concentration Camps." *Phylon* 45 (September 1985):220–233.

Park, Andrew Sung. *Racial Conflict and Healing: An Asian-American Theological Perspective.* Maryknoll, N.Y.: Orbis Books, 1996.

Park, I. H., and L. J. Cho. "Confucianism and the Korean Family." *Journal of Comparative Family Studies* 26(1) (Spring 1995):117–134.

Poonsakvorasan, Apichart. "Perceptions of Educational Needs Indicated by Thai Laity and Church Leaders." Ed.D. dissertation, Trinity Evangelical Divinity School, 1995.

Powell, Melvin Cecil. "Nichiren Shoshu Soka Gakkai of America in Tucson, Arizona: Portrait of an Imported Religion." M.A. thesis, University of Arizona, 1985.

Schachter, Hindy Lauer. "Public School Teachers and Religiously Distinctive Dress: A Diversity-Centered Approach." *Journal of Law and Education* 22(1) (Winter 1993):61–69. Includes a case involving Sikh dress.

Scott, George M. "The Lao Hmong Refugees in San Diego: Their Religious Transformation and Its Implications for Geertz's Thesis." *Ethnic Studies Report* 5(2) (July 1987):32–46.

Shimada, Shigeo. *A Stone Cried Out: The True Story of Simple Faith in Difficult Days.* Valley Forge, Pa.: Judson Press, 1987.

Stokes, John F. G. *Heiau of the Island of Hawaii.* Honolulu: Bishop Museum Press, 1991. Sacred structure of Hawaiian religion.

Tamashiro, John Gerald. "Konkokyo, a Japanese Religion in Hawaii." Ph.D. dissertation, University of Hawai'i, 1985.

Tran, Luat Trong. "A Theology of *dan chung:* A Humanistic Approach to the Ministry for the Vietnamese Refugees and Immigrants in the United States." Ph.D. dissertation, Claremont School of Theology, 1993.

Tran, Peter. "The Pastoral Care and Challenges of the People from Cambodia, Laos and Vietnam in the United States." *Migration World* 18(2) (1990):17–22.

Watkins, Joanne C. *Spirited Women: Gender, Religion, and Cultural Identity in the Nepal Himalaya.* New York: Columbia University Press, 1996.

Watkins, Keith. "Multi-Language Congregations: A Field Study of Los Angeles 1993." *Encounter* 55(2) (Spring 1994):129–153.

Weightman, Barbara A. "Changing Religious Landscapes in Los Angeles." *Journal of Cultural Geography* 14(1) (Fall–Winter 1993): 1–20.

Welcome into the Community of Faith: A Report on the Cambodian, Hmong and Laotian Apostolate, 1986. Washington, D.C.: USCC Pastoral Care of Migrants and Refugees, 1986.

Westermeyer, Joseph, and Sean Nugent. "Religiosity and Psychosocial Adjustment Among 100 Hmong Refugees." *Asian American and Pacific Islander Journal of Health* 2(2) (Spring 1994): 133–145.

White, John. "Separation of Church and Liquor Store: Korean American Merchants in L.A." *Rice Paper* (University of California, Irvine) (June 1994):6–7. Christianity and Korean immigrant liquor stores.

Wimberly, Anne E. Streaty. "Christian Education for Health and Wholeness: Responses to Older Adults in Ethnic/Racial Contexts." *Religious Education* 89(2) (Spring 1994):248–264.

Winland, Daphne N. "The Role of Religious Affiliation in Refugee Resettlement: The Case of the Hmong." *Canadian Ethnic Studies* 24(1) (1992):96–119.

Wooden, Wayne S., Joseph J. Leon, and Michelle T. Toshima. "Ethnic Identity Among Sansei and Yonsei Church-Affiliated Youth in Los Angeles and Honolulu." *Psychological Reports* 62(1) (February 1988):268–270.

Woodrum, Eric. "Religion and Economics Among Japanese Americans: A Weberian Study." *Social Forces* 64(1) (September 1985): 191–204.

Woods, L. Shelton. "Ilocano Immigration and the Attitudes of American Missionaries." *Filipino American National Historical Society Journal* 4 (1996):19–28.

Contributors

Meena Alexander is professor of English and women's studies at Hunter College and the Graduate Center, CUNY. She is the author of numerous books including *The Shock of Arrival: Reflection on Postcolonial Experience*.

Rudy V. Busto is assistant professor of American ethnic religions at Stanford University.

Allan DeSouza is an artist and writer based in Los Angeles.

Heinz Insu Fenkl is the author of *Memories of My Ghost Brother* and an assistant professor of English at Eastern Michigan University.

Jung Ha Kim is a 1.5 Korean American woman who teaches at Georgia State University. She is cochair of the Asian American consultation at the American Academy of Religion.

Vinay Lal is an assistant professor of history at UCLA and was a senior fellow at the American Institute of Indian Studies.

Marjorie Lee is librarian of the UCLA Asian American Studies Reading Room.

Sang Hyun Lee is K. C. Han Professor of Systematic Theology at Princeton Theological Seminary.

Russell C. Leong is editor of UCLA's *Amerasia Journal* and series editor of *Intersections: Asian and Pacific American Transcultural Studies*.

Index

Index

Kong, H. H., 20
Koran, 237–239
Korea, Christianity. See
    Christianity, in Korea
Korean Americans: autobio-
    graphical reflections by,
    194–198, 218; Christianity of,
    174–175, 179; response to
    Los Angeles civil unrest by,
    222. See also churches,
    Korean American
Kyo-whe, history of, 204–205

La Brack, Bruce, 102–103
Lai, Him Mark, 19–20
Layman, Emma McCloy,
    135–136
Lee, Mabel, 36, 48n. 67
Legionarios del Trabajo, 54–55,
    81n. 6
Lem Chung, 28
Leonard, Karen, 10
Lipman-Blumen, Jean, 209
Livingston Union School Dis-
    trict. See *Cheema, Rajinder
    Singh, et al., v. Harold V.
    Thompson, et al.*
Lockyer, Bill, 116
Longowal, Harchand Singh, 99
Los Angeles, 1992 civil unrest,
    222, 274–277
Mamiya, Larry, 188
Manshin, 190–191
Mariano, Ansie Lara, 77
Marxism, 8–9
May Fourth movement, 22,
    32–35
missionaries: in Asia, 9; in
    Hong Kong, 29–30; in the
    United States, 23, 25, 34–35

model minority stereotype,
    178–180, 219
Moncado, Hilario Camino: as
    charismatic figure, 62–63; as
    founder of the Filipino Fed-
    eration of America, 57–59;
    postwar activities, 76–77;
    relationship with Lorenzo
    de los Reyes, 65–66, 70. *See
    also* E. F. B. religion; Fili-
    pino Federation of America
Moncado religion. *See* E. F. B.
    religion
Muslims: autobiographical
    accounts in America,
    250–255; childhood recollec-
    tions in India, of circumci-
    sion, 237–238; —, of fasting,
    238, 242–243; —, of hypoc-
    risy, 246–249; —, of Idd,
    242–246; —, of Koran
    study, 238–239; —, of Rama-
    dan, 242–243; as defenders
    of faith to Americans, 254;
    raising children in America
    as, 255
mutual aid societies, Asian
    immigrant, 54–63. *See also
    under individual organiza-
    tions*

Nagal, Alfonzo, 63–64, 75
Nanak, 90
Nationalism: of Chinese
    American Protestants 19–39;
    of Filipino Americans, 55–57;
    of Korean Americans, 174;
    of Sikhs in India, 95–96; of
    Sikhs overseas, 101–102, 117
National Rifle Association, 120

Index

321

322